BELOVED  KW-220-472
Mary Moffat of Kuruman

by

MORA DICKSON

ST. MARY'S CONVENT CHISWICK SISTERS LIBRARY

On September 7th, 1819, Mary Smith of Manchester sailed from Cowes for Cape Town in Southern Africa, on her way to marry the young nursery gardener Robert Moffat, who had gone out three years previously with the London Missionary Society. For the next fifty years Mary and Robert Moffat worked as pioneer missionaries in the lands north of the Orange River. It was a harsh, demanding life in conditions of physical hardship and spiritual barrenness far removed from the picture accepted back in England of rewarding missionary activity. In the midst of drought, famine, tribal wars, vast raiding migrations and the strife caused by Boer pressures on the northern frontiers of the Colony, Mary Moffat built a home, taught the Gospel, bore her children and ran the infant mission station while her husband travelled.

Twenty-five years later, when the fascination of African exploration was just beginning to make itself felt in Europe, Kuruman had become a flourishing centre of missionary activity. In 1845 one of the young recruits fresh out from Britain, David Livingstone, married the Moffats' eldest daughter. It was an unexpected match and Mary Moffat, while loving her son-in-law as one of the family, nevertheless strongly disapproved of much that he did and never hesitated to make her views known to him.

Mary Moffat was a remarkable woman in her own right. She went out to Africa to be not only Robert Moffat's wife but a partner in his missionary work, and neither ill-health, disasters nor family pressures deflected her from this aim. 'Would that some knew,' her husband wrote to her in 1859, 'even were it a tithe, of what you have had to suffer for the cause, for Christ's sake among the Bechuanas.'

Mora Dickson has drawn a moving and detailed portrait of a most dedicated and faithful woman.

This biography has won for Mora Dickson a Scottish Arts Council Award.

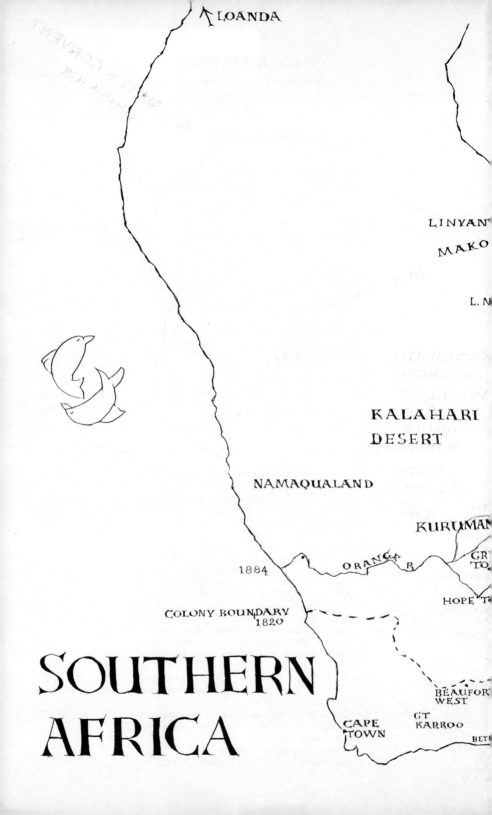

LOANDA

LINYAN'

MAKO

L. N

KALAHARI
DESERT

NAMAQUALAND

KURUMAN

GR
TO.

ORANGE R.

1884

HOPE T

COLONY BOUNDARY
1820

BEAUFOR
WEST

SOUTHERN

CAPE
TOWN

GT
KARROO

BET

AFRICA

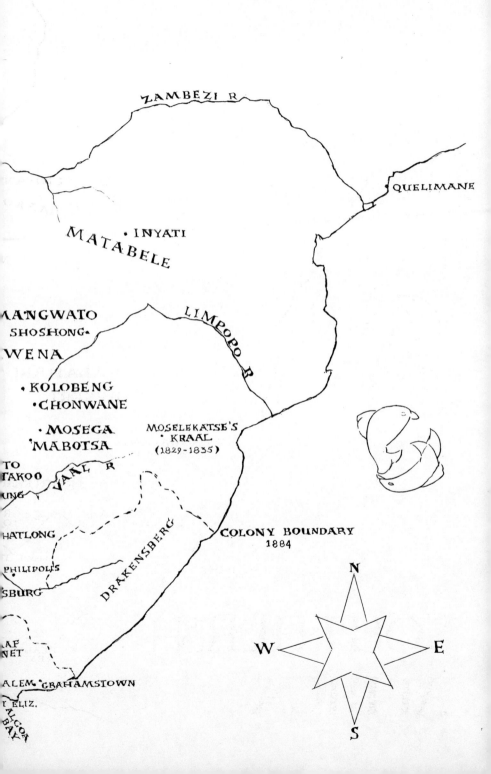

BELOVED PARTNER
Mary Moffat of Kuruman

By the same author

NEW NIGERIANS
A SEASON IN SARAWAK
BAGHDAD AND BEYOND
ISRAELI INTERLUDE
A WORLD ELSEWHERE
COUNT US IN
(A Community Service Handbook)
LONGHOUSE IN SARAWAK
THE INSEPARABLE GRIEF
Margaret Cargill of Fiji

A CHANCE TO SERVE Alec Dickson
Edited by Mora Dickson

KURUMAN CHURCH

BELOVED PARTNER

Mary Moffat of Kuruman

by

Mora Dickson

LONDON
DENNIS DOBSON

© Mora Dickson 1974, 1976

First published in Great Britain in 1974 by Victor Gollancz Ltd
This edition published in Great Britain in 1976
by Dobson Books Ltd 80 Kensington Church Street,
London W8
Printed and made in Great Britain by Billing & Sons Limited,
Guildford, London and Worcester

ISBN 0 234 72015 8 Hardback

ISBN 0 234 72017 4 Paperback

For Archie,
who would so much have liked
to see this book.

Contents

Illustrations

Acknowledgements

I AM MOST grateful to the Rev. Stuart Craig of the Congregational Council for World Mission who allowed me to make use of the library and the London Missionary Society Archives at Livingstone House, where the bulk of research for this book was done. At a time of considerable upheaval and reorganisation I was always greeted with kindness and help. Both the David Livingstone Trust at Blantyre and the Trustees of the National Library of Scotland supplied me with material; as did the Rhodes Library at Oxford. Mrs Sheila Moffat and her daughter Mrs Mary Philip very kindly let me see and make use of Mary Moffat's letter to her granddaughter Agnes. Finally, and by no means least, the London Library has been a most valuable source of printed material.

The majority of the material quoted from printed sources is from publications already out of copyright. I am grateful, however, to Chatto & Windus for permission to quote from David Livingstone's *Family Letters* and *Private Journals 1851–1853*, edited by Isaac Schapera; to Edward Arnold for extracts from the *Journals of Elizabeth Lees Price*, edited by Una Long; and to the Central African Archives for quotations from the Oppenheimer Papers.

M.D.

PART I

PARTNER

Chapter 1

IN SEPTEMBER 1819, the year that Queen Victoria was born, Mary Smith set sail for Cape Town. It was no light undertaking for a young woman of twenty-four, who had rarely travelled further south than Manchester, to start off alone on a journey of several thousand miles to meet—in a strange and savage country—a fiancé with whom, because he was beneath her in station, she had had 'only occasional intercourse', and since September 1816 had not seen at all.

It was true that when he himself had left Britain she had wanted to accompany him, being herself drawn to Southern Africa by the same missionary fervour as he was, but she had found it impossible to persuade her parents to give their permission. Unsurprisingly, although they admired the young man and had done all in their power to help him, the Smith parents were reluctant to let their only daughter, the apple of their eye, go off to the other side of the world with one of her father's employees—and a very temporary one at that. It was not that they doubted the young man's integrity, or sense of responsibility, or absolute Christian commitment; on the contrary they greatly respected Robert Moffat. But Mary was a different matter. For Mary there were surely other ways, nearer home, to serve the Kingdom of God.

Mary Smith was born on May 24th 1795, the daughter of James Smith of Dukinfield, near Manchester, and his wife Mary Gray of York. James Smith or Gow was a Scotsman from Little Dunkeld in Perthshire. His father owned land and the family consisted of five sons and a daughter. Some of the family were ardent Jacobites and in those troubled times the Gow house was burned down and their land lost. The sons being forced to find work elsewhere, James Gow drifted south, anglicised his name to Smith and eventually started a nursery garden at Dukinfield. There was a family legend which said that one of the brothers, Alexander, changed his name to John Adams and became one of the ring-leaders of the mutiny on the Bounty, and the last survivor of those who landed on Pitcairn island — but this, in fact, was not true.

Be that as it may, James Smith had done well for himself. He was a nursery gardener in a good way of business, a stout non-conformist, a man of principle and a committed Christian. His wife was an Anglican, devoted and dutiful. Mary was their eldest child, the only girl among three boys.

She was a pretty child and grew up into an attractive girl with dark curly hair, bright blue eyes and a fresh complexion. Both her parents adored her and she was closer to them than were her brothers because she shared their religious faith in a way that the sons did not. But she was not a docile, pious, insipid young thing; on the contrary, along with her rich colouring went considerable force of character, a quick temper, a sensible, practical outlook on life.

She was sent to a school run by the Moravians at Fairfield, one of their original settlements in England. The Moravian church was one of the earliest Protestant churches, having its origins in Bohemia and Moravia in the fourteenth and fifteenth centuries. John Huss and Count Zinzendorf were among its great names, and both John and Charles Wesley had been much influenced by their early connection with the Moravians.

They were a strongly evangelical missionary church. From the very outset the congregations had been dispersed through persecution, but their desire to take the Gospel to unknown lands was more positive than this. In the 1730s, as well as a deputation to England, they sent missionaries to the West Indies, Greenland, Georgia, North America, Swedish Lapland, Guinea, the Cape of Good Hope, Ceylon and South America. They laid stress on order and discipline, and the simplicity of the Gospel. Their church life was based on a deeply spiritual, emotional, Christian fellowship and upon the centrality of Jesus in all teaching and preaching—with special emphasis on the education of children and the establishment of schools. They loved singing and held that it was not lawful to bear arms. Theirs was a humble, joyful life and Mary's schooldays were very happy. She never forgot the Moravians and it was they who first aroused in her an interest in missionary work overseas.

Life, however, was not all serious study. One day the young ladies of Fairfield school had an argument as to which of them was the possessor of the most perfectly shaped leg. Long skirts were pulled up to scrutinise, measure and parade these members—and it was Mary Smith who won this beauty competition. She was not vain, but she remembered this incident. Many years later, in another country and a totally different situation, a distinguished son-in-law, watching her bustling about in her kitchen with her sleeves tucked up above her elbows, said, 'Mother, do you know that you have a perfectly symmetrical arm?' She retorted, 'Indeed! I did not know it.' But later she told her daughter of the competition at Fairfield.

The girl, Mary Smith, was given to sleep-walking. In both the instances recorded it seems to have been of an unusual character, as she remembered the next morning what had happened. Once, at school, she discovered the servants having a midnight carousal—as a result of which they were subsequently dismissed. When consternation was caused at home one morning on finding the front door of the house wide open, Mary recollected that she had gone out in the middle of the night to feed her rabbits.

She did not have much sense of humour, though her brothers —like all brothers of an only sister—enjoyed playing practical jokes on her. Mary suffered from an inability to distinguish one tune from another, though she loved singing hymns and had a good voice so long as she was surrounded by a congregation. One of her brothers, who played the fiddle, was fond of teasing her by asking which of her favourite hymn tunes she would like. Usually she replied the Old Hundredth, at which he would very solemnly play a jig—rejoicing in her inability to tell the difference.

This then was the young lady, of good position, well educated, serious-minded, pretty, with polished manners, a number of suitors and the expectation of some fortune, who had reached the age of twenty when, in January 1816, her father took on a young Scotsman, also aged twenty, to work in the nursery garden.

Robert Moffat, though coming from a family as devout and

devoted as Mary Smith's own, had had very few of her advantages. His father was a ploughman in the Lothians in southeast Scotland who, when his son was two, transferred to the salt tax office in Portsoy, Banffshire, to better himself. In 1806, nine years later, the family moved south again to Carronshore, near Falkirk.

Robert was a restless, adventurous boy, who went off to sea at the age of about ten, did not like it much and returned to go to school at Falkirk for about six months. This was virtually all his formal schooling. But he came from Scottish Lowland stock where there was at this period a universal respect for literacy and learning, which meant that material poverty and lack of opportunity were no barrier to a continuing and wide-ranging education. When Robert Moffat, at fourteen, became apprenticed to John Robertson of Polmont as an under-gardener, he also learned Latin, mensuration and black-smithing in his spare time.

Like James Smith and other young Scots before him, Robert Moffat, at the age of eighteen, moved down to England in search of wider horizons, to take up a position as under-gardener in Cheshire. It was a lonely life. He lived by himself in a bothy on the estate, his chief job being to stoke the nineteen fires in the many greenhouses. He worked by day and read avidly at night, walking fortnightly to the cottage meetings of the Independent Methodists to whose fellowship he was drawn. One evening he walked to Warrington and, by the Town Bridge, saw a placard for a missionary meeting to be chaired by the Rev. William Roby of Grosvenor Chapel, Manchester. He went, was caught up by the personality and appeal of William Roby and determined to meet him.

William Roby was forty-nine at this time. He had begun his career as a schoolmaster, also teaching religion. The parish priest objected to this combination of activities and had him removed from his job, which led William Roby to look closely at the articles of the Church of England into which he had been born—and ended in his becoming a Congregationalist minister. He was a man of consuming passions sustained and fed by an orderly theological mind. He saw the church as missionary, both at home and overseas, and was one of the first to respond to the appeal in 1794 to set up the London Missionary

Society, of which he became a Director. He also retained all his life a warm interest in young people. His Sunday school in Manchester was crowded with scholars, 1,280 of them, and, through the generosity of an individual patron, an academy for the training of men for the ministry was also under his charge.

He was impressed by the young man who found his way into his presence. Robert Moffat was not only physically fine-looking, over six-foot tall, dark haired; he had also a personality which was to attract and dominate other people all his life. Eager, outgoing, he immersed himself totally in those things which captured his interest. For all his lack of schooling he was plainly able. He stated without much ado his desire to be a missionary.

William Roby was willing to put his name forward to the London Missionary Society. The LMS was ecumenical, sending young men out to preach the Gospel rather than to propagate any particular denomination. In 1815 they asked very little in the way of training or academic background or pastoral experience. Their policy was still to send practical men—'godly men who understood mechanic arts'. It seemed to William Roby that Robert Moffat fulfilled this ideal. The Society did not agree and turned Robert Moffat down.

He was not discouraged. He knew now where he was going, and he had the patience to work steadily towards this goal. The first step was to move nearer to Manchester and William Roby, so that he could study with him and begin to ground himself in theology. Mr Roby found him a job in the nursery gardens of James Smith at Dukinfield and he went there on January 1st 1816.

At the same time William Roby began to give this young man the only formal theological training he ever received. It was based on the curriculum of the training college of which he was a director, and consisted of grammatical construction of English, composition of sermons, logic, ecclesiastical history, geography, use of globes, first principles of natural and moral philosophy, Greek, Hebrew, and a course of eighty theological lectures which each student copied out for himself.

For the next few months Robert Moffat worked in the Dukinfield gardens, attended tutoring sessions with William Roby,

17

was caught up in the religious life of Manchester—in particular a great missionary festival—and made the acquaintance of his employer's daughter, Miss Smith. When, in July, he finally heard that the London Missionary Society would accept him and went back to Scotland to say goodbye to his parents, he and Mary Smith already knew that they wished to spend their lives together in Southern Africa and had had to face the fact that it was unlikely they would ever be able to do so.

It was not his physical handsomeness that attracted Mary Smith to her father's young employee—there were a number of good-looking young men among her acquaintance and she was not without offers, it was the discovery that he shared with her a passionate concern for the missionary cause, particularly in Africa. She had come to this concern early. Many years later she wrote to her father, reminding him of the time that he had taken her 'to be present at the first missionary meeting to be held in our part of the country. . . . My mind was powerfully affected. I was very young and had not the slightest prospect of joining the missionary band but I felt the cause was worth a thousand lives.' The Moravians had nourished and extended this interest but, until this moment, it had had perforce to be a passive one—reaching little further than missionary collecting boxes. It was inconceivable that any young woman could go alone to London—far less Africa. Her role was to support at home, by prayer and practical assistance, those who answered the call to go overseas.

Now the situation had entirely changed. She had found a young man who not only shared her vision but wished to offer her the chance to go out with him and put it into practice. She longed to accept. She made it plain to him that she was willing to leave her comfortable, secure home and go with him to whatever hardships he might encounter, but when they approached her parents it was to meet with an absolute prohibition. Under no circumstances would they allow Mary to leave them in this way. Her father, in particular, was adamant.

Any decision was not made easier by her devotion to her parents. She knew very well the sacrifice that she was asking them to make, and understood their reasons for refusing to make it. When Robert went north to Scotland to say goodbye to his mother and father he did so in the knowledge that he might never see them again. Missionaries returned home only after long intervals—ten, fifteen, twenty years (and then only for good reason)—if they lived to return home at all. Mr and Mrs Smith were being asked to give up their daughter for ever, to deny themselves the pleasure of her company, the delight of future grandchildren around them, the comfort of her care in their declining years. Sons could never compensate for this kind of loss. Mary loved them, and accepted that their veto came from love of her—but it did not alleviate the anguish in having to let Robert Moffat go off alone, to face what dangers he must. Nor, though she urged him to take someone else, did she consider her parents' decision necessarily final. If she had sufficient strength of faith to see the hand of God in it, she also had confidence enough in the power of prayer to believe that the Lord could, ultimately, change her parents' minds.

In September 1816, nine months after he had arrived at Dukinfield, Robert Moffat travelled south to meet the Directors of the London Missionary Society in London; on the 30th he was ordained in Surrey Chapel on the South Bank, given three dozen shirts, £10 for books, £5 for other things, and his boots. At the end of October he sailed for South Africa on the *Alacrity*. Back in Dukinfield Mary Smith settled down to wait, and hope, and pray. Though the future was often to look very bleak she was never to be daunted by it.

Life went on as usual, the Smith parents no doubt hoping that, as time went by, Mary would forget the young man whom she was unlikely to see again and accept a more satisfactory suitor nearer home. A cotton manufacturer, who had had his eye on her for a long time, renewed his suit when it began to seem that she would never get her parents' permission to sail for Africa. As she sat sewing he would plead with her, meanwhile fiddling with her reel of cotton in his nervousness and leaving it blue from the dye ingrained on his fingers. He had no success. Patience and determination were qualities that Mary Smith possessed in as full a measure as Robert Moffat. She had no idea how things were ever going to be changed, but she was prepared to wait until they were.

The long, frustrating years ground slowly by. Letters took months to arrive and when they did the contents did not ease her painfully torn heart. Robert was away in the remote interior at the kraal of an outlawed Hottentot chief. He was 'carpenter, smith, cooper, tailor, shoemaker, miller, baker and housekeeper', the last the most burdensome chore. He was happy, committed, stretched to the limit. He was doing the work that she longed to do beside him, and, reading his letters, the reality of the missionary field was sharply—and magnetically—brought home to her. And he needed her—this too was very plain.

She suffered from headaches, which were to dog her for the rest of her life. Although she had been convinced when they parted that it was right to obey her father's decision whatever the consequences, as time went on and it became clear that in the isolated, arduous, lonely life which he was leading Robert Moffat longed for a wife, she began to suffer from a strong sense of sin that she had let him go alone. Her health deteriorated. No doubt her parents told her that she would have been unsuited to life overseas. At any rate she found a medical man to consult who assured her that the climate of Southern Africa would probably agree with her and that 'the delicate often survive the strong and robust in that country'.

For the parents too it cannot have been an easy time. They loved their daughter. In their desire to keep her, selfish motives had been mixed with genuine anxiety to do what was best for her own good. It must have been plain to them, as the months went on, how much she was suffering. Clearly the alternative suitor, whom they had hoped for, was not going to be accepted; equally clearly Robert Moffat continued to feel for their daughter an undiminished affection. He had said that if he could not have her he would have no other—and this added to her feeling of guilt in consigning him to a solitary life. His loneliness called out to her.

But, though as time went on she came to feel that there was no alternative to Africa except to go into a decline and die, her strong affection for her parents did not allow her to concentrate solely on her own desires. She began to fear that circumstances might compel them to let her go, unwillingly, and that she would then be cut off from them and burdened with a sense of guilt on their account which would shadow all her happiness in a new life. To her friend, Miss Elizabeth Lees of Manchester, she poured out her anguish, often convinced that she was peculiarly marked out for suffering; that in all the world it was only herself, Mary Smith, whose prayers were not answered. Torn between breaking her mother's heart and deserting the man she loved and the cause she felt called to serve, she could not view either course without misery. She tortured herself by imagining in detail her mother's old age and death, bowed down by sorrow and without a daughter's love and affection to console her. Her thoughts dwelt on Robert, surrounded by dangers, giving everything to the cause that was central to both their lives, and she accused herself of betraying him.

The situation, so painfully deadlocked, remained unresolved until December 1818, two-and-a-half years after Robert Moffat had left Dukinfield. Mary was staying in Manchester, probably with Miss Lees, possibly because it had become unbearable for her to continue to live at home. At the beginning of the month, letters, dated April and May, arrived from Robert Moffat. They related the details of his daily life, the work of the Society, the slow progress of the kingdom of God. They were no different in tone from the letters which she had received from him at infrequent intervals over the years— his heart remained set on her but meanwhile he was not neglecting the Lord's work because of her.

Nevertheless, Mary felt that a crisis had arrived. Unless now she could persuade her father to give his consent and her mother to agree to let her go, she could no longer support this agonising life. Her body would not be able to endure the tremendous nervous strain to which it was being subjected. She took the letters and went home, determined to exert herself to the utmost to convince her parents that they must, willingly, relinquish her to Robert and to Africa.

She went with dread—and was astounded when her father, after reading the letters, calmly assented. He too had anguished and prayed and sought for a sign. Now, with a suddenness that Mary could only attribute to the direct intervention of the Lord, the obstacles that had for so long frustrated her were removed. If a ship and a suitable escort could be found, she had her parents' permission to sail to join Mr Moffat in the spring.

She wrote at once to Robert Moffat's parents in Scotland. She was not sure whether they even knew of her existence or of

21

their son's engagement. Now they were the first to be told of the dramatic turn of events.

Dramatic it may have been, but heartache still remained.

The die was cast, but, certain though she was that the course she was now taking was the proper one, Mary nevertheless dreaded the parting with her family. Her mother, particularly, though she had resigned her right to control her daughter's life, had not been able to do so without showing clearly how deeply Mary's desire to leave hurt her. It was natural she should feel like this. She may have admired her future son-in-law, but she can hardly have known him at all. For her it was inconceivable that Mary could not have found as rewarding ways to serve the cause of Christ in Manchester as in an unknown heathen land. James Smith, whose own father was reputed to have been a Covenanter, understood the magnetism of Faith, but Mrs Smith mourned overwhelmingly the loss of an only daughter. Mary was constantly having to reassure her that this choice of path did not mean any diminution in her love for her family, and she was distressed that even her father took the view that, in one sense, she would be dead to them when she married Robert Moffat. Her own conviction was much more positive and robust. They were sending her out to be the partner of a devoted servant of God and of some use in the world—and, after all, written communication, though slow and hazardous, was not impossible.

There was, however, a further consolation, one which set the seal on Mary's conviction that her prayers were now being answered. It was a cause of concern and anxiety to her that none of her three brothers shared the Christian faith which was the mainstay of herself and her parents. When she left the latter they would have no child able to share the deep spiritual beliefs which were the foundations of their lives. They would have to go alone to the central act of worship at the Lord's Table, and would feel this loneliness the more because this was a service whose significance lay precisely in its ties of spiritual communion between God and man, man and man, loved ones near and far. But she herself, in her long anguish, when she had tried to fulfil all the obligations of love and duty and had survived and triumphed only through a steadfast faith in the ultimate goodness of God, was instrumental in now bringing one of those brothers to make his own declaration of belief. On May 1st 1819 Mary wrote to Miss Lees, 'And now! my dear friend, how shall I tell you? Now I can depart in peace . . . for my dear brother John . . . was last night proposed to the church. . . .'

Mary was still at home when this happened. Although it had been decided that she should seek a ship in the spring, this was sooner said than done. The combination of a ship going to the Cape and a suitable couple to chaperon Miss Smith was not easy to come by. The months passed. Mary was given presents to take out with her by her friends and relatives; no doubt the long prelude to leave-taking produced its own tensions and anxieties. Constantly too in her mind, now that she was actually going to him, was the fear of some crisis or disaster in Robert Moffat's life. With news taking many months to arrive, she had to make her preparations always conscious that the situation which she knew had existed four, five or six months previously might now be totally changed. His affection she never doubted; his physical safety she could only pray would be preserved. These last months, with her object now gained, must have been in many ways harder to bear than the years of frustration which had gone before.

At last, however, circumstances joined to release her. A Mr and Mrs Beck were going out to the Dutch Church in Southern Africa in the autumn and, on being approached, agreed to take Mary Smith with them.

She left Dukinfield on August 6th 1819, going with her father by coach to London. The parting was painful. Africa was still many months away in a future full of uncertainties; the present horizon was filled with the sorrow of a mother whom she had no hope of seeing again, and all her efforts were employed to convince her that it was not want of love but the joyful acceptance of a fuller life which took her daughter from her. She wrote from London, where she was boarded with Mr Lewis the pastor of Islington Chapel (her father having to return home), 'I have sent you a small token of affection, I thought it would be better calculated to communicate pleasure and comfort to your heart than any article of dress. As for having my portrait taken, I cannot now, as my father is leaving, and I should have to pay for it myself; and that you know would not do. Whatever I possess now I must husband well, remembering that I am now supported more peculiarly out of the sacred treasury. . . . O my dear mother! do be happy as you value my peace of mind, the honour of religion, and my credit in the world. Do not let me be reflected on for want of affection to the best of mothers. You know it is not want of affection. O! do not allow the world to think so. . . .'

She was to sail on the *British Colony* and on August 24th left London for Gosport to join the ship. Weather, however, was of paramount importance. For two more weeks, while the wind backed and veered, the captain fumed and the passengers waited with patience and apprehension, the *British Colony* was unable to leave port. Mary stayed with a Dr and Mrs Bogue in Gosport 'in excellent health and spirits . . . and in a very happy and suitable frame of mind', no doubt relieved that the ties with home had finally been severed and the tensions which had so long troubled her were eased. She looked forward to the voyage. She was fond of reading and had books with her, work to do and, now that she had got to know them a little, pleasant travelling companions.

Nevertheless, waiting in limbo, on the threshold of a new life, committed to the perils of a long sea voyage and an unknown future on achieving a landfall, her thoughts turned often home to the quiet, ordered, comfortable existence in the house at Dukinfield and the parents who mourned for her. When at last, on Tuesday September 7th, the passengers received orders to go on board at Cowes, she wrote a final hasty note home: 'Do not be anxious about me. The Lord is going with me. Do not be long before you write to me at the Cape—conceive how anxious I shall be to hear; and be sure to send good full letters, or they will only set my teeth on edge. The wind is quite unfavourable, but the captain is tired out, and we are to sail at twelve today.'

They did sail but the omens of bad weather and the captain's temper were both to be fulfilled. For the first few days they got nowhere; the wind changed, then there was a dead calm and an adverse tide, then fair weather but the wind against them and their speed only one mile an hour. In her first hours on board Mary felt squeamish and had to stay on deck, 'but only sick once, ate a hearty dinner afterwards of goose and apple pudding'. Sea-sickness was a natural hazard of sailing; less easy to accept were the bugs. She had been warned about them, so examined her mattress on boarding—to find it swarming. She took it off, determined to have it well cleaned, and made up a bed of books, linen and blankets on top of which she slept. Even after this, however, she did not sleep well, imagining all night that the bugs were finding their way back. She had a small cabin on the lee side in which it rapidly became impossible to exist unless actually in bed with the porthole closed: heat, stench, constant drenchings by sea water all combined to make life below decks a misery.

At first, however, the excitement, the novelty, the relief at having at last set sail outweighed the discomforts. She kept a diary to send home to her parents when she arrived at Cape Town, telling them of the noise, pigs squeaking, geese gabbling, ducks quacking, sailors bellowing; of fellow passengers (who looked at the Becks' small party somewhat askance as being religious characters): Mrs Loudon who was delicate and paid 250 guineas for the state room, in spite of which she had all her linen spoiled by the sea, Mr Prince, a stiff little man who bickered, Mrs Johnstone, the widow of an old sailor, and others: of food, goose, duck, fowl, ham, tongue, salt beef, apple after dinner, and drink—she sat on the deck before dinner with a tumbler of brandy and water 'as bold as if it were milk'. She needed it to settle her stomach which was again queasy. At the same time she regretted that she had not taken her mother's advice and brought more things to eat, such as raisins, hard spicy cakes and ginger bread.

As time went on, though, and nerves began to fray in the confined space, the voyage grew less pleasant. Unfortunately, on closer acquaintance, she did not greatly care for the Becks. Mrs Beck was always poorly and was in any case 'a woman I cannot love', and Mr Beck, Mary considered, pandered too much to his wife's whims. Suffering from headaches, seasick and homesick, she felt lonely and isolated. One of the sheep died from want of water and the poultry wasted away (as opposed to being killed) all the time.

The captain, an autocrat of very uncertain temper, surprised them all by giving Mr Beck permission to preach on Sunday. The other passengers avoided such a display of religious fervour and Mary suggested that the sailors should be given a chance to come to the service. She had been watching the crew and had come to admire their uncomplaining hard work and to worry over their safety when they had to climb the rigging to reef the sails in bad weather. To her anger the captain forbad the sailors to attend the service. Undeterred, she took a handful of tracts and went round the decks handing them out. One of the crew then told her that they were forbidden to read, which roused her natural instincts to champion the underdog. She had a ready tongue and was not afraid to say what she thought, so no doubt she made her displeasure plain. It did not, however, change the captain's mind.

There were other, more unpleasant, incidents. On board was a 'virago who loved the bottle' and was very ill-tempered. She chose to vent her spite on Mary Smith, pretty, young, a missionary—and much of the time unchaperoned as Mr Beck was occupied below comforting the miserably sick Mrs Beck. One day, because the captain happened to say something pleasant about Miss Smith at table, the virago leapt up from her seat, rushed on deck and attacked the unsuspecting Mary, reducing her to tears from terror. Fortunately public opinion was entirely on Miss Smith's side and next day the virago, no doubt through pressure, apologised and the two ladies shook hands. They had been three weeks at sea and it seemed to Mary that her sense of purpose was escaping from her, the reality of both England and Africa disintegrating. It had become very hot, she suffered from prickly heat and violent headaches; the sailors had caught some sharks and killed them on deck and the smell which pervaded the ship was nauseous and offensive.

On October 2nd they passed the island of St Jagers. Some of the gentlemen wanted to land, anxious to stretch their legs after a month's confinement. Although the ship was taking on water from the island the captain absolutely refused to allow his passengers off. There were words, and Mr P. left the captain's table and took his meals on deck. After that relations with the captain deteriorated. Three days later there was a terrible quarrel about a servant maid and the cook—some of the passengers had their own servants with them. The captain threatened to blow one of the male passengers' brains out and forbad Mr Prince ever to have a dish served at table. He raved like a madman, made fresh rules in every department and created such a row as to frighten every soul on board. Mary prayed earnestly that they might run into a squall so that he had something to do. It was her brother James' birthday and she was homesick.

On the 7th of October they were passed by, and spoke to, a whaler, the *Griffin*, which had left England two days after the *British Colony*. It was only the second ship they had seen since the voyage started. At the same time a good breeze sprang up—accompanied by thunder and lightning—and the captain's temper improved. On her father's birthday, having slept fitfully, dreaming about the parting from her parents, Mary had a conversation with Mrs Johnstone, the widow travelling with one daughter, two children left in England, a son in Calcutta and a mother also in India. Hearing of this dispersed family, Mary, thinking of her own close-knit circle so recently torn apart by her departure, pitied this other mother with her children in far-flung places. She said as much. 'Mrs J. your family is much scattered.' To which Mrs Johnstone replied robustly, 'Yes, but there's no getting on in the world without it.'

Mary was greatly struck by this answer. She felt suddenly ashamed for her parents and herself that they should have found it such a piercing trial to part. Especially when their motives as Christians should have been so much more powerful than 'getting on' to a worldling. She had often thought that the world sometimes shamed the disciples of Christ, and here indeed was an instance of it. She was to remember Mrs Johnstone in the years ahead, when her own turn came to be parted from her children.

As they neared the equator the weather worsened. Lightning played around the ship; wind and rain beat down on them. The passengers were confined below decks, miserably hot and airless. In her cabin Mary left the porthole open and in consequence both she and her possessions were soaked; she shut it and the stifling heat was unbearable. The whole ship stank with the unendurable smells—human, animal and rotting food —of long confinement in tropical heat. Mary's headaches continued, but otherwise her health was good and her appetite voracious. Each day that passed her fears about her own ability to face hardship receded. Consciously she thought of this voyage as a training-ground for the life she might have to face in Africa, and rejoiced when she found herself able to withstand it. Her hands and feet were bitten raw by bugs, every morning she conducted an organised hunt for them; each evening they returned undefeated to the attack.

On October 19th, the day before they crossed the equator, she had a private anniversary to celebrate. Three years ago that day Robert Moffat had embarked at Gravesend for Africa. How little then had she expected to follow him. There was a fair wind and the ship was making good progress, but her thoughts were still tied to the home she had left. There were moments when the sudden realisation of what she was actually doing overwhelmed her and she wondered, panic-stricken, if she had made the right decision. She could not bear the thought that she might be forgotten in the years to come by those whom she so dearly loved at home. When her headaches troubled her she saw herself as being a burden and a hindrance to Robert and the work in Africa. Then she would calm herself with the remembrance of past mercies and a strong sense of the love of God.

Then the ship was discovered to have a leak and all hands were set to man the pumps. Next day the carpenter was put overboard and lashed to the side to see whether he could effect any repair. He lost two hammers and spent himself—but the leak could not be stopped. Mary, watching over the rail with the other passengers, was terrified in case sharks should discover the wretched carpenter and was struck afresh by the realisation of the harshness of the sailor's life.

Bickering and squabbling among the passengers was a daily occurrence, the result of too long and too close association in disagreeable circumstances, and aggravated by the very real fear that the ship might now be in some danger. 'A jangling company', Mary called it. Unfortunately Mrs Beck, a woman very tenacious of her rights, was often deeply involved in the friction, and Mr Beck, who was devoted to her, defended her hotly. In turn the other passengers made snide remarks about persons professing godliness. Mary, very conscious of her position as the future wife of a missionary, did her best not to become involved in these quarrels and so bring reproach on the Gospel.

28

It was not only among the passengers, however, that there was dissension. Between passengers and crew arguments also broke out. One evening the ladies wished to dance. The captain refused permission because Mrs Loudon, his first-class passenger, was not among the deputation that came to solicit his permission. The men joined in and there was a stiff quarrel which put the captain in a violent humour. This was probably not helped the next day by a change of wind which blew the vessel back two hundred and ten miles on her course before noon. Though the wind continued contrary, the captain recovered his temper, but the passengers were so offended that they refused to heal the breach. A dead calm fell on November 12th, and Mrs Beck confided to Mary that the captain had loaded his pistols and had been heard to say that if there was any more unpleasantness the cause of it would be sent forrard to live with the men and forbidden to come aft. It was said that the officers were being set on the passengers as spies; that the sailors were in a mutinous state; that the captain was meditating the blackest revenge.

In all this hullaballo of frayed tempers, stretched nerves, rumour and suspicion, Mary, rather to her own surprise, managed to remain uninvolved. Even when she was teased about her Lancashire accent and provincial outlook she maintained a calm demeanour, reminding herself that she could take a joke—though neither her brothers nor her future husband would have said this was one of her stronger points. The fact was that, though the headaches still persisted, she was sleeping well, getting stout and brown, and had an appetite that could devour salt beef or ham for breakfast, which she used to dislike at home.

On November 13th water became scarce and they began drinking salt water. There was a fine breeze, however, and everybody's thoughts were now, longingly, reaching forward to Africa. It had been over two months since the *British Colony* had sailed from Cowes—and England seemed a lifetime away. But there were still trials in store. As they ploughed south they ran into squalls and heavy seas. The ship began to roll and bucket so violently that they feared it would sink. Everyone was very conscious of the leak which the carpenter had failed to plug. The top mast split and a sail was carried away, Mary, thrown uncontrollably about her cabin, was bruised and sore. Her spirits had sunk to zero and she had become so nervous that she expected momentarily to be precipitated into disaster. Perhaps it was as well that Mrs Beck was now pregnant and needing a great deal of attention.

Nevertheless, they made a landfall, though almost immediately driven off again, and Mary began to prepare her things to go ashore. Now that the moment was actually at hand she was beset with doubts and fears. The reality of all that she had struggled towards for the last three years loomed up before her and terrified her. The irrevocable nature of the decision she had taken struck her with a force that was fresh and appalling. This was the land she would die in. What trials awaited her before that happened? Of Robert she could hardly bear to think. It was months since she had had any news of him, and years since she had seen him in the flesh. Was he even alive, or had he died while she was on the way to join him? Could she expect to see him when she landed—or must she still travel hundreds of miles to reach him? How could she do this? Who would help her? Though outwardly she remained calm, efficient, resourceful, inwardly her thoughts were in turmoil, her heart trembling with agitation.

On December 6th, at 4 a.m., a cry sounded through the ship. 'Land! Land!' She went on deck, prepared to rest on the strong arm of the Lord, and found Mr Melvill, Government Surveyor and warm friend to the London Missionary Society, had come on board to meet her.

She hardly dared to ask him the question that meant life or death.

'Is all well?'

'Well.'

'About 1 o'clock I went ashore and clasped my Robert in my arms. I was tolerably composed! To the last I was kept so by endeavouring to soothe his feelings which were very strongly manifest.' 'But oh! my cup of happiness seems almost full; here I have found him all my heart could desire, except his being almost worn out with anxiety, and his very look made my heart ache. Our worthy friend Melvill met me on board, and conducted me to his house, where a scene took place such as I never wish to experience again.'

Chapter 2

THEY WERE MARRIED on December 27th 1819 in St George's Church, Cape Town. Mr Melvill, the soul of kindness, gave his house for the reception and Dr Philip, who had been sent out from London by the Society to report on the state of the mission (and later became its superintendent in Southern Africa), gave the bride away. After the ceremony was over she cut off her dark curls and tucked her hair under a matron's cap—as became the wife of a minister. The pattern of their lives together had been set in those first few moments when they remet after long separation: Robert, individual, independent, given to moods both visionary and depressed; Mary, steady, disciplined, patient and organised, with a faith in the future that never wavered, ready always to comfort and support.

She had prepared herself, during the interminable voyage, for an existence of hardship and reproach at Moffat's side. No doubt the stories of the struggles of the Moravian brethren, when they first set foot on St Thomas in the West Indies and on Greenland, were much in her mind. In the relief of a safe landfall and the euphoria of high endeavour for Christ she was ready to bear any sufferings, while at the same time she could not but believe that the Africans would hear their message joyfully. But life is more complex than visions; reality harsher than dreams.

The first shock was to find that missionaries were greatly despised by the English of the Colony, 'and indeed it is not to be wondered at after the conduct of some'. There were both public and personal reasons why the London Missionary Society was at this moment in some disarray in Southern Africa. No doubt it was the latter that struck the newly-wedded Mary Moffat with most force. Two of the missionaries had married Hottentot wives and this was a cause of scandal among the white community. There was also dissension among some of the missionaries themselves, which must have seemed alarming and

31

saddening to a young bride fresh from England, where the image of missionary endeavour confronting heathen darkness had been unsullied by political difficulties and human weakness.

It was not an easy situation in which the missionaries found themselves and, being men like other men, they reacted in divergent ways. Cape Town in 1820 was still mainly a trading and victualling station, more Dutch than English, although following the Napoleonic wars power now lay with the British. The town also supported a garrison of four-and-a-half thousand British troops.

Beyond Cape Town the rich hinterland of the Colony stretched northwards some three or four hundred miles to a fluid, gradually expanding frontier, still well south of the Orange river. In this vast emptiness the Dutch farmers established and extended their farms, and small isolated trading towns struggled into being to service them. Though slavery had been abolished in Britain in 1807, the economy of the Colony in 1820 was still slave-based. Trade, the rights and freedoms of Dutch farmers, and supplies of cheap Hottentot labour were the chief concerns of the administration in Cape Town.

The LMS missionaries, strong-willed, independent young men burning with eagerness to spread the Gospel to the heathen, had seen their immediate task to lie among the Hottentots— poor, dispossessed and without rights. Working from their scattered mission stations, they set about this work with dedication; teaching reading and writing, gathering some of the wandering Hottentots into settlements, imparting simple skills and agricultural techniques, above all telling the Hottentot that in the eyes of God he was also a man with an immortal soul.

It was not long before this concern for these people led to charges being made against Boer farmers of ill treatment of their Hottentot servants—and even, openly, of slavery.

In 1812 this culminated in an official investigation into accusations brought by James Read—one of the missionaries who had a Hottentot wife—against Boer farmers of the Graaff Reinet and Uitenhage areas. The assizes took four months, and a thousand witnesses were summoned to be heard. Twelve charges out of thirty-six for murder and violence were proved— but the general indictment was not upheld. For both Boer farmers and British administration, the London Missionary

Society and its servants became objects of calumny and hatred.

The Government saw the missionaries as troublemakers, disturbing the delicate political balance of the Colony, bringing new ideas to those whose place was to accept and serve. Besides, the young men were not content to remain within the jurisdiction of the administration. It was part of their calling, basic to their reasons for being in Southern Africa at all, that they longed to carry their message further and further into the unknown lands to the north. They brought words of hope for all men, and many of them were unwilling to settle for a life within the confines—and restrictions—of comparative, if limited, civilisation while thousands beyond the boundaries of that civilisation perished in ignorance. In Government eyes this movement north posed insurmountable and unwelcome problems of control.

The situation of the Boer farmers was more complex. For the Boer farmers were Old Testament Christians and their religion was part of their whole ethos and way of life. But this religion had social as well as spiritual consequences. They believed, literally, in the curse of Noah—that the sons of Ham should be slaves for ever—and this fundamentalist belief made it possible for them, in their own eyes, to live upright Christian lives and yet treat the Hottentots like dogs. That the missionaries should bring in radically different ideas about the brotherhood of man was bad enough, but that these ideas should be inextricably linked to a new brand of Christianity was an affront to all that the Boer farmers held dear.

The husband whom Mary married in Cape Town was already showing himself to be among the most strong-willed, independent and far-seeing of the younger missionaries. Though he came from a warm and affectionate family, Robert Moffat had always been a 'loner', making his own decisions. The trade which he had first learned, that of a gardener, gave a man direct responsibility for the fruits of his own actions and long hours of solitude in which to come to terms with the quality of his nature and beliefs. He knew Whose he was and Whom he served. Though his loyalty to the London Missionary Society was to remain absolute and unwavering during the long years that lay before him, it was a loyalty *in absentia* rather than in close co-operation. Many of the young men who came out with the Society to Africa had in greater or lesser degree these initial qualities. Robert Moffat had already shown himself to have something more: the ability to master new disciplines and a personality which inspired trust and affection in Africans. He was not a young man whose religion made him either pompous or gloomy; on the contrary his cheerful, outgoing manner, his ability to use plain words in speech with other men, his enjoyment of his own and other people's essential humanity made him immensely likeable.

He had learned Dutch, to the extent that he could now speak and preach in it, and in 1817 permission had been gained from the Governor for two of the Society's new young missionaries to make a journey into Namaqualand, the arid, desert country which lay to the north-west of the Colony's borders well away from the fertile Boer farmlands of the north-east. After a journey full of trials, excitements, surprises, and hardships, Robert Moffat at last found himself alone at the remote kraal of Afrikaner, an outlaw Hottentot chief with a price on his head for murder. The older missionary who had been for some years with Afrikaner's people left very shortly after his young colleague arrived. Perhaps it was as well; relations with the chief's family were strained and the isolated, harsh life had begun to take its toll of body and spirit.

Left to himself, full of the enthusiasm of youth and his very first missionary endeavour, Robert Moffat laid the foundations of a friendship that was to last till Afrikaner died, and came to the conclusion that life in a country as barren as this was insupportable and that it was as much part of his duty to effect a change in this way of life as to look after the spiritual concerns of its people. He travelled widely—and painfully—to see if there were more fertile country within reach of the tribe and, finding none, was forced to conclude that any move would have to be either some hundreds of miles to the east or south towards the Cape.

It was then that he conceived, quite suddenly, the idea of taking Afrikaner back with him to the Cape, an idea which the chief—with a price on his head and miles of Boer territory to traverse before reaching Cape Town, immediately rejected. Nevertheless, in 1819, Robert Moffat, to the amazement of friends and enemies alike, arrived in Cape Town in company

34

with the outlawed chief. What was significant was not the triumphant reception given to the young man, nor the pardon granted to Afrikaner, but the astonishing friendship and confidence that the twenty-four-year-old Scot inspired in the elderly, wily, hardened Hottentot.

One other thing Robert Moffat discovered in the wilds of Namaqualand—the nature of his need for a wife. His was a love match. At Dukinfield Mary Smith had shared his passionate interest in missionary work and he had fallen in love with her. Although at first the necessity of providing himself with a wife in the harsh life to which he was going may have been uppermost, in the end he knew that—whatever the pressures—it was this young woman or no other. In Namaqualand, when it still seemed to him that any future together was doomed, he found that he wanted Miss Smith of Dukinfield not only to look after his material needs—at which he was bad—nor solely to be a bulwark against the temptations of the flesh, but to be a partner in the work, someone whom he could talk to and pray with, who would support and sustain him, with whom he could share his hopes and aspirations and his profound love of God. In an age when marriage was often a contract, with severe lines of demarcation drawn between the roles of husband and wife, Mary Moffat was fortunate that hers was not only a love match but a partnership.

There had been some dissension as to where Mr and Mrs Moffat were to go once married and ready to start work. Robert wanted to go back to Afrikaner, but he was dissuaded by Dr Philip and Mr Campbell, the two members of the deputation from the London headquarters of the Society. They saw Lattakoo, on the inhabited road to the north-east, as being a more important station, and to this Robert Moffat agreed, on condition that another missionary went to Afrikaner. Unfortunately there was a snag to this plan; the Government would not give permission for the young man to be stationed at Lattakoo, six hundred miles north of Cape Town, well beyond the Orange river. A Mr Read was already there and the excuse given was that 'Read and I could not reside together without dividing the affections of the people.' It was possible, however, that the Government might be persuaded to change its mind, and meanwhile the Moffats accompanied by Mr

Campbell, were to set out for Griqua Town, the nearest mission station to Lattakoo.

The Directors, many months away in London, might have some difficulty in controlling their young men on the African continent, but they took their parental role seriously. Though it was natural to think of women as the weaker sex and young women of good family were hedged about by protective prohibitions which must for many have resulted in fatal nervous frustrations, the LMS in its early years expected its missionaries to have wives and families, and took it for granted that the women would endure whatever hardships were to be met alongside their men. There were reasons for this policy, more profound than the obvious one that bachelor missionaries could turn to local women for aid and comfort and sexual fulfilment. The man who travelled into remote country among strange and savage peoples accompanied by his family signalled to them in a way that was unmistakable in any language that he came in peace, desiring to make a home among them and to establish stable contacts with them. The outlaw, the marauder, the pillager, the enemy, did not travel encumbered by women and small children.

Mary Moffat accepted that her place was at her husband's side, even if it killed her—as it did kill many wives. Indeed she would have been outraged at the suggestion that Robert Moffat should have pioneered alone. It was only a later generation that began to question whether the sacrifice was not too great.

The Directors gave her a letter to take out to Robert. It contained advice and practical hints on entering the matrimonial state. Realistically also he was told to acquaint himself with the hard facts of childbirth. 'Obedient to the request of the Deputation I have during my stay in this town made considerable proficiency in midwifery under one of the most eminent physicians in this town who has kindly and disinterestedly instructed me void of experience. You will conceive from this how great a favour you will do to procure an approved volume on that subject with plates and send to me. The sooner the better.' He was indeed to find this knowledge invaluable, not only to his own immediate family but, as experience added to his medical ability, to a 'practice' of many thousands.

They left Cape Town for Lattakoo on January 18th 1820.

36

Mary Moffat had been married just under a month, so it was in some respects a honeymoon journey for her and Robert—though somewhat constricted by the presence of John Campbell. He was considerably older, had little in common with the Moffats and had proposed himself for this trip to the north. Nevertheless even the seemingly pedestrian Mr Campbell concealed an adventurous spirit beneath his pedantic exterior and good relations were preserved until, towards the end of the long trail, a natural irritability began to magnify for each the faults of his fellow traveller.

It took seven weeks. Travel was by ox-waggon, slow, ponderous, subject to maddening delays, but in the end reliable. It had its charms too, and for Mary these must have been uppermost on this first journey. She had tried on the ship to prepare herself for the hardship of sleeping on boards, the rolling motion, the restricted space and all the other peculiarities of ox-travel that Robert had written about. Now she found herself mistress of a compact small home on wheels, behind twelve pale brown oxen driven by a Hottentot. The waggon was packed not only with all that was needed to make it a reasonably comfortable habitat while travelling but also with possessions and provisions to ensure self-sufficient living for many months to come.

Fortunately Mary was naturally tidy and well organised. Robert, who found it difficult to control his possessions, all of which he liked to be always where he could lay his hands on them, must have resigned the packing of the waggon to her with a sigh of relief. There was a forechest across the front, forming the driver's seat, in which were kept supplies of tea, coffee, rice, etc. in canisters and bags. Across the back was an afterchest filled with bulk stores, from which the forechest was replenished weekly. Lining either side were smaller chests for crockery and utensils; at the back of the forechest room for trunks containing clothes. Over the space in the centre there was a stretcher on which the mattress went and under which numerous boxes and containers were packed away. During the day a movable back was put up to make a seat and a small table could be let down from one of the sides. Underneath the waggon itself were slung the pots and pans, and round the sides sailcloth bags held provisions.

The oxen were slow, stupid, often temperamental beasts; the

waggon immensely cumbersome. The hazards of heat, lions, lack of water—or too much water—were always present, and both the route and the times of travelling had to be geared to cope in the best way possible with those natural enemies, crawling from waterhole to fountain, moving in the dawn and at dusk, herding and guarding the nervous, easily stampeded beasts when they were out of the yoke.

Nevertheless this first journey was idyllic. Not only was it the real beginning to their married life together, in an establishment, however small, of their own, but they were at last moving towards the reality of the work—away from the scandals and sophistication of the town. From Beaufort West, 350 miles north and close to the Colony boundary, Mary wrote home on February 17th, anxious to reassure her parents that all was well.

'My beloved Parents. . . . We are all well and excepting a little headache, my health is extraordinary. It is true I feel a little feeble and languid in the very heat of the day, but am not sickly as I always was at home in warm weather. I never was more vigorous than I am now in the cool of the day; and when I consider the manner in which we live, just eating and sleeping when it is convenient, I am truly astonished. It is frequently one or two o'clock when we outspan. I like waggon travelling better than I expected. It is not so fatiguing. I have none of those hardships which I looked for. Our table is generally well-spread, better than we shall look for when poor missionaries; this is partly owing to Mr Campbell being with us, and partly to Moffat's being well-known in the country, and receiving liberal presents. . . . I have never met so much hospitality in my life as I have witnessed in Africa, though the Dutch are considered fond of saving.

. . . I trust you will have received a letter from Robert, dated 31st ultimo, at the Hex river. Since that time we have been in a perfect desert called the Karroo, and in the last ten days we never saw but one house till last night, about two hours ride from here. For eight of those days we have been on the banks of the Gamka river. . . . The banks are thick with the long-thorned mimosa, which is certainly very beautiful. In some places I have seen the old tree fallen with age, and from the root a young flourishing large tree, and both attached to each other. There are few other things except succulent plants and everything in the desert, except the mimosas, has a blue and yellow sickly hue with the saltpetre. We have scarcely seen any grass for a fortnight. . . . The roads have been very good indeed—in many parts as fine as any turnpike road in England. . . .

Some persons thought it imprudent of us to travel at this season of the year; but from all we see and hear, we think it by far the best, notwithstanding the heat, for the rivers we have to cross are at present chiefly without water, except a little stream the same as your river in summer. . . .

We have seen no beasts of prey. . . . M saw the footmarks of one about a mile from where we outspanned one day; and at the farmhouse we saw last week we were informed that sixty lions had been killed in six years in that neighbourhood. At that farm we saw two tame ostriches, which to our great surprise devoured pebble stones like bread. . . .

The place where we are now is the newly-formed district where our missionary Taylor has accepted of a church—which bye-the-bye is only a room in a farmhouse, with two beds in it. I have been in many odd-looking places to worship, but never one like that. There are only about six houses in the place and the Landrost's is one of them. . . . He visited our tent on arrival here and courteously invited us to his house to eat. . . . We go to every meal, and then return to the waggons. . . . He supplies us plentifully with delicious fruit from his garden, though we eat it three times a day at his house. . . .

We leave this place today for Griqua Town, which is ten days comfortable journey from here, good roads, plenty of water the most of the way, and a fine moon which is valuable to African travellers.'

Beaufort West was not only the frontier of the Colony, it was also the end of the honeymoon. Although Mary wrote cheerfully of conditions on the road to the next major stopping place, the mission station at Griqua Town, it was the optimism of reassurance and inexperience. However arduous journeys might be within the Colony—and they could be arduous—once over the border the kind of life which bore any resemblance at all to what she had known disappeared. No longer was there the possibility of finding remote, settled homesteads, seeing white faces, whether friendly or hostile; the tenuous contacts with home and friends, which had been gradually spun out ever

39

thinner and thinner as they progressed north, now almost vanished. 'Poor Mrs Helm has not had a letter for five years.' The pleasant, picnic-like stops beside mimosa-laden river banks were only memories. It was nineteen days to the Orange river, across Bushman country, desert, the haunt of lions, and the weather was very warm. Water, after all, was not so plentiful or so easy to come by as she had anticipated, and unending days in a confined space had contracted the waggon which had once seemed such a comfortable little home.

Tempers frayed, habits and opinions, human and insignificant at the start of the journey, began to assume unpleasing importance. Robert Moffat and Mr Campbell fell out over a number of issues. The former thought the latter prejudiced and quarrelsome; the latter, no doubt, thought the former a smug, self-opinionated young man. Mary began to learn one of the hard lessons of missionary life, that the nature of man, obstinate and often unregenerate in the best of circumstances, can be a constant stumbling block, even to those who live in Faith and with love, in the worst. She had married a pioneer, a young man with fire in his belly and a single-minded spiritual vision. Such men do not look for an easy life; nor do they always make life easy for others. But they are the men who change the world—in great or small degree.

They crossed the Orange river, a quarter of a mile wide, easily because it was still the dry season, and arrived in Griqua Town on March 13th. Griqua Town was a Hottentot settlement, the interior headquarters of the mission. Beyond that, four days further on into the unknown and unsettled country lay Lattakoo where for some time there had been an unsuccessful mission station, rent with internal quarrels and with little sign of external influence. In the vast stretch of country with a scattered turbulent population which lay before them, Lattakoo was a tiny, insignificant outpost set down beside a section of the Bechuana tribe. It had the grave disadvantage of not lying near an adequate supply of water, although there was just such a fountain about a day's journey away at the source of the River Kuruman. But the mission had to be where the people were and to the tribesmen it was of more importance to be able to find thorn bushes to make kraals to protect the cattle from lions, and of this material there was still an abundance at Lattakoo.

Robert Hamilton was at Lattakoo; a gentle, industrious good man considerably older than the Moffats. He had been there for some years, but with little to show for it. Unfortunately he was burdened with a family problem which must have affected the whole atmosphere in which he worked. Mrs Hamilton, who had followed her husband out to the mission field, had not the nature or temperament to meet the demands of this rigorous, dedicated life. Confronted by it she became bitter and discontented, blaming her own unhappiness on her husband. For Mary, who had fought for two-and-a-half years to join Robert Moffat in work which she felt to be of immense importance, to find herself at close quarters with open marital strife must have been a shock and a great trial. She was to have to endure it, with increasing intensity, over the next three years.

She did not tell her parents about it. It was, in any case, one of the subjects about which the less said the better—though Mrs Hamilton herself was both voluble and articulate. There were many things Mary did not tell her parents in those early days, and what she could not disguise she wrote about with cheerful briskness. Over one thing, however, she did not need to dissimulate. She was happy, whatever the material conditions, 'remarkably happy'.

The material conditions were very different from what she had envisaged. The vision of a neat little mission house of her own shared with Robert, in the midst of a community of smiling 'sable' Africans all eager to learn what they had come to teach, vanished without trace. Griqua Town had been a disappointment and to Mary, herself efficient, industrious, responsible, the local people seemed woefully indolent and feckless. They did not care, that was the truth; they did not care at all about any of the things that she held dear.

The last part of the journey, from Griqua Town to Lattakoo, had been terrible. She was exhausted, no doubt not only from physical tiredness but also from the nervous tension of discovering reality. The country, dry, flat, frighteningly vast, in no way resembled the English landscape which was her only yardstick: except at one place, the Kuruman fountain, where they outspanned for the last night. Here an abundance of water gave encouragement to some trees and plants.

It was not even as though Lattakoo was the final destination and she could begin, however precariously, to set up a home. Permission had not yet come through for Robert Moffat to stay in Lattakoo, and it was by no means certain that it ever would. This visit, to what they both hoped would ultimately be their station, was in the nature of a temporary inspection. They lived in the vestry room of the mud-walled, thatched church, their possessions still packed in the waggon. There was curiosity, a kind of condescension, in the way people came—occasionally—to look at them or listen to them, but certainly no piety. It was a world of very different values, and the task of changing these values appeared dauntingly huge. The reversal of work roles between men and women struck Mary forcibly, especially as it seemed to make impossible one of the projects which she had visualised for herself—a girl's school.

She took it for granted that the gift of the Gospel which they had brought was of overriding importance. The self-analysis and questioning of later generations had not yet been born. What she saw of physical harshness, discomfort and insecurity in the lives of the people around her must have given her a frightening glimpse of the struggle that lay ahead to maintain her own oasis of civilisation, far less spread it to others. Robert might be content to live in a domestic muddle paying little attention to the niceties of home-making—she could not. On her would devolve the whole weight of the civilising side of the mission which would enable Robert to impart his great spiritual vision. She noted, with acumen and disapproval, that so far none of the missionaries at Lattakoo could speak the local language.

In July, after three months of this insecure, unproductive life, they returned to Griqua Town, where—quite suddenly and surprisingly—permission had just been granted by the Colony Government for Robert Moffat to remain. They were to be there for another ten months, living in a kind of vacuum, uncertain where their real work was to begin and take root; in the midst of a community of half-breed European, Hottentot, Bushman, Bechuana, with whom they did not feel wholly in sympathy. Both of them during their time at Lattakoo had become convinced that it was with the scattered, feckless, unvalorous peoples of the Bechuana that their mission lay. Robert Moffat, this self-taught young man, started to study

Greek and Sechuana, and probably made himself unbearable to his older colleagues by making no bones about his disapproval of their misuse of some of the Society's property. He was a man of practical ability with a craftsman's respect for tools. He could not bear to see them neglected. He felt it his duty to let the Society know what was going on. He disagreed strongly with Mr Campbell that the missionaries had any right to interfere with the political affairs of the people they had come to work with, a view which he held to the end of his life and which frequently brought him into conflict with those who felt that spiritual and political change must go hand in hand. He took a sweeping look round the position of the mission in Southern Africa in 1820 and decided that the foundation on which it stood was rotten. He longed to get in and build afresh. He was arrogant, priggish, at a loose end, conscious of his own strength and the power of the Lord in him, itching to take charge, to put things in order, to get on with the job.

Mary Moffat, while supporting and consoling Robert, helping him through the fits of depression to which he was always prone, set herself to master the new skills of house-keeping and home-making required of her in these very different circumstances. She was planning always for the return to Lattakoo, noting how the missionary families in Griqua Town managed their households, commenting that her 'good man has promised to order matters differently when he builds'. She did not like the lay-out of the ordinary mission house with the kitchen separated from it at the back. 'If one turns one's back, perhaps half of the food is gone and spoons, knife, fork, or what-ever lies about is away.' The stores too stood apart from the main house and this she would alter. It encouraged thieving to have them out of sight. 'No servant will like it as she will not then have an opportunity of displaying her liberality. They seem to account all Europeans stingy.' The houses were norm-ally built with a forehouse into which one entered directly and which was the large living space for the family. At each end doors opened into a small room, the one a bedroom, the other a study.

All washing was done in the river, beating the clothes against the stones, until the substance as well as the dirt was beaten out of them. Robert had promised that when they were settled he would make her tubs. In the meantime he had made her sieves of all kinds, for meal and corn and flour, and had built her a brick oven. 'We leaven our bread always keeping a lump of leaven, and the bread is as sweet as any yeast could make it. . . . We have the wheat all ground down together.'

Each week the missionary households killed a sheep to feed themselves and their servants. The fat was melted and used in cooking. Soap and candles, a long troublesome job, were made from the hard fat. Mutton was salted for the summer, and some meat smoked to keep the moth out of it. The cows, in contrast to the English cows she knew, gave only a thin trickle of milk. But the Bechuana would collect this over a period in a scraped goatskin and hang it in a warm place until it curdled. At first Mary shrank from this delicacy, but she quickly adapted herself and found it delicious.

There was another local custom which she resisted, until circumstances forced her to admit that it suited the place and the climate better than any she could import. This was the habit of smearing the dirt floors once a week with cow dung. She said to herself—and probably to Robert—that she could do without that dirty trick. But she could not. In a short while she found that it was the only way to lay dust and fleas, and presently she was viewing her 'fine clear green cow dung floors with as much complacency as the best scoured'.

Then two things happened, one she must have anticipated with pleasure, the other she dreaded. In July she became pregnant for the first time; and in December she fell so seriously ill that her life was despaired of.

Death was not something to shrink from with averted eyes. To see the doorway of death as the threshold of a better life in a world to come was not to abdicate from the responsibilities of the present. On the contrary, the reality of the world to come gave sharpness and urgency to the tasks in hand. Robert Moffat's strong sense of hell caused him anguish and sorrow when he contemplated the millions who had not heard the good news, and drove him relentlessly, with compassionate concern, to try to bring it to them. Mary had faced many times the possibility of her own death, the death of her parents, never seeing Robert again. Grief was not lessened by a readiness to prepare for the next world; but the sense of continuity brought consola-

44

tion to those who were constantly reminded of the transience of life and saved them from the sin of fatalistic despair.

She remained desperately ill throughout the rest of her pregnancy. Robert tried to conceal the situation from her parents in Dukinfield, aware of the burden of responsibility that their grief would cast on him. There was no professional medical man for hundreds of miles and, with the help of Buchan's Domestic Medicine and the accumulated wisdom of older missionary wives, he struggled to save her. The Chief and his wife from Lattakoo, who had been taken with the young couple during their stay on the station, several times sent messages commanding her not to die. Permission came through for Robert to return to Lattakoo after all, but he could not move so long as his beloved partner was so heavily afflicted. Mary prepared herself calmly for her deathbed and the parting with her dear Mr Moffat.

But she did not die. Contrary to all expectations, on April 12th 1821, the baby was born: Mary, a sturdy, placid child who had been given very little chance of being anything but sickly. On the 17th of May 1821, the Moffat family finally returned to Lattakoo.

Chapter 3

THEY DID NOT go alone. Mr and Mrs Melvill, their good
friends from Cape Town, and a Wesleyan husband and wife
went with the party. There was the advantage of friendship and
experienced support at a time when Mary, coping with a new
small baby, needed it; but the disadvantage of continual distraction from being able to settle down to tackle the arduous
responsibilities of her new domestic life. With her long illness
and the arrival of her first baby, it seemed to Mary that she had
got nowhere during her sixteen months as a missionary wife.
Now at last there was the opportunity, but temporary visitors
did not make it easy to grasp.

The very arrival at Lattakoo was unnerving. Chief Mothibi's
junior wife, a woman of about forty-five, daughter of a Korana
chief, hastened towards Mary as she alighted from the waggon,
gave her a hearty handshake, grasped the baby out of her arms
before she quite knew what was happening, pressed it to her
breast and kissed it. Several of the other Bechuana women
followed suit. Robert, its father, thought this 'truely interesting'.
Mary probably had rather different feelings at the sight of her
month-old darling clasped to breasts smeared with fat and red
ochre and subject to indiscriminate embraces. She believed,
however, that it was not just herself and her husband but her
whole family whose lives were given to the Lord in service to
these people, so she refrained from snatching the baby back.
The infant, with no such concepts of love and duty, nevertheless seems to have behaved admirably and not protested at all.
At this moment Mary became MaMary to the Bechuana, a
name she was to bear to the end of her life—MaMary, mother
of Mary, her first-born.

They came back to a multitude of tribulations. Robert had
waited a long time for a station and responsibilities of his own.
It seems to have been accepted from the day of his arrival in
Lattakoo, although Robert Hamilton had already been there

some years, that the driving force was Robert Moffat's. He was determined to examine and cleanse the church, so as to have a worthy instrument upon which to build. The trouble was that there was virtually no church, in the sense of a body of worshippers, and what there was consisted solely of the missionaries and the Hottentot workers whom they had brought from the Cape. And even within this small band there were grievous iniquities.

For Mary there were the equally difficult, though perhaps less searing, problems of home-making. Some of their heavy baggage, over which there were often long delays in unloading from the ship and then bringing up country, had arrived during the months of waiting. She knew enough now of life in the wilds to be grateful for that, 'though they had left behind what was most needful, the drawers containing all my useful clothing pieces of fabrics, linen haberdashery, etc. etc. and it puts me a little about'. Robert set to, almost immediately, to build a decent house, but until it was ready they lived in a one-room hut, the roof supported by pillars made of the trunks of trees, the walls of reed daubed inside with clay and a thatch which offered no protection from wind or rain. The drudgery was terrible. All her life Mary had been accustomed to servants who knew their work, and here such a luxury was impossible. She wrestled with a wood fire on a flat hearth, filling her eyes and the hut with smoke. She had no furniture and very little space to stow her possessions; every household chore had to be accomplished with the maximum labour and the minimum help.

As if this were not enough, she was never alone. A new, young, pretty missionary wife with a baby was a matter of tremendous interest and excitement to the local people. The women were inquisitive, fascinated, suspicious, afraid. That they might help her never entered their heads—and indeed much of what she did must have appeared incomprehensible to them. All day groups of women, who in Mary's view should have had better things to do, crowded round her door, peeping in, chattering, exclaiming, shutting out the light and filling the tiny room with the smell of their greased, unwashed bodies. She was desperate to be able to speak to them, to have some communication, some way of telling them why she was here and explaining what she was doing.

Sometimes, instead of trying to ignore them, she would ask them in, arranging the boxes and stools which were all the furniture she possessed so that they could sit round and be friendly, and perhaps help her to learn some Sechuana. She visualised a time when they might sit in a class like this while she taught them to read their Bibles. But they chatted and laughed together, touched and examined everything in the room—ignoring their hostess. She tried to amuse them but they took no notice; they were amused enough already by the fascinating strangeness of this little house with its foreign occupant. She had asked them in because she longed to come to some sort of terms with them, to work with them in the way that she had always hoped to do; but after a short while she longed equally passionately for them to go away, to leave her in peace. When they did go she would fetch a bucket of water and soap and scrub her stools and boxes to rid them of the grease. After a while she discovered that they preferred anyway to sit on the floor.

It was a back-breaking, despairing, seemingly endless struggle. Robert was fully occupied with struggles of his own, for he had to turn his hand to all the basic chores that would make it possible for them to live there at all—building, the problem of water, starting a garden, which meant clearing and preparing ground to grow crops and vegetables, repairing, carpentry, making vessels and utensils. He was a devoted husband, but the reality of the ideal of partnership—which both so much cherished—meant for Mary that she had to solve the problems of baby, household and wanted/unwanted visitors alone. She could not show herself unequal to the task and so add to Robert's burdens by appealing to him for help.

Once the Melvills and the Wesleyans had departed there was no one whom she could trust with the baby. Mary junior, who had started life robust and flourishing, was now a sickly little thing whose constant wailing added to her mother's trials. MaMary often looked with envy at the Bechuana women with their babies tied on their backs and was sometimes tempted to copy them. It would have comforted the child and simplified her work. But she refrained. She felt that to be seen accepting such a custom would indicate that she approved of other practices which were heathen.

So she battled on, rebellious, depressed, stubbornly determined, till one day, trying vainly to light the wood fire, with smoke in her eyes the baby keening on the mat beside her, it all seemed too much and she burst into tears, crying out, 'Is *this* the sort of work I've left home and friends to spend my life doing, in this uncongenial heathen land?'

And inside her, out of the strength of her faith and the depth of a commitment which she had almost forgotten, a voice said, 'If I may be a hewer of wood and a drawer of water in the temple of my God, am I not still blessed and privileged?'

It was a turning point. Nothing was changed as far as the physical efforts were concerned, but her sense of priorities was restored. She was able to recognise that she could make this as much the Lord's work as the spiritual teaching that she had most ardently—and so far unavailingly—hoped to be engaged in. Yet there were still times of depression, chiefly when letters arrived—either from family and friends in England or other missionary wives at the Cape—for on these occasions her correspondents took it for granted that she was actively imparting the things of the spirit to eager listeners and drew rosy pictures out of their own imaginations of her circumstances. She knew that their ignorance made it impossible for them to understand the true situation—yet still the letters seemed to reproach her. 'The time will come,' she wrote to one such friend, 'when I shall do something, especially when I get a little of the language, which with the help of God I will do my utmost to obtain. I conceive conversation with these people is a most likely means for usefulness. I trust the Lord will not disappoint my hopes but will yet grant me the honour of doing something for Him in Africa.' It was a far cry from the dreams at Dukinfield.

She was not content, however, just to leave it to the Lord. It was not in her nature to resign herself to adverse circumstances. She set herself to consider seriously every part of her daily work to see what, if any, of it could be dispensed with to give her more time. Here she found herself in an area of controversy. There were some among the missionaries, and it would seem likely that these were to be found more among the men than the women, who felt that they should live as close to the manners and customs of the local people as possible, including eating

49

local food: others considered that, on the contrary, it was part of the function of the mission household to provide new patterns of domestic living.

Mary Moffat took an entirely practical view, that it was time enough to alter her own customs when there was absolutely no other alternative, but 'it appears to us that European constitutions require tolerable good living in this climate. I am convinced there is a necessity for missionaries to have wives to cheer them under the multiple sorrows and trials of their lives, to provide comfortable food for the support of their bodies under hard labours, and to enable them to set before the heathen an example of cleanliness and decency.' Robert Moffat heartily agreed with her.

He had his troubles too. He also was overwhelmed by hard physical work, and he had constantly to strive for the welfare of the infant church. Here all was not well. It was of supreme importance that the church, the visible body of believers, the only witness that the Africans had to the truth of the new Gospel that was being preached, should be seen to live up to its own demands. Robert Moffat believed that the Bechuanas knew nothing of God and did not credit them with any religious beliefs of their own. To preach about a spirit was complex and difficult, but this Spirit had become man and laid down guidelines for His followers and it was through those followers that something, however dimly, could be perceived of the love and mercy and justice of God. The church had to accept within its fellowship only those who gave real evidence of a changed life—and it had to cut off, temporarily at least, those who departed from the way they had chosen.

Mrs Hamilton, the other missionary wife on the station, was such a one. She was a woman of much stronger mind than her gentle, retiring husband, who might in other circumstances have successfully managed committees and run women's meetings. But the life at Lattakoo and her husband in his acceptance of it drove her mad. She had a fearful temper—had even been known to tell a missionary to go to hell—and some thought her insane. Indeed it may well have been that the appalling frustrations of a life she hated temporarily upset the balance of her mind. One of her complaints against Mr Hamilton, which clearly was of great importance to her, was that he fell asleep and snored while she was talking to him. She wanted to leave him and go back to England, an unheard-of situation and one that caused great scandal. She abandoned his bed, contrary to his will and when he timidly proposed a reconciliation she said, 'Never.' Everyone knew what was going on and something clearly had to be done about it.

It was an appalling dilemma for Robert Moffat. He was a man of peace who, though he did not hesitate to stand up for what he considered right, took no pleasure in rows. For Mary too, forced by circumstances to see and talk to Mrs Hamilton constantly, it must have been one more almost insupportable trial to add to those she already had to bear. Robert Moffat decided, with the concurrence of her husband, that Mrs Hamilton must be separated from the church, and this was duly carried out. She accused him of being a man without understanding or pity and told his wife that she would never belong to any church of which he was in charge.

As if that were not enough for the wretched Mr Hamilton, his son William, quite a small boy, was one day accused of pushing a Bechuana girl off the end of a waggon. The girl, unfortunately, was the daughter of a chief. Robert and Mr Hamilton went to see the parents and found the child upset but unhurt. Mr Hamilton apologised, trying to explain that it was only children playing; there had been no evil intent. The chief agreed; but the women were unappeased and it was feared that William might be in danger of some retaliation. So a decision was taken, no doubt with considerable relief, that Mrs Hamilton and the children should retire for a while to Griqua Town.

Language was an extremely important issue. Robert preached in Dutch, because the Hottentots who formed a large part of the church membership spoke Dutch; or in English, for the missionary families. But he and Mary recognised at the very beginning that there would be no progress until they were able to speak to the Bechuana face to face in their own tongue. Robert had imagined that he could do this without much difficulty—as he had so far acquired every other language—Dutch, Hebrew, Greek, Latin. But the situation was very different. There was no time to sit down and study, hard physical work and constant problems saw to that. Neither did he have books or a teacher to help him. All his communication

51

with the local people had to be through interpreters, and these proved to be very unsatisfactory go-betweens. No interpreter would admit to misunderstanding the original concept in English or in Dutch, so that it was sometimes only much later that Robert discovered how wildly his teaching had been misinterpreted.

The interpreters, too, who had come with them from Griqua Town and the Cape, did not always provide the Christian witness that was expected of them as well as their technical skill. There was one major scandal, involving a young Hottentot in the service of the mission and an African interpreter, which must have rocked the whole station.

For some little time Mary had feared that Bonsenye, a young Bechuana girl whom she was trying to train as a servant, was pregnant. The Bechuana held very strong views on adultery and fornication, and a girl in such a situation would be driven out into the wilds and forced to kill the child when it was born. The father was a Hottentot. He admitted his responsibility but was quite unrepentant. Robert Moffat wanted to drive him away from Lattakoo but here, to his surprise, he came up against opposition from Mr Hamilton.

The girl had at one time been in the household of Cedras, an interpreter. Cedras must have been a man of strong temper: he had already been cut off from the church because of mis-behaviour. Now he insisted that he, rather than the Moffats or her chief, had the right to decide what happened to Bonsenye. He went to her hut one day, bound her hands and took her back to his own house where he tied her to a post. She screamed. The station was roused. The two missionaries hurried over to see what was happening and found Cedras with a sjambok in his hands. They asked him what he was going to do. He refused to reply. Robert was convinced that as soon as his back was turned Cedras would assault the wretched girl. He strode into the hut, untied her and brought her out. Cedras seized her from him and they struggled. He would not listen to any arguments nor heed the warning that he might be guilty of murder if he carried out his threats. Someone called the chief, Mothibi, who came and took hold of the girl, insisting that her bound hands be loosened. Cedras refused, and again there was a struggle during which Bonsenye was at last freed. Escorted by the missionaries and the chief—and no doubt a good many fascinated spectators—she was brought back to Mary's safe keeping.

The matter, however, was not finished. Cedras still threatened and the missionaries were impelled to go to the chief, who agreed to order him to leave the girl with the Moffats. Then the Bechuanas began to mutter that Frederick, who was the cause of all the trouble, had got off too lightly. Frederick was again spoken to and was told that he must go back to his own country. He agreed also to give the girl a cow in compensation. The missionaries called on the Bechuana chief to tell him of this result. The chief agreed that it was just and, on their pleading with him, told them that the child's life would be spared and it was theirs to do with as they liked. The climax of this affair, the scene with Cedras, took place on a Sunday and so upset were the Moffats and Robert Hamilton by it that they felt unable to hold the Communion service in the evening.

Two things about Robert Moffat are illustrated by this incident. He was a man of peace with great physical courage. In circumstances much more alarming than this which he was presently to meet, he never carried a weapon, relying on the strength of his faith, his conviction of the rightness of the action he was taking, and his own personality. And the only times that he interfered with the ways in which people governed themselves were in particular cases of injustice or cruelty—when he did not hesitate to intercede through the chief. He believed strongly in political non-interference; his work was to preach and teach the new way of the Spirit, from which other changes would flow. Not only to preach and teach the Gospel, but also to live it. Though for him, as for the Bechuana, Bonsenye's situation was one of sin—and on this his stance was absolute and undeviating—where their response was rejection, his was to care. Mary, overburdened as she was, immediately took the girl back into her protection.

Relief from the overworked, harassing—and on the whole depressing—life of every day took the form of itinerating. John Campbell, on deputation, had been struck by the 'fortress' mentality of the mission at Lattakoo and had written Mr Hamilton some very sensible and practical instructions about getting out and about. 'Novelty and curiousity may induce to

53

regular attendance at the commencement of a mission, but as force of these fail indifference will prevail. Continuing to give regular daily addresses in an empty place,'—and, he might have added, in a strange language—'may be some labour to the missionary, but alone it is of little use. . . . When the heathen will not come to the missionary, the missionary should go to the heathen. To the man who has come ten thousand miles to teach the heathen, it will not be considered very irksome to walk a thousand steps further to reach their ears.'

It was good advice and it accorded with Robert Moffat's own inclination to seek out the people, but it perhaps took too little account of the realities of life beyond the boundaries of civilisation. Mr Campbell went home to Britain, to write two interesting books about his African travels; the missionary families, left beyond the frontiers of the Colony, needed courage and faith in unusual measure to stay and maintain their precarious foothold in the mission field—far less venture out from it into the unknown. As always, in similar circumstances, when between those who work in the field and those who direct from headquarters there is a gulf of distance and perspective, a certain amount of irritation began to pervade correspondence dealing with how matters should proceed on the ground. When into the bargain letters between Lattakoo and London could take many months—and a year or more to receive an answer— and visits from the regional superintendent of the Society at the Cape were perforce few and far between, it is not surprising that Robert Moffat early made it plain that the work of this mission station would be run as the missionaries on the spot thought best.

Robert did itinerate, and Mary went with him. 'It is a rule of mine that when my husband goes with the waggon for more than two days I go with him, unless circumstances render it very improper,' she wrote to her parents—that was unless she were obviously pregnant. It was a relief to get away from the station and its problems, but she also did not trust him to look after himself if he went alone, 'he will not be at trouble to make himself comfortable'. She could do that—even with long, tiring rolling stretches of eight to twelve hours travel, a child to keep amused and soothed, such heat by day that the men had to run over the sandy soil to prevent their feet being burned, or bitter cold by night.

54

The first thing on outspanning was always to make a fire, for protection from lions, for warmth, and for the first cup of tea or coffee. It was Robert's job to make the domestic fire and put the kettle on. Mary would not emerge from the waggon until this was done, and indeed she thought any missionary a poor sort who did not take this much thought for his wife's comfort.

The hazards were considerable. They were many miles from any form of assistance if something went wrong and their only transport was painfully slow. Strange diseases could strike suddenly and run a swift and terrible course. Robert, with great self-confidence, had taken on the doctoring of the little community, with copious laxatives and bleeding, but many illnesses lay outside the scope of even professional medical knowledge. Wild animals, particularly lions, were common and could be aggressive. Natural disasters, drought, famine, tempest, abounded. On one occasion, on the way to Griqua Town to collect their goods, after they had been overtaken by a terrible storm of thunder, lightning and rain, it was discovered that a blind Bechuana woman who was travelling with them had somehow been left behind when they inspanned. Searchers returned to look for her, but with no success. Seven days later, on the way home, she was found. The people, owners of great herds of cattle, were subject to constant tribal warfare, raids and counter-raids, the whims of tyrannical chiefs. Rumours of catastrophes flew about the country with a speed only possible in places where there are no mechanical devices for transmitting news.

In the midst of all this, pregnant with the Gospel that they longed to bring to as many perishing souls as possible, confident in the faith that their destiny was in the hands of their God, and serene in the love they bore each other, the Moffat family itinerated. When, out on the open veldt, the little group, unprotected except from wild beasts, sat together, white and coloured, round their fire conducting their evening worship, it must have been plain to any watcher that something new had entered Africa.

Chapter 4

WHAT EXACTLY IT was all about, however, was not clear to anyone, and the difficulties of communication were still immense. 1822 dawned. Robert had made very little progress with the language; there were no local converts, and Mary's life was no easier. It was true that she had gathered a few more possessions, Robert had made a bedstead and shelves for their books, and her household had grown. She had three Bechuana girls now, to look after the abominable wood fire, grind corn, wash linen, and so on; but they were difficult and choosy and if worked too hard they left immediately. Many years later her daughter was to say that Mary Moffat had a real talent for training people in household work. She acquired it slowly and with much grief.

Theft was an everyday occurrence. Every kind of possession was stolen, tools, household goods, cattle, produce. Once Mary, carrying her baby, begged the woman who was helping her in the kitchen to go so that MaMary could lock up and get to church for the service, whereupon the woman seized a piece of wood and prepared to hurl it at her employer's head. Mary escaped hastily, leaving her victorious opponent in the unguarded kitchen able to appropriate anything she wanted. It was not unusual for thieves to take advantage of the church services to break into the houses of those who were engaged in them.

Mary still suffered from the constant presence in her home of unruly visitors. Access to the people was all-important to the Moffats. It was for the sake of the people that they had come to Africa, but to keep connections open Mary had to pay a high price. Anybody who liked, men and women, could come to her hut to touch and stare. Sometimes the room would be so crowded that she and Robert could barely get in. Some of their visitors talked, some slept, some pilfered openly. Everything was covered with the red ochre of their body grease. When Robert was out working, which was a major part of the time,

Mary was a prisoner in her own home—unable to leave because there was nowhere else for her to go and afraid that if she did everything they possessed would be stolen. She would delay the meals, hoping that the audience would leave, but when they did not she and Robert would eat hastily in the midst of an indifferent crowd sitting round and despatching lice.

Perhaps this torment would have been easier to bear if she could have seen her husband's work prospering. But it was not, and she had Robert's burdens also to share with him. There was a total indifference to his real message, and no willingness to listen to him unless it were in return for a gift or service. Knives were coveted, metal spoons could be melted down, tobacco, cloth, medicines. When these were refused he suffered ridicule and abuse, and often lost them anyway by theft. His practical skills were much in demand to make or mend tools and household articles. He was expected to. be at everyone's beck and call. The Bechuanas thought the missionaries' possessions endless, their time unlimited, their energy inexhaustible—and all of it at their disposal.

The Moffats were only too urgently, and frustratingly, aware that possessions were precious and could be ill spared on a salary of £80 a year—even if it had been possible to replace them; and of the transience of time and energy, both being, perhaps fatally, consumed in the vital but spiritually unproductive work of building and planting. The site of Lattakoo was on a light sandy soil and nothing at all grew without irrigation, a science until then unknown among the Bechuanas. With enormous effort Robert Moffat and Mr Hamilton, with what help they could get, dug a water ditch which led from the Kuruman river for some miles to the mission garden.

The effect on the garden was predictable, the effect on the Bechuana women was not. Seeing that the water actually made things grow, the women cut open the irrigation ditch as it passed, flooding their own patch of ground, dissipating the water, depriving the mission of any at all—even for cooking. In vain the missionaries pleaded with them to leave the channel intact; either Robert Moffat or Mr Hamilton would have to walk several miles, often in the hottest part of the day, to make repairs. The women watched, and as soon as they left broke open the breaches again. At last they were obliged to irrigate at night, keeping watch, if they were to produce any food at all.

When they tried to explain to the women the reasons for what they were doing the only result was the destruction of the dam so painfully built to feed the irrigation ditches. In February, Mary wrote home, 'After our hearts had both been often excessively pained at Robert being obliged to spend so much time in the garden, we have had four dishes of vegetables out of it this year.' Their diet consisted mainly of meat, sheep that they had to buy at a distance, many of which were stolen on the way to Lattakoo.

It had been a season of blazing heat and long drought. The cattle died from starvation and the people, who depended on them, fed on the flesh of their corpses. The rainmakers were called in and when their rituals met with no success chose as a scapegoat the presence of the missionaries. For everything that went wrong the missionaries got the blame. It was said that they were to be killed, or driven away. Privately the rain-maker visited Robert Moffat, curious to cross-question his rival; publicly he condemned him as the bringer of trouble.

One day a deputation, a chief and a dozen attendants, came and sat under the shadow of a large tree near to the Moffat's house. Robert was repairing a waggon, Mary stood at the door with her baby in her arms. Mr Hamilton was called. The chief stood up, quivering his spear in his hand—a sign of war—and told the missionaries that they must leave the country. Because they had chosen to take no notice of threats, they must be prepared for violence if they still refused to go. Robert, mag-nificent now in a long black beard, stepped forward and replied that they intended to stay. They knew that the people did not really understand why they were there or what they were doing, but they would remain until they did and it would be necessary to kill them, or burn them out, to get rid of them. But in any case, he added, accepting them as men like himself, he knew that whatever happened they would not harm the wives and children. This speech, delivered simply, without bravado or fear, bewildered the chief. Perhaps, after all, there was some-thing in the immortal life about which this man so often spoke, for he could not conceive that otherwise the missionaries would be willing to face the risk of death. He looked at Robert Moffat, at MaMary and her baby, and walked away.

But the drought went on. Public opinion turned against the rainmaker and another council decided that the penalty for his failure was death, to be astonished when Robert burst in on them to plead that his enemy should be allowed to return to his own country a free man. They let him go, more than ever convinced that they had within their midst a man of strange powers and influence. The rainmaker left, to be killed by another tribe before he reached home.

These were the years of sorrow; the years when Robert Moffat's days were spent standing in the saw-pit, labouring at the anvil, treading clay, cleaning a water ditch, and Mary's salting meat, tending children, scouring, cleaning, cooking, supervising other women who found her instructions ridiculous. The household had been joined by two small Bushmen children, brother and sister, whom Robert had rescued when he had found their kinsman about to bury them in their mother's grave. Mrs Hamilton came back from Griqua Town, but nothing was resolved and she decided to go with her children to Cape Town. Poor Mr Hamilton, ashamed and harassed, petitioned to be allowed to leave Lattakoo for the sake of peace. In any case he felt himself a failure because he had not been able to learn any Sechuana. His request was refused—unless Robert Moffat endorsed it. The Moffats did not, and he stayed on to become a faithful worker and friend.

He was not the only one who was finding the language difficult. Robert was struggling with it, with no privacy, no room to study, no proper interpreter, and the added disadvantage that all his daily intercourse was in Dutch, a language which the people were suspicious of for they feared and disliked the Dutchmen. He wanted to undertake a journey, to get away from the station among people where his only recourse would be to speak Sechuana—but every time arrangements were made something prevented their fulfilment.

Of the spiritual progress, which for both Robert and Mary was the only reason for their presence in Africa, there was no sign. Indeed the Hottentots whom they had brought with them quarrelled among themselves, were offended at being disciplined, and fell away from the church—a fact which was not lost on the watching Africans.

Mary and Robert read the Bible together and prayed. The

sense of being pioneers for the Gospel sustained them, but Robert was often filled with the frustration and gloom of a man left alone to fight against overwhelming odds. It was Mary, with a long discipline in patience and faith behind her, who supported him during these moods and gave him the strength to carry on.

The Bechuanas watched and waited and speculated, and tested these strangers out. Some thought that their real purpose was to trade, others that they were runaways from their native land who dared not return to the Colony. They demanded tobacco for coming to hear them preach in the villages; at Lattakoo itself congregations varied between one and forty and were often unruly, snoring, laughing, working away at removing lice from their ornaments and deliberately letting them run along the bench where MaMary sat. They perched with their feet on the stools and forms, their knees tucked under their chins—and when they slept, as often happened, they fell sideways and toppled off amid universal amusement. There was a wooden Dutch clock on the wall of the little church and out of a box above the dial two soldiers marched when the hours struck. The Bechuana were afraid of this clock and rumours spread that those who went to church would be turned into small soldiers.

Some chiefs from outlying villages, seeing the material advantages of having a missionary who would dig ditches, mend tools, carpenter and blacksmith, came to ask Robert if they could have one too, bringing with them a daughter to offer him as a bribe. He was embarrassed when this happened in Mary's presence, but it is doubtful if she felt anything but desperation at another sign of their lack of understanding. Her baby was fifteen months old, she was pregnant again and would have her second child, delivered by Robert, at Lattakoo.

She wrote home to her parents with calm good sense, mentioning few of the daily trials which must have made her life at times a nightmare, but not disguising the difficulties in the way of their ultimate objective. 'We have no prosperity in the work, not the least sign of good being done. . . . Five years have rolled on since the missionaries came, and not one soul converted, nor does anyone seem to lend an ear. All treat with ridicule and contempt the truths which are delivered.' There was no sign of wavering or regret. Their desperate need was for news, to receive letters, to know what was going on elsewhere, to feel that they were not abandoned and alone; the reassurance that among those whom they loved and whose faith they shared neither they—nor Africa—were quite forgotten.

BECHUANA HUT

Chapter 5

MARY'S SECOND PREGNANCY ran the same unpleasant course as her first. With the coming of the summer heat in October she was again attacked by a return of the fever and sickness that had prostrated her at Griqua Town when carrying her first-born. For three or four months she continued to suffer greatly then, towards the end of January 1823, her symptoms disappeared quite suddenly and her health returned to normal. It was a trying time. She was incapacitated and unable to do more than the minimum to help her overburdened husband; it was not fears for her own, or the baby's, safety that beset her but frustration at her inability to make any contribution to what she considered the real work of the mission station. The lack of a sympathetic female ear was also a great trial. Robert's medical skill was unable to deal with the complications of her condition and they decided, if circumstances made it possible, to try to visit the Cape at the end of the year to get proper medical attention.

Nevertheless, in spite of all the hazards, the baby was born at Lattakoo on March 23rd 1823. She was called Ann, after Robert Moffat's mother—a name which he had already given to the six-year-old Bushman child who had been rescued with her brother, Dicky, and acted as playmate and friend to the toddler Mary.

With the arrival of a second child, a growing household and the knowledge that her health had certain strict limitations, Mary's role in the partnership imperceptibly changed. It was not without considerable anguish of spirit that she saw herself forced to relinquish the active travelling and teaching vocation at Mr Moffat's side which she had originally visualised. Though she recognised the value of good domestic management, she accepted that the real work lay elsewhere. Her daughter later described the role of a missionary wife as 'being an organ-blower to a musician'.

Robert Moffat, however, though he would not have contested this view, in fact recognised how much more evenly the scales were balanced in the mission and the marriage of himself and his 'beloved partner'. He was often sunk in gloom, close to despair; she it was who restored him and gave him the stubbornness to carry on. During the barren years that still lay ahead, the Bechuana, while listening unheeding to his preaching, watched closely the loving, unremitting, hopeful building of a home and a family in desperate circumstances. It was a time when actions said what words were often incapable of conveying. When Robert left the station to itinerate, so far as he was concerned he left it in Mary's charge. It was to her that he wrote by every opportunity, and much that was later transmuted into official reports was originally addressed to MaMary. Whatever masculine presence there might be guiding the destinies of the mission at Lattakoo, Mary's was the judgement Robert Moffat trusted.

The mission was now about to enter the most precarious period of its existence. These were the years of change and expansion among peoples in Southern Africa, of displacement and tribal war, vast raiding migrations, wild, hunting, outlaw bands. Pushed by fear of losing their independence and greed of land, the Boer farmers were pressing outwards the frontiers of the Colony to the north; pushed by fear of the maelstrom in Zululand and greed of cattle, the Bantu tribes were whirling out of the east, across the Drakensberg, towards the north-west and the Zambesi. In the vortex of these movements, under the momentum of upheaval, vast hordes of men, with their women and children and animals, moved and pillaged and plundered; forming and re-forming as groups broke away and then coming together again, slaughtering, massacring, laying waste with a total disregard of life or land. And like outriders, far preceding the host itself, even more terrible in its unidentifiable horrors, flew a multitude of rumours.

For more than a year these had concerned the Mantatee, a mighty woman at the head of an invincible army, numerous as locusts, marching among the interior nations carrying ruin and devastation. She nourished the army with her own milk, and sent out hornets before it. This horde became known as the Mantatees; some said it took its name from a warrior widow of

63

the Batlokoa, some that the word Mantatee simply meant marauder. Whatever the truth the name Mantatee became synonymous with pillage and terror, and was used of many different kinds of marauding bands.

In the early part of 1823, preoccupied with the internal problems of the station and concerned with plans to move it to a more potentially prosperous site by the Kuruman fountain eight miles away, it did not seem to the Moffats that these rumours threatened them. Language was still a major worry; indeed as time went on the need to speed up the process of learning Sechuana became ever more pressing. As soon as Mary was able to travel after Ann's birth, Robert wanted to go on a journey, to visit Makaba, chief of the Bangwaketse in his town at Kanye, 280 miles to the north-east. It was clear to him now that only by getting away from the arduous daily toil of Lattakoo and the mixed Dutch, English, Sechuana background would he make any real progress. The journey would also have the secondary object of checking on the rumours of the approach of the Mantatees. Mary would dearly have loved to have gone with him, but when the time came she felt that the presence of a wife and children—talking in his native tongue—would be a further barrier to Robert's acquiring fluency. So she decided to stay at home. It must have been a difficult decision for her to take.

Robert went off on May 14th, wearing trousers of prepared antelope skin and a Bechuana cap of fox fur. The stock of clothes he had brought with him from London, not large even in 1816, was by now quite exhausted. He had taught himself to make his own leather shoes, and indeed those of the family too. Mary was in somewhat better case sartorially, for not only had she come out with a bigger wardrobe but her mother renewed the supply from time to time by sending a trunk full of necessities.

Clothes were a bone of contention on the mission station itself. While admitting that lustful glances were unknown and that there was probably less sexual titillation than in Britain, the nakedness of the Bechuana women was still abhorrent to Robert Moffat. Mary particularly disliked the grease with which they smeared their bodies. Mahuto, the chief's wife, promised that if MaMary made her a dress she would wear it.

64

Mary did so, but Mahuto never appeared in it. However the Moffats did not demand, as sometimes happened at a later date, that the women clothe themselves straightaway in European fashion. Indeed, when the time came that they wanted to do so Mary insisted that they first make themselves a prepared skin dress of the kind that might naturally have evolved out of their own karosses.

It was not long before Robert arrived back. On June 4th, weeks before he was expected, he returned to Lattakoo with very alarming news. The Mantatees, far from being many hundreds of miles distant, were in fact on their very doorstep and marching towards the mission station. At this news there was widespread alarm among the Bechuana, never a very brave people and certainly not fighters. The station was virtually defenceless and it was only too clear, from the rumours which had now become painfully relevant and from the killing and devastation which Robert had seen, what would happen when the Mantatees arrived. In a panic the Africans began to drive their cattle off into the desert country to the west, hoping to save them from the invaders. Others clamoured round their missionary who, while he may have been an object of ridicule and contempt for his ideas, had nevertheless shown himself to be a man of resource and courage and above all somehow on their side. Robert set off for Griqua Town to summon a commando to their aid. It took him three and a half days—because even in such an emergency he did not think it right to travel on the Sabbath. On the afternoon of Wednesday June 11th, on a borrowed horse, he left Griqua Town with a Mr Thompson to return to Lattakoo. The commando was to follow immediately. On the evening of the next day Robert and Mr Thompson rode into Lattakoo.

Mary in the meanwhile, with a child of two and a baby of three months, was left with Mr Hamilton in charge of the station. It was to her house, rather than Mr Hamilton's, that the agitated local people came, feeling no doubt that this was the centre of their source of courage in this crisis—even if its master was absent seeking help—but certainly recognising that MaMary had a fearless spirit of her own.

The commando was slow to appear and in the meantime, like a cloud of locusts on the distant plain, the Mantatees could be seen approaching. On the night of June 21st, a Saturday, Robert and Mary packed up and buried their most valuable possessions prior to leaving with their people a station that could not be defended. The next day the commando of about 180 men arrived, and on the Monday Mr Melvill, the Government agent, and yet more horsemen rode into Lattakoo. On the Tuesday at 9 a.m. they all set off to meet the Mantatee horde.

Left at home with her babies, her faith to sustain her and her courage to hearten those who remained, Mary Moffat waited four days while rumours of a bloody battle gathered force and detail about her. She knew that Robert would take no part in the fighting, but she knew too that he would be in the forefront of the opposing forces hoping to be able to parley, regardless of his own safety, in his conviction that it must be possible to avert slaughter by the power of words and prayer. She believed this too—but she had no illusions that the Lord necessarily protected his followers from mutilation or death.

At six o'clock on the 27th Robert arrived home. There had indeed been a battle. All attempts to parley had met with failure and the Mantatees had not been intimidated, as Robert had hoped they might have been, simply by the sight of mounted men armed with guns coming against them. At last, outgunned, they had retreated. He estimated about 40,000 of them—and the Bechuanas had then begun to slaughter the wounded, including large numbers of women and children. He had ridden about the battlefield rescuing the enemy from such a fate whenever possible, and many were being brought in later to the station by Mr Melvill.

Flushed with success and anxious to get back to their homes, the Griqua commando left on June 30th. Mr Melvill and Mr Hamilton took a waggon and went out to look for any of the abandoned or wounded Mantatee women and children. Four of these joined Mary Moffat's family: two women, an eight-year-old boy and a girl of about four. Mary immediately made the younger woman cook, the older nurse and washerwoman, while Robert took the boy, who seemed clever, as a kind of apprentice. Mary was thankful for the help, particularly with the washing, which was a heavy chore, and seems not to have had the slightest hesitation in accepting the women as part of her domestic menage.

All, however, was not settled. News came that, now the Griquas had gone home, the marauders were threatening to revenge their defeat by a fresh march on the mission. The rumours grew to frightening proportions and, as night fell, a panic fear took over the town. No lights were lit. Families trembled round doused fires. Hearts leaped when the dogs barked. Imagination painted the town surrounded by enemies. In the mission house Mary put warm clothes on the babies. Robert hung a gun and a cloak on the door. They sat down to read and pray. A woman, who had escaped from the previous battle, ran the whole night and arrived in the centre of the town fainting, gasping 'The Mantatees'. The crowds were electrified. No one knew—or was calm enough to discover— where she had come from. The terrifying, uneasy night wore on.

In the morning it was seen that the town was not surrounded, though the rumours still persisted that the Mantatees were not far distant and bent on reprisal. A waggon was got ready, Mary and her babies and the other women and children of the mission left for Griqua Town.

It was the first of many retreats, and subsequent returns, during the next two years. The returns were important. Somehow, somewhere, in spite of hardship, depression, exhaustion, ridicule, disregard, exploitation, isolation, there had grown up in both the Moffats a stubborn belief that this was their home, this was where their lifework lay, these were their people; and in the Bechuana a rising astonishment each time the little family returned, and a slowly dawning recognition that this man and this woman cared what happened to them, although why they should do so and in what way still lay outside their comprehension.

After this first withdrawal Robert went back alone to see how things stood, and also once again to make an attempt at language study. 'He writes me that all our buried things are taken up in excellent order, but the garden is completely destroyed by the oxen. Some of the Bechuanas made attempts at robbing the houses, but Mothibi had acted honourably. . . . Were these people idolaters, I should be afraid of them deifying Robert now. . . . They say it would have been easy for us to decamp, with all belonging to us; but are surprised at the promptitude and activity which Robert used in warning the

Griquas of the approaching danger,' Mary wrote to her parents.

Although this appeared to be a moment of extreme peril for all that the mission stood for, it was also—as so often happens—a moment for looking forward. In the aftermath of battle, when they had more in common than ever before, Robert came to an agreement with Mothibi, the chief, to move the mission station to a new site, and completed a transaction to lease to the London Missionary Society, for the equivalent of fifty pounds, the valley below the Kuruman fountain eight miles from Lattakoo.

It was hoped that the chiefs and most of their people would follow the mission and set up a new town in the vicinity of Kuruman, and that the abundant water, which would make agriculture possible, would attract other peoples to come and settle. The Bechuanas needed some persuading about this, water in their view not being so important as wood for houses and cattle kraal fences.

Robert was a gardener, and Mary was the daughter of a gardener. With a source of water secured they had a vision, even in this their darkest moment, of the valley blossoming and becoming 'a magazine of provision', both physically and spiritually, for a multitude of infant mission stations spreading up into the far northern interior.

They left for Cape Town, a two months' journey, on October 22nd 1823. It must have been a relaxation and a pleasure to be again in the safe, slow security of the ox-waggon, with time to play with her babies and teach the alphabet to the other youngsters whom she had now gathered about her. They took with them Mothibi's son and heir, Peclu, partly as a witness to their good standing among Europeans—for they were still suspected of being runaways—partly because Robert foresaw that this young man could have a great influence for good among his own people in the future. But the main object of the journey was to seek medical advice for Mary, to restock up with supplies, and to get official permission from the representatives of the Society at the Cape to complete the transaction with Mothibi and change the site of the mission.

Mary's health certainly improved from this visit, but it is likely that the relief from constant tension afforded by the journey and the knowledge that her husband was safe and at her side did more to restore her than any medical advice.

Certainly, while appreciating the kindness of friends and the conveniences of civilisation, she found that the four years since her last stay in Cape Town had altered considerably both her own attitudes and, it seemed, those of her acquaintances. She now knew what it was to labour in an interior mission and she recognised how great a gulf there was between those who had this experience and the others, with their pious hopes and respectable congregations, who had not. For a long time she was to feel that only lip service was paid to the importance of the Bechuana mission, for which she and Robert were wearing out their lives, instead of the urgent practical help they so badly needed.

They did, all the same, travel back with Mr and Mrs Hughes, who were to be stationed at Kuruman; though, owing to Mrs Hughes' pregnancy, they had to leave them at Griqua Town and so arrive, on May 4th 1824, at Lattakoo alone.

But they came back to a warm welcome and renewed health, hopes and plans. For Mothibi and Mahuto they brought back Peclu, full of stories of the things he had seen and done in the Colony, and with Peclu the respectability of the missionaries was finally established.

The arrangement for the new land at Kuruman was ratified, and the two missionaries went over and surveyed the sites for the first houses and marked out the course of the irrigation channel. There seemed to be a new willingness on the part of the people to listen to them, although as yet it showed no signs of bearing any fruit. Yet again, Robert arranged for a journey north, to Makaba, whom he had not reached in 1823, to prospect for the Gospel.

He left on July 1st. The country was still very much disturbed with rumours of wars and raidings, but they had come to accept this as normal and not a situation that should interfere, except in times of extreme danger, with the work of strengthening the mission and spreading the Word. Nevertheless Mary was a prey to anxiety and very much alone. Not only was Robert gone, Mr Hamilton was now over at the new site along with the Hottentot workers supervising the building of the houses. They came back to Lattakoo on Saturday evenings and stayed over Sunday, but during the week Mary was by herself. 'We are surrounded on every hand,' she wrote in July 1824.

69

'It requires some little fortitude to live at rest in such a tumultuous land.' She was, however, persuaded of the absolute
importance of Robert's journey to the north, recognising as he
did that to remain embattled in Lattakoo was no way to reach
the heathen.

She saw too, all round her, compelling reasons for preaching
and teaching with all the energy they could muster. There had
been discussions in the drawing-rooms of Cape Town in which
it had been made clear to her that missionaries were considered
busybodies upsetting the peaceful, harmless native going
quietly about his own business with his flocks and herds,
making his life miserable by introducing him to the burdens of
refined society. She was scornful of such arguments. 'The
hundreds who annually perish from hunger in this state of
society is another argument against such reasonings. . . .
Horror and devastation reign over the whole land. The longer
we live in it the more convinced we are of the necessity of
missionaries being here.'

Almost immediately she was to see more of the horror and
devastation. About ten days after Robert left, two notes came
from the missionary in charge at Griqua Town to Mr Hamilton,
saying 'that an immense body of Mantatees was rapidly
approaching Griqua Town, the Koranna mission was destroyed,
that Mr Edwards had been to call a commando, that Edwards
and Melvill were going out with the Griquas and had been
three days away.' It was disastrous news, not so much because of
what might be happening at Griqua Town, though that was
bad enough, but because she feared that the marauders,
sweeping back on their return journey to the north, might
intercept Robert and his single waggon on the road.

Her suspense was made the more acute by his not arriving
back at the time that he had said he would. She wrote him a
letter and sent it by a group of men going north, in the hope
that somehow he might get it. 'It is with a faint, faint hope that
you will ever see this, that I take up my pen, it being so very
improbable that you will meet with the Barolong who take
it. . . . Oh, my dear, I find it requires the exercise of some fortitude to be calm and serene under such a separation, in such
circumstances and at such a time in a land of barbarians. In
vain has my heart fluttered when I have seen a strange face,

hoping he would pull out from under his kaross a letter, no post yet having arrived from you. . . . You know I dreaded your departure exceedingly. I had many fears about your health from that ugly cough. I had also fears on account of the tumultuous state of the land. I expected also to suffer a good deal myself from low spirits in my great solitude, but in this I was mistaken, having been remarkably composed and very seldom in a melancholy mood. When I feel it come on I make great efforts to dispel it, and have been successful. . . .'

She went on to give him news of the children, of Mr Hamilton and the new station, and of the marauders. 'Since you left, Jacob Cleote (a renegade Griqua), with a number of armed Korannas and Bushmen, has been making terrible ravages at a town beyond Lehaise's, has taken a great number of cattle, killed eight chiefs, besides others and women and children. By all accounts he has acted most barbarously; the people here were much alarmed, as he threatened to come here to get powder. Of course I had some fears, but am happy to say he has gone back to his place. . . .'

As always she rose to a crisis. She was alone in her house with the children. Her neighbour was a young Hottentot woman. A party of marauders collected about forty miles west of the station and attacked some villages along the Kuruman river. Reports began to come in of a possible attack on the mission. Mary was alarmed, knowing that there was a certain amount of ammunition on the station and fearing an attempt to capture it. However she calmed herself; such rumours were usual and not necessarily based on fact.

One evening the Hottentot girl rushed in to say that the marauders had been seen on their way. By herself, with two babies and the two Bushman children Dicky and Ann, Mary could see no way of escape except to take them and flee with the other women into the bushes. She sent a message to Mothibi to ask if the news were true. He replied that it was, but he did not expect danger before morning. Filled with fears, Mary commended herself and the children to the protection of Providence and lay down to get some sleep.

At midnight there was a loud rapping on her door. She got up, not knowing whether it was Jacob Cleote or news of the horde, and asked without opening the door who was there.

'Mothibi,' the chief answered.

When she unbarred the door he thrust his way in, followed by as many men as the room would hold, and announced that the Mantatees were approaching. In this emergency the moral support, as well as the downright common sense, of MaMary were clearly felt to be of great, perhaps even of supernatural, importance.

A candle was brought. Mary, in her night-cap with a wrap hastily flung round her, seated herself in the middle of the noisy council and listened intently to the reports, the rumours, the alarms and advice that flew from mouth to mouth. It was no time for arduous translation and, while no mention is made of what language predominated at this midnight conference, it can be presumed that Mary was by now sufficiently at home in Sechuana that, with the help of Dutch, she managed to be informed of what was going on.

When she had disentangled the situation she took ink and paper and wrote a note to Mr Hamilton at Kuruman, urging him to return at once with the men. This was sent off by messenger and for the rest of the night MaMary's house remained a scene of universal confusion, for those who had sought her protection—under whatever pretext—were not going to leave it till daylight. Curiously enough, the activity, Mary's own strength and her obvious confidence in a higher power, and a general feeling of having reached a decision, raised everybody's spirits. When daylight came they were prepared to face whatever it might bring.

It brought Mr Hamilton and the men from the new site. They arrived at 8 a.m. and immediately advised on preparations for flight. Warriors were assembling; thousands of people were hiding their property or packing up to leave; every messenger that came in brought fresh alarms.

About noon, however, a change in the rumours began to make it clear that the enemy had swung away from the mission station and was instead preparing to fall on the Barolongs to the north-east. Instantly the mood altered. Mothibi and his people, who had been in a state of despair an hour before, were flung into a paroxysm of rejoicing. Not so poor Mary, who realised at once that this new route must bring the marauders on a collision course with Robert. She voiced her fears and was surrounded by

72

sympathisers, but nothing that she could say would induce a single man to go out in an attempt to warn Mr Moffat and give him some help.

For three weeks Mary lived in a state of continual anxiety, not knowing what had happened or was happening to her husband, though constantly regaled with 'news' of him by strangers and travellers. One said that he had been cut off. Another had seen a piece of his waggon, which could only mean that he had been attacked and captured. Yet another had found part of his saddle. Someone had picked up fragments of his clothing stained with blood. At last, desperate, she persuaded some men to go out to try and find the truth—and on the morning of the very next day Robert arrived home.

After all he was well and had encountered no dangers. Owing to the disturbed state of the country he had had very little news and, as it happened, his road had not crossed that of the marauders. For his part he found Mary in good health and spirits. Far from sinking under the weight of anxiety, she had accepted the challenge thrust upon her and the Bechuanas expressed astonishment at her courage.

She was prepared to die with them, if necessary for them—and her children too, for they were missionary children and must accept the same risks as their parents. She had come to Africa out of a compulsion to spread the news of the Gospel of love, and she could love the souls of the Bechuanas. But as yet she did not like them. Perhaps it is hardly surprising. 'It is not conferring with flesh and blood to live among these people. In the natives of South Africa there is nothing naturally engaging; their extreme selfishness, filthiness, obstinate stupidity and want of sensibility, have a tendency to disgust, and sometimes cause the mind to shrink from the idea of spending the whole life amongst them.' Nevertheless, with God's help she intended to do just that, but she did not deceive herself about the task that lay ahead and her attitude towards it was without the hypocrisy and sentimentality that she found so hard to sympathise with in the sitting-rooms of the Colony or the church halls of Britain.

No sooner had Robert returned home than he fell ill with anthrax caught from eating an infected animal. A large boil developed above his right eyebrow and his head and neck swelled up. Seven months later Peclu, on whom they had set such store, was to die of a similar malignant boil. Robert, however, recovered. Mr Hamilton returned to work at the new Kuruman site, to be joined there by Mr Hughes who had at last come up from Griqua Town. An effort was made to go on as though things were returning to normal.

But they were not. The surrounding country was now in a state of civil war in which Mothibi, greatly against Robert Moffat's advice, became embroiled. He wanted his missionaries to join with him and was angrily embittered when Robert refused, accusing the missionaries of being unable to control or reform the renegade Griquas who had once been under their influence.

Twice during the next few months the Moffat family had to retire to Griqua Town seeking shelter from the bloodbath and chaos which swept the country. Makaba, whom Robert had gone to visit, was slain. Mothibi, after an initial sortie, was routed and thousands of Bechuanas, who appeared to have been afflicted with madness, wandered about hungry and desperate. The country was in a state of devastation, hundreds were killed or died of starvation, disease, despair.

The wars swept back and forward, abating for a time in one place only to break out with renewed fury in another. At Griqua Town in December 1824 Mary, again pregnant and suffering greatly from the heat, felt, as did her husband, that at the age of twenty-nine her productive life was almost over and ardently regretted that she had been able to do so little for the cause. '. . . if we go where our hearts are, to the Kuruman, we may scarcely be there before we are recalled, and then narrowly escape with our lives. . . . Thus every purpose of our lives is broken, our minds are racked between one prospect and another. We resolve and re-resolve what to do, but all our determinations are frustrated.'

Chapter 6

WHEN, ON MARCH 18TH 1825, the Moffats returned to the new site at Kuruman which was to be their permanent home, they were determined this time not to flee again if it was humanly possible to remain. Quite apart from the constant setbacks to the spiritual work, the drain upon both their physical and material resources was severe. Each time they left, a certain amount of irreplaceable property—tools, books, clothes, utensils, building materials, cattle—was lost, and the frustrations of defeat took their toll upon the health of both Moffats.

There was much, however, about the new station to raise their spirits. First and foremost water, the one essential element which had been missing at Lattakoo and which now meant that Robert's green fingers could start to turn the desert into a true garden. Until this happened supplies of food were so short that a hunter had to be employed to go out and kill game.

Mr and Mrs Hughes came back with them to rejoin Mr Hamilton, who had faithfully retained the link with Kuruman, and in May Mr Millen arrived. He was a mason from the township of Bethelsdorp, engaged for two years to help with the mission buildings. Hugh Millen was one of a number of men of humble origin who, in those days, made their way to the more remote parts of the world in search of freedom and a better life. He was not and never became a member of the London Missionary Society, offering his technical skills directly to the mission in the field when he found a need. An excellent craftsman, he refused to build in clay brick and used the local stone. Mary Moffat grew very fond of him and treated him as a member of her family.

Among the Bechuana, although there were still no converts, there was an increasing respect for the missionaries, and a good number of people followed them to the new station and began to establish a small town near by.

Troubles, however, were not over. Peclu's death soon after their return was a blow to his parents, for he was the eldest son; it was also a set-back to the mission, for hopes of a brighter future had been pinned on the increasing influence of this well-disposed young man. Mary did her best to comfort his mother, Mahuto. In a very short while she was to have more in common with her than she realised.

They had been back less than two months when fresh trouble threatened from groups of marauders in the west. This time they barricaded the reed walls of Mr Hamilton's house— the one good building on the station—with chests and sacks, determined to make a stand rather than again abandon their people. Mr Hughes was prostrated by a severe attack of nervous fever; Mrs Hughes dangerously ill. Mothibi's family came to the Moffats' temporary house; men were armed; a watch set. Work, building and making a water system went on, under a burning sun, with guns laid beside them in case of attack. Some of their assistants, Hottentots from Bethelsdorp and the Colony, were not prepared to accept the privations of the station and left. Each day brought a fresh crop of rumours and alarms.

In the midst of all this, attended by her husband, Mary Moffat bore a son, Robert, on May 16th 1825, and five days later the baby died of convulsions. His was the first grave in the little cemetery of the new station and Kuruman acquired a special significance for the Moffats. They were both very fond of children and looked forward to sons who would follow their father in his work. Though the precariousness of their situation faced them daily with death, and Mary recognised that every confinement 'renders my decease so very probable' this was, in fact, the only close bereavement that either of them had so far suffered. It added a new dimension to the uncertainties of life.

There was little time to grieve. In spite of armed robbers constantly threatening, the work of the station had to go steadily forward. Planting, building, carrying, creating, salting, storing, sewing, cobbling, carpentering, blacksmithing, butchering, preaching, teaching, exhorting, pacifying, supporting, cleaning, feeding, praying, writing; they were carried forward relentlessly by the momentum of providing for the necessities of life and the conviction that they had something to bring to Africa. To all this Robert had begun to add another contribution—the one which was, above all others, to do most for the spread of the Gospel that he cherished. Slowly, painfully, with a language as yet only partially assimilated, he had translated a spelling book, a catechism and some small Scripture portions into Sechuana. It was a task not made easier by the fact that he undertook his full load of the day's hard physical labour and came to this extra work already fatigued in the evenings.

While they struggled, almost beleaguered, to cultivate their insecure foothold at Kuruman, digging a water-ditch two miles in length, erecting a row of temporary houses, fencing in gardens and laying them out, planting trees, edible roots and seeds, the lure of the far interior, which was later to make Kuruman a centre for many traders and travellers, was beginning to make itself felt. Towards the end of 1825 visitors arrived at the station, some in connection with the mission, others not. While they brought with them news, fresh faces, and stimulating conversation which were very welcome, their ignorance of the true nature of daily life must often have irritated the missionaries almost beyond enduring. Dr Philip came from the Cape on his first pastoral round, bringing with him a Mr Bartlett and Mr and Mrs Melvill. They stayed from Saturday to Wednesday and, hardly surprisingly, Robert Moffat ended at loggerheads with his superintendent, each man feeling that the other had little grasp of the real situation. More strangely two gentlemen arrived out of the blue one Sabbath evening. 'The one a Mr Gleig from the East Indies and his colleague a Captain Warren from Grahamstown.' It was a pleasure jaunt for the benefit of their health—ironic in view of the constant battles with fevers, exhaustion, cold, and heat which Mary waged. The Moffats entertained them and Robert wrote, with almost saintly charity, 'Our house is their home, which of course takes up much of my time as well as much fatigues Mary.' Mary herself did not record her feelings.

In October 1825, though she did not know about it at that time, an event occurred which Mary had long been dreading. Back in England her mother died. Unknown to Robert too his elder brother died in the same month. Mrs Smith had been painfully ill for more than two years and every letter that Mary received in her father's handwriting was opened with a

77

'palpitating heart' in case it should carry the news of her mother's death. Though she knew of the distressing symptoms which accompanied Mrs Smith's illness, she had nevertheless retained hope that she would live long enough to let them meet again. In the event Mary was not to see England for another thirteen years. That her usually clear-sighted, sensible assessment of personal circumstances deserted her in this instance was a measure of the depth of her feeling for her mother and an acknowledgement that the latter had never really become reconciled to the loss of her only daughter.

The news arrived in the following April, by the same mail as a letter from Robert's family telling him of his brother's death. It was a melancholy time. In February Mary had had a miscarriage, brought on by fatigue caring for Mrs Hughes during the birth of a son. To recover from the after-effects she and the children went on a visit to Mrs Melvill at Griqua Town, travelling with Mr Hamilton and Mr Millen who were in search of timber for buildings. While she was away Robert suffered from insomnia and depression. After several years of drought rain had fallen plentifully in the early part of the season, but the benefit was wiped out by clouds of locusts—a phenomenon not seen in this district for twenty years. They devoured all the vegetation, but in turn themselves became food for the starving Bechuana. Robert Moffat watched them being prepared, boiled, spread on a mat to dry and then pounded in a wooden mortar like meal. He tried them and found them very tasty. The country remained uneasy and alarms kept coming in of raiding parties threatening to attack both Kuruman and Griqua Town.

There was an addition to the Moffat family, a compensation for the two lost babies, and for the future children that Mary now had begun to fear she might never have. This was a new little baby girl who came into her care in very strange circumstances.

One Sunday, while they were getting ready for church, one of the children of the household, maybe Dicky, the Bushman boy, rushed in to say that he could hear a child 'crying among the stones on the side of the hill about a quarter of a mile away'. Robert and Mr Millen went out to see what was the matter and Mary followed more slowly. When she arrived at the spot, she saw, with a sense of shock, that they were un-covering a shallow stone grave in which lay a tiny baby about five weeks old. The large slab set over the hole in which it was buried had rested on its face, making an unpleasant wound. There was extensive bruising on its limbs where it had kicked against the hard sides of its prison. It was deadly cold.

Mary picked the little thing up and took it straight home where she fed and washed it and bathed its wounds, while the Bechuana women looked on in astonishment. 'They viewed it with indifference; said the mother was a rascal, but wondered much that we should love so poor an object.' It then appeared that the mother, a poor soul who was in the habit of begging food from MaMary and who had told her that her child was dead, had gone out on the Saturday, accompanied by her own mother, and buried the baby. It had lain all night, in the cold that accompanied heavy rain and with the constant risk that hyenas might scent its presence. When they heard that the baby had been discovered both mother and grandmother im-mediately left Kuruman.

The infant was so tiny that it might have been new-born. Mary did not care to trust it to any of the women she knew to act as a wet nurse, so she looked after it herself, feeding it minute spoonfuls of milk with infinite patience. At about this time she had her miscarriage, and handed over the care of the resurrected baby to a good-natured Hottentot woman, whom she paid well to look after it. She felt, however, a special affection for this child, who had been so strangely given to them, and with the loss of her own baby she decided to adopt it. It was baptised in March and named Sarah Roby after the wife of the man who had so greatly influenced Robert Moffat during his time at Dukinfield. The baby soon lost its desperate and forlorn air, and in April, when Mary described the incident to her father, she was able to say, 'It is coming on very well and is considered a very pretty child.'

After this things took a turn for the better. It was true that there were still many alarms about marauders, but several thousand people had come to settle on the opposite side of the valley to the mission station; the little school, which Isaac Hughes conducted at the same time as being the mission carpenter, had about forty pupils; there were even three hymns

79

to be sung in Sechuana, first fruits of Robert's translation—
though the spelling book and catechism, which had gone down
to Cape Town to be printed, had never arrived back. The
station itself had about fifty families from seven different tribes
grouped round it. In a moment of optimism, for there were still
no converts—'as to the Bechuanas, I am sorry to say they are
much as usual, equally careless about spiritual things, and
evidently as much attached to their old superstitions'—Mary
wrote home to friends in Sheffield asking if they could send out
a set of communion vessels for the church at Kuruman. The
new house was going up, a well-designed permanent stone
structure of four small rooms and a hall, with a kitchen and
pantry behind. Mary watched its progress with impatience.

She was pregnant again—after all her fears—and hoping
that all would go well and the infant be a boy. With this
pregnancy her health had taken a turn for the better 'and
could I regain my strength should be as well as in my native
land'. Robert too was well, even though terribly harassed by
manual labour. As soon as the house was finished he intended
to try to dissociate himself from this side of the work—with the
exception of blacksmithing which nobody else could do—and
apply himself yet again to a final effort to master the language.
'You may form some idea of what missionaries have to put their
hands to when I tell you that Robert was a fortnight every day
up to the middle in water cutting thatch for the house . . .' Mary
wrote to her father.

Her baby was born in January 1827. It was a son, Robert, a
fine, strong child, to his mother 'a great treasure which the
Lord had vouchsafed to us'. Mary Moffat, the only girl in a
family of boys, while too devoted a mother to make distinctions
between her children, undoubtedly had a partiality for her
sons.

When the baby was eight weeks old, and there seemed to be
a lull in the sometimes turbulent affairs of the station, Robert
managed at long last to carry out the project that so often
before he had been deflected from—a study trip. With a kind of
desperate determination, aware that time was running against
him, he set out, alone except for a driver, a small boy to lead the
oxen (perhaps Fahaange, the boy who had come into the Moffat
household after the Mantatee battle) and two men from the

tribe with whom he hoped to live, the Barolong. He journeyed about a hundred miles to the north-east and settled down among them to an intensive period of talking, listening to and writing down Sechuana. He did not anticipate having an easy time—and he was right. Quite apart from the difficulties of living entirely among the Barolong, he was going to miss Mary. 'One thing I do anticipate, that is low spirits, which has hitherto been my constant companion in your absence.' However, this time it was imperative that he succeed. To help him he instituted a postal service, with one of the Kuruman Hottentots as runner, which kept him in touch with Mary and she with him. He suffered from flies, lice, incessant begging, drought, ridicule, a sense of frustration in language learning, the excessive noisiness of the Barolong people. There were many moments when only the letters from Kuruman and Mary urging him to persevere kept him going.

Mary and the three children drove out some way to meet him when, after ten weeks, he was due to return home. The children loved the waggon journeys and some of their happiest memories in later life were of the little house on wheels, with their mother relaxed and unharried, ready to tell them stories and play with them. Neither Robert nor Mary had enjoyed the separation but it had been well worth it. When he preached, in the temporary building that did duty for a chapel, on the Sabbath after he returned home, the congregation was electrified to 'hear the gospel direct from Moffat in their own language'.

At last a break-through had been made, progress seemed possible. But, as had so often happened before, no sooner had they settled down again than fresh alarms of raiding commandos all set to attack Kuruman and to seize powder and ammunition, came to their ears. 'On receiving this intelligence, we were thunderstruck, as we were at the time indulging pleasing hopes with regard to the strength of our mission, and Mothibi was just on the point of removing his town close to the station in order to cultivate the valley below.'

They were determined to remain, but this decision was received with alarm and astonishment in Griqua Town, so with very great reluctance they agreed to leave. The moment they arrived in Griqua Town they regretted having come, feeling certain now that it was an unnecessary journey. When they returned, a few weeks later, it was to find that the drought had been excessive; nearly all the cows and calves, which they had had to leave behind, had died of want and half of the oxen, and many of the people were scattered. They could hardly forgive themselves for having fled, and resolved there and then never to leave again. They brought back with them the first Sechuana books, written nearly two years before, which by some oversight had gone all the way back to England instead of being printed in the Cape.

Chapter 7

EIGHTEEN HUNDRED AND TWENTY-EIGHT, though it was hardly apparent at the time, was the turning point. Mary had been in Africa eight years. During that period she had borne four children, three now living and one dead: she had a trim, secure home on a mission station that had begun to have the appearance of 'a little paradise in this wilderness country', with fruit trees starting to bear, grapes, figs, peaches, apricots, apples, melons, and good harvests of wheat, tobacco, Indian corn. Her marriage had ripened into a partnership of mutual dependence and trust developed through years of shared hardship and danger; the mission had gathered round it a community of Africans, many of them from the poorer, slave peoples of the Bechuana, who looked to the missionaries for defence and support. Robert had at last mastered the language and had opened a day-school conducted in Sechuana.

Yet nothing seemed to have been accomplished of the work which had been the purpose of their coming to Africa and, though they toiled on in faith, there was little apparent sign that it ever would be. In all these eight years there had not been one single Bechuana convert.

Robert was in a dilemma over the language question. Now that he was fluent in Sechuana he had before him the grand vision of a complete translation of the Bible. But, while he was willing to undertake whatever labour might be involved, he shrank from the task of doing so unaided. At this point he felt his own academic inadequacies. He needed a companion with some literary ability. He needed books on philology and Biblical criticism. On the other hand, as the only missionary at present at Kuruman who spoke Sechuana, he saw the importance of his being able to travel further into the interior, able at last to speak the message of the Gospel directly, ungarbled by interpreters. He could start to set up a network of smaller mission stations, served by Kuruman, round which he could try to persuade the tribes to settle. But he needed to know that the Directors would support this work by providing missionaries to man these stations once he had set them up.

He wrote of these matters to the Directors in London and was exasperated because he could not get a satisfactory reply out of them. The long delay between question and answer occasioned by the slowness of the mail, and an element of ambiguity in the letters that did come from London made him feel that Kuruman was being deliberately neglected. 'Do the Directors view this mission as a forlorn hope and intend to leave it to die a natural death? Is it of so little importance? Truly to be told that Elliott spent 30 years to translate the scriptures into a language which is now extinct and the translation useless! is not calculated to diffuse much zeal, but I can assure you that it has not done much towards quenching it!' he wrote to London.

Mary too felt that they were unsupported. At this moment she and Robert were alone against the world. Mr Hamilton had gone to the Cape for leave, the first in twelve years. To his horror Robert heard that he had sent for his wife (who had left for England in March 1823) to return to him. Robert could not believe it! 'I cannot solve it on any other ground than that his intellect must be impaired, which however does not appear in his general deportment,' he wrote to the Directors, ending with the threat that if Mrs Hamilton came he himself would leave for a desolate place.

Mr Hughes had asked to be transferred, because he did not like being an assistant and felt that his talents were not properly used. He and Mrs Hughes had gone to Griqua Town. There had even been a suggestion mooted in Cape Town that the Kuruman mission be closed down. Dr Philip was going back to England. Mary disliked him heartily, sharing her husband's view that his interest in political matters was wrong for a missionary and that he was neglectful of the interests of Kuruman. In a letter to her father she indulged in a rare, and human, fit of malice: 'We feel gratified that our Dr is not likely to return, and though we do not rejoice that he has met with such humiliation, we hope it will do him good.' He did, however, return, and later on relations were restored to a more amicable level.

Mary, however, had a more personal reason for feeling that the Directors back in England were against them. Of her three brothers only one, John, shared her spiritual convictions and her interest in missionary work. Indeed it had been his sister's courage and dedication during the trying years of her engagement which had brought John Smith into the church. The other two brothers seem to have been both worldly and extravagant, a constant source of worry to their father. Now his business had failed, which caused Mary much anxiety, particularly as it was in some way connected with the general unsatisfactoriness of his son William's behaviour. Mary could hardly bear to look at this brother's portrait, which hung with John's over the chimneypiece in her new house, because it so distressed her to think of what he had done to their father.

John Smith had offered himself to the London Missionary Society for work overseas. He was greatly influenced by his sister and brother-in-law, and they certainly took it for granted that he would come to Kuruman. The prospect of being reinforced, not only by a close and dear relative but by a fellow-worker who from his constant communication with them knew exactly the problems and difficulties of the mission, delighted the Moffats. It seemed, at last, to offer a real chance to build up the work.

Mary especially was overjoyed. More than Robert she suffered from a sense of isolation. She felt that the friends she had at home were gradually forgetting her. The gaps between letters became longer and longer, and when, from the unremitting toil of Kuruman, she viewed the comparative ease of life back in Manchester she could not but feel that it was lack of interest, rather than lack of time, which made them such poor correspondents.

Since her mother's death she had been oppressed by a sense of the transience of life when it came to her own circle of friends and relatives. Where, in ordinary circumstances, she would have been making new friends to take the place of those left behind, in her situation this was impossible. They went so seldom to the Colony that there was no chance to develop any close friendships and 'as the missionary spirit does not run high at the Cape we may emphatically say that there are none there who care for us, or who will care for ours when we are gone!'

The African women, of course, she did not consider in this context. They knew nothing of her background or customs, family, thoughts or feelings. At a later stage she was to become attached to one or two of the missionary wives, but she did not make casual friendships easily and, in the early days, the forced contact under very difficult circumstances of women who often had little in common except their husband's work can only rarely have been conducive to close personal relationships.

So the news that brother John anticipated coming to Kuruman overwhelmed Mary. In the light of this addition to their family circle the whole future was transformed. Because she so keenly anticipated John's coming, the blow when it fell was all the greater.

The Directors in London, with an expanding mission field to look after and no doubt having weighed the priorities carefully, decided that John Smith was more urgently needed in India, and he sailed for Madras. When the news came to Kuruman Mary was devastated. 'I need not say that his change of destination has proved one of the severest disappointments of my life.' It was not only a personal disappointment; it was also, she felt, a 'slight thrown on the Bechuana mission by our Directors who instead of discouraging him ought to have rejoiced with us that at length one was found willing to encounter the privations and hardships of an interior mission.' She still had a temper and she was very angry with the Directors. Contrary to her normal inclination to make the best of a bad job, she even hoped for some divine intervention—that like Jonah brother John might yet be halted in mid-ocean and returned to Kuruman, though not of course in the belly of a whale! At this moment she was perhaps more depressed than at any time since she had landed in Africa eight years before.

There were other family problems. Little Mary was now seven, her sister Ann five. The perennial dilemma of overseas families—education—was looming up. Mary was finding it impossible to do the job herself, as she had originally visualised. She was already overburdened by cares and responsibilities and again pregnant, but she was also now increasingly aware of the difficulties of bringing up children as she wished to in surrounding circumstances of such turmoil and savagery. Except by hearsay they knew nothing of the customs and institutions of

86

their parents' homeland. It was becoming clear too to Mary that the major, perhaps the entire, responsibility for decisions about the children's education was going to fall on her. Robert was preoccupied with a myriad other affairs: he trusted her implicitly and had absolute confidence in her judgement and abilities.

He was, however, concerned with one aspect of this approaching family commitment: finance. Later on the Society made an educational allowance for each child and there were schools in England which made special provision for the children of missionaries. At this stage, 1828, no provision was made for daughters—though by inference there was some for sons. Considerable pressure was brought to bear on the Society to set up a school somewhere in Africa to take missionary children, but nothing came of it.

Though there had been some small increase in salary since the Moffats first started to work in Africa, they were still receiving only about £100 a year, and much of this had to be spent on replacing essential equipment, including oxen, lost due to constant attacks and upheavals. Into the bargain Mary's father was no longer in a financial position to give any help, and after her mother's death the regular boxes of clothing and provisions had stopped. Nevertheless, they intended, 'God willing, to take them to the Colony and place them at school within two years from this time,' Mary wrote to her friend Mrs Wrigley in December 1828. Her daughter, Mary, was a sturdy, thoughtful, placid child. There was an occasion, on a journey, when the waggon overturned—a not infrequent occurrence— and in all the hurly-burly of getting oxen, stores, spilled provisions, sorted out it was suddenly discovered that both Mary junior and the latest baby were missing. In the agitation of the search it was noticed that a rolled-up mat appeared bumpy. Unrolled, it revealed Mary, clasping the baby in her arms to keep it from harm and patiently waiting to be rescued. Ann was a normal, healthy child, but Robert was the apple of his mother's eye. She had breast-fed him, as she did all the children, till he was over a year old, because of shortage of milk in the ravaged countryside, which made weaning difficult. At the age of eighteen months he was 'rather gross and fat'. However he then began to suffer from an irritable skin disease, which reduced his fat but made him rather troublesome. He was 'a bright, lively creature and is clever for his age'.

During the greater part of this year attacks on the station by roving marauders continued. In March a band of Corannas, a Bastard tribe, arrived at Kuruman and rambled about the mission station haughty and menacing. At Robert's insistence they were treated calmly and with kindness. They encamped in a natural entrenchment within a few yards of the houses and shook their clubs threateningly. Robert had difficulty restraining some of the Griquas, who were on the station, from attacking them. Mary's opinion of the Bechuanas in this emergency was less than complimentary. 'You are probably aware that no dependence can be placed on Bechuanas who fly before such people in battle like chaff before the wind.'

Robert, his strong black beard flowing over his chest, stood out between the two sides and resorted, as always, to the persuasive power of the spoken word. A shot was fired, then a second which whistled over his head. He walked slowly back to his house. Seeing this the Griquas instantly attacked and drove the enemy off. Five men were captured—and were brought to the Moffats' house to be fed!

A considerable impression was made on everybody engaged in this fight by the victory and the humanity displayed after it. Usually the victors indulged in ruthless killing and maiming, and in rounding up women and children as slaves. For some months there was peace.

Then a fresh commando appeared in the north-west. The alarm was given by a boy, a prisoner, who escaped and sought shelter in the station. Once again all was confusion. An attack was expected hourly. A guard was set to keep watch. Cattle were collected and driven off to the Bushman country to protect them from the raiders.

This time the station had very few men capable of defending it. The Griquas had gone home or into the interior on their hunting trips. 'We had not more than 2 or 3 good shooters on the place and the enemy consisted of 80 or 90 with 30 guns besides bows and arrows.'

Through that night, the next day and yet another night, Mary and Robert Moffat, sickened by the thought that the mission might become a battleground yet again, prayed fervently together and as they went about their tasks. In the early morning the commando emerged, a confused rabble, from behind rising ground half a mile away and advanced towards the mission. Begging his own men to refrain from firing, Robert climbed to the top of a small hillock with his telescope, to see if any of the enemy were familiar to him. For some time they milled about, taking some of Mr Hamilton's sheep and goats which had not been protected.

Then a man was seen to be advancing under a flag. Robert walked out to meet him. The messenger said that they were going to attack the station, but one of the chiefs wanted first to see Mr Moffat to get some tobacco. Robert agreed to go with the man to meet the chief. He then found that the real leader was a man whom he had known in his early years in Namaqualand, and who had vowed not to meet Mr Moffat— probably because he both feared and respected him and knew in his heart that he would be shamed if he did so. In fact, 'Mr M was enabled to persuade them to relinquish their vile intentions and depart in peace having first restored some flocks of sheep and goats which they had got into their hands and remained 4 days about the station,' Mary reported laconically.

'A party of the latter [Corannas] not being willing to return entirely without booty, went further to Barolongs and succeeded in getting away a good number of cattle but were most of them (18 out of 27) treacherously murdered by a party of Bechuanas headed by Mohura the king's brother who lay at Old Lattakoo, two of these escaped fled hither for protection one of them with nothing on but his shoes. A short time before 30 out of 40 Corunnas were killed by another party of Bechuanas near the same place—but they were previously half dead with hunger—indeed the judgements of God are abroad in all the country. I suppose many hundreds of these depredators and their families have perished with hunger in the course of the last year and many more must die, because there is not food in the country the drought having been excessive for some years. The Batlapees, Battareres and Barolongs are entirely scattered and impoverished—some who possessed many hundreds of cattle have not now a single head. The interior are in a similar condition from the incursion of their more powerful neighbours the Baqueans—we have just been informed that the Bowankete have been driven and that the Bahurutse chief or king possesses 5 goats!! Where or how these things will terminate we know not . . .', Mary wrote to Mrs Wrigley. The mission was saved, but the country continued disturbed. The Bechuanas, made desperate by bloodshed and poverty, had become brave because they had nothing to lose.

Very little had changed, it seemed, except perhaps the physical landscape about Kuruman and their own determination not to be driven away. Accustomed to the long years of indifference they were taken by surprise when, at this moment, for Mary perhaps the blackest of her African life, their work began to blossom and bear fruit.

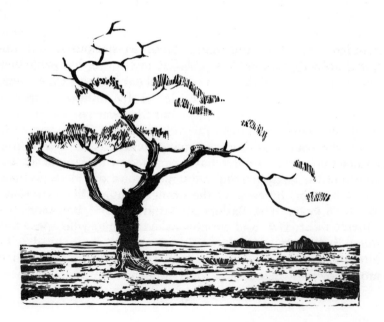

Chapter 8

THE TIMING OF such an awakening is as mysterious as the event itself. It coincided in this instance with the beginning of an exhausted and devastated peace in the country. Manifestations of this kind are not unconnected with the gift of tongues, signifying a sudden ability not only to hear but to understand what is heard. Undoubtedly Robert Moffat's final mastery of Sechuana had a powerful effect upon the people; the impact of his personality was the greater because the flow of his words was unimpeded by the barrier of interpretation. Mary too could now speak directly in everyday conversation with the women, as she had once longed to do.

But language itself is not enough. To be believed, the words that are spoken must come from a source that carries conviction. Through a long time of testing the Bechuana had come to trust their missionaries. They had watched them live up to their own precepts. The uncompromising toughness of Robert Moffat's moral standards, private as well as public, combined with an undeviating belief in an immortal African soul, commanded respect in this harsh land. Mysteriously, but unmistakably, Robert and Mary Moffat had shown that while they might in many ways despise the Bechuana, yet they loved them. After the most stringent of trials they were still there to prove it.

Evangelise before civilising, Robert Moffat believed. It was a point on which not everybody agreed with him. The hard manual work of building and growing, irrigating, cultivating, creating a home in which children could live and flourish had all been done simply to make living and evangelisation possible. But it provided a powerful witness. Kuruman with its trees and crops, its neat row of houses, its air of modest prosperity presented a miracle in this destroyed land and men were astounded when they saw it. It reinforced, powerfully and visibly, the Moffats' claim that the Lord protected and provided for His own.

Undoubtedly Robert Moffat had charisma. Tall, black-bearded, direct, untiring, with an urgent simplicity, he drew Africans to him. He possessed in abundant measure the virtue which is perhaps most immediately attractive—courage! A total self-disregard if what he had to do was in his eyes right. He believed in trusting Africans, as he trusted his God, with his life, and, both for the valorous Matabele (whom he later met) and the timid Bechuana, this was an astonishing trait. Nor could they eventually resist the knowledge that it was in their interest and on their behalf that he used it.

Robert and Mary Moffat made no effort to understand the Bechuanas. In one sense they were not concerned with their daily lives or their physical well-being, seeing only that in terms of urgent spiritual priorities much must be changed. Mary frequently complained of the Bechuanas' lack of energy and initiative. It seems never to have occurred to her that it might be connected with the starvation which she also noticed. She suffered herself from much ill-health, but would have died rather than let it prevent her doing her utmost. She was driven mad by constant begging and had no time for the somewhat specious argument that to be begged from was a sign of chieftainship. Her views on clothing, food, the position of women, the upbringing of children, the values of society remained unchanged. She neither accepted nor absorbed anything from her surroundings. Yet this very rigidity was strength. Refusal to compromise was essential to their survival. Had they taken on local colour, the tide of African humanity would have washed over and obliterated them. But, like a great rock, when the tide retreated and the sea calmed the Moffats were still there, unchanged, unassailable, stable, protecting. The church members were a 'separate' people. When they did wrong they were separated from the Church. It was very important that the Christian should be seen to be different, and the standards were rigid. But it was not a sterile rigidity, rather a demanding, loving one. At this moment in time it was exactly what was needed.

As so often in the early history of Christianity, it was among the poor people (those of the downtrodden tribes among the Bechuana) that the message first began to be heard. It started quietly. Now that there were lessons in Sechuana a number began to make progress in reading and writing. It became noticeable that behaviour improved during the services and that they listened to Robert's preaching with a fixed attention which was new. He had translated some hymns and the singing became a joy. Then, on a rising tide, a surge of feeling swept over the station, bursting out in revivalist fervour; a kind of religious hysteria took hold, 'a commotion in the minds of the people'.

It surprised the Moffats. They did not damp it down, neither did they encourage it. Neither Robert nor Mary was going to accept conversion based on emotion alone. They needed more than that—proof, evidence of a changed life not arrived at quickly but sustained over months. Those who were likely to be overcome during a service were asked to retire—or to sit near the door.

Nevertheless Mary began to hope. There was one firm candidate for baptism 'who tho' not a Mochuan we hope will prove a kind of first fruits of the mission—his name is Arend, formerly a slave who ran away from the Colony, sojourned many years in the interior and some years ago by means of the missionaries purchased his freedom with ivory and has since lived about 3 miles from the station and has lately seen the necessity of a decided profession.'

On February 27th 1829, Mary gave birth to her third daughter, Helen. On a Sabbath in July this baby shared with Arend, the ex-slave, his wife Rachel and four other candidates, the first public baptism that the Kuruman mission had seen.

Arend, a builder and thatcher by trade, had come with two other men and offered to construct a schoolhouse. They asked of the missionaries only plans and dimensions, door and window frames. The building was ready and opened and, for the time being, doing double duty as a church. As if to confirm the miracle, on the Friday before the baptismal service the communion vessels, ordered by Mary in faith so many years before, arrived. The station happened to be crowded with Griqua hunters passing through and other transient strangers. For weeks there had been a spontaneous, and quite new, interest in the subject of clothes. Mary was besieged with requests for help and advice and demands for instruction. A sewing class was started with a motley group of pupils, both men and women. Materials were pitifully scarce and they were six hundred miles from any kind of market, so she set to, designing jackets, trousers, dresses out of prepared skins. For two of the women she provided dresses from her own wardrobe.

The service was crowded. It was conducted by Robert in Sechuana, and for many of the strangers present was the first time that they had heard a man preach in their own tongue. For the sake of Rachel and some of the Griquas and Hottentots who did not understand, Mr Hamilton also gave a short address in Dutch. Robert took as his text John 1.29. the baptism of Christ in the Jordan. In the evening twelve communicants gathered round the table for the Lord's Supper. It must have been a celebration of tremendous emotional significance for the missionaries.

Of course it was hard to retain the high point of intense and practical commitment. There were backslidings and lapses. One of the greatest stumbling blocks was monogamy. A people accustomed to polygamous marriage did not take easily or kindly to putting away some of their wives, and for many of the women it could have been close to disaster to find themselves unsupported. Sometimes, pathetically, a man found that he simply could not live with only his senior wife, who now had the right to legality, and would cut himself off from his new-found fellowship and responsibilities rather than desert a younger wife whom he loved.

It was a situation which could have led to many crises, but the Moffats, while admitting no deviation from the strict rule of 'one man, one wife' for church members, were not unsympathetic to the human dilemmas which this involved. Robert Moffat would not countenance a man driving away his second wife. She was to be given a free choice as to whether she would return home to her father. If she did not wish to, then her husband had to support her until she found another husband or ceased to be in need of his protection. While for a long time there continued to be hardship and suffering in this respect, it is also true that the number of second wives who remarried gradually increased.

In this same month, July, Mary received two boxes from home. They contained portraits of her father and mother, and at the sight of them, after so many years of what still felt like exile, she was overcome by a turmoil of feelings. Unpacked, she hung them over the fireplace in the living-room of her house. That evening there was a church meeting held in this room and Mary, with a full heart, watched her husband sitting on one side of the fire with Mr Hamilton on the other, surrounded by the growing company of the infant church, all under the thoughtful gaze of the parents whom she so much loved. It seemed, after all, that she had not put her trust in the Lord in vain.

Towards the end of this year, which had seen many significant changes—including the first translation of the Gospel of St Luke—an event occurred which was to affect Robert Moffat's life and the future of the mission. In the same way that rumours of the Mantatee invasion had spread immense distances with great rapidity, news had now begun to go through the country that something strange was happening at Kuruman.

One day two strangers arrived at the station seeking hospitality, and explained that they had come to examine this new way of life. The Bechuana were shocked at the appearance of these men, tall, fine-looking—and completely naked. They were Matabele, *indunas* or councillors of the absolute monarch Moselekatse, whose people, with their enormous herds of cattle, occupied at this time the country to the north-east, round what later became Pretoria in the Transvaal. The Matabele were a warrior Zulu tribe owing rigorous obedience to their king, and a source of fear and terror to their neighbours.

The Moffats were extremely impressed by these messengers, their politeness and good manners. With great dignity the Matabele agreed to accede to their hosts' wishes and cover some of their nakedness. They were shown everything, the houses; the gardens with their wheat, maize, pumpkins, tobacco, beans, Indian corn, water-melons; the fruit trees; the irrigation channels and water ditch; the smith's forge; the carpentry shop; the walls of the cattle folds. They looked and touched and it was plain that, while astonished at what they saw, they were men of intelligence storing up this experience to tell their king. 'You are men, we are but children,' one of them said to Robert.

Mary showed them her house, its European furniture—most

95

of it made by her husband—the portraits on the wall, a looking-glass. She gave one a present of the glass, but he returned it saying that he could not trust it. The more he saw of them the more Robert Moffat's admiration grew.

As the time came for them to return to Moselekatse various considerations began to preoccupy the missionaries. The Matabele were not loved by the Bechuana tribes through whose lands they would have to travel. They had risked considerable danger by coming and this might well be doubled when it was known that they had started home. There began to be rumours of a plan to murder them, and the Moffats were very aware that if this happened the Matabele would avenge the killing with ruthless slaughter.

Again and again Mary and Robert, with Mr Hamilton who had by now become an accepted member of their household, discussed what was to be done, and at last the decision was made that Robert should travel back through the Bechuana tribes with them, using his personal prestige to avert disaster. It was an arduous prospect, a journey of two or three months, and Mary must have known that for all his growing reputation it held many hazards for her husband.

Then there was the mission, just beginning to take root and grow, which would have to be left in the hands of herself and Mr Hamilton, of whose management ability she had a low opinion. Also she had four young children and Robert was the only person for a hundred miles with even rudimentary medical skills if illness threatened.

But it was also a challenge. Moselekatse was an infinitely more powerful chief than any they had yet encountered. He was already intrigued by the work of the mission or he would not have sent his *indunas*. There might be an opportunity here to extend the work mightily and open up a road into the interior for the Lord.

After much discussion and prayer, it was agreed that Robert should accompany the messengers—at least to the borders of Moselekatse's lands, and on November 9th, laden with presents for the king from many people on the station, he set off in two ox-waggons with the *indunas* and a number of Bechuana volunteers.

Chapter 9

ROBERT MOFFAT WAS away for two months. When he
reached the boundaries of the Matabele chief's lands the
indunas pressed him to continue on to greet their king, saying
that they themselves would not survive if they arrived without
him. It was a journey that was to lay the foundations of a most
remarkable friendship, between Robert Moffat, dedicated
Scottish missionary, and Moselekatse despotic Matabele monarch. Each found the other's beliefs incomprehensible—and
yet fascinating. Moselekatse possessed his subjects and their
goods and controlled them absolutely: men trembled at his
slightest breath. Robert Moffat abhorred everything that
Moselekatse stood for, but he was scrupulous in his determination to avoid any political involvement. He was not afraid to
tell Moselekatse the enormity of his guilt before God, but only
on rare occasions did he use his influence to interfere in the
course of daily life as he found it in the king's kraal. There is no
doubt that Moselekatse's fascination with this stranger grew
into a genuine love for him which lasted forty years. Moshete
he called him, and he gave him also the name of his own father,
Machobane—though the two men were exactly the same age.
He questioned him closely about everything that went on at
Kuruman and wished that next time he might also see MaMary.
Deliberately, Robert Moffat was unimpressed by the honours
paid him and the barbaric displays of drilling and dancing, but
he admired the Matabele as people and he reciprocated
Moselekatse's personal liking.

He came back in January 1830, rather anxious about how
things had been in his absence with Mary and the children and
the infant mission. He need not have worried. Indeed seeing it
again he was struck by the station's air of prosperity. A second
house was finished and the church, which was to be the magnifi-
cent focus for the mission, had been started. The buildings
were in blue dove-coloured limestone thatched with reed or

97

straw. It had been a good season with plenty of rain and the Bechuana had begun to imitate the missionaries both in the crops they grew—tobacco, vegetables, maize, barley, peas, potatoes, etc—and also in the tools they were using. Progress in reading continued and the services in the temporary church were well attended. Mary and the children were healthy.

The matter of education, however, was now becoming pressing. The little girls, Mary and Ann, were aged nine and seven, and increasingly their mother felt the responsibility of making arrangements for their schooling. Their father, who enjoyed his children and loved to have them about him, would have been content to bring them up in Kuruman had it not been that Mary was too overburdened for such a task. She, however, remembered her own happy schooldays with the Moravians and did not intend that her children should be denied such advantages.

They discussed the possibility of a journey to the Colony. Robert had his own reasons for welcoming the idea. He had finished his translation of the Gospel of St Luke into Sechuana, also a hymn book, and he wanted to get them printed. He was becoming obsessed by the importance of translation and there was some talk of a printing press for Kuruman itself. So on June 15th they packed up the waggons and left on the long trek south.

They arrived at Grahamstown on the first of August. Robert wanted some action after the slow six weeks on the waggon. He borrowed a horse and went off to see some of the mission stations in this district, leaving Mary and the children to proceed to Theopolis, where she was able to make purchases and outfit the girls for school. Mary had chosen a 'Wesleyan establishment' at Salem, quite near Grahamstown, and Robert joined her there on September 1st to say goodbye to his daughters.

Leaving the little girls, from whom they had never been separated, was a severe wrench; 'a new sort of trial', Mary called it. However, she was pleased with the school. It paid strict attention to religious instruction, it was cheap, and, all things considered, it was not impossibly far away from home. She saw it being practicable for herself to make the long journey to visit them in two or three years, though 'we purpose calling to see them as we return, after which it is probable Moffat will be many years before he sees them again'. Whatever the heartbreak she did not regret her decision, being quite certain that 'keeping them at home is beyond all doubt highly improper'.

No sooner were the girls settled and Mary, with Robert and Helen, staying in the mission at Bethelsdorp than Mr Moffat was off again. The intention had been for the whole family to take a ship at Algoa Bay for Cape Town. However no ship was scheduled when they arrived there, so Robert, impatient to reach a printing press, again took to horseback and set off to ride the last lap. Mary was to follow as soon as she could get a ship making the fourteen-day, four-hundred-mile voyage round to Table Bay. She was pregnant again and no doubt glad to have a few weeks without responsibility to compose herself and gather strength for the future.

Temporarily she was in a vacuum. News of the death of William Roby had cut one more thread which bound her to her native land. She wondered now whether, if the time ever came, she would wish to return to a place where so much had changed. Yet Kuruman was still the sphere of her duty and her toil—not her home. Though she shared Robert's hopes and vision, and he expected full partnership from her when he needed it, with his increasing immersion in translation and the growth of her family their priorities had imperceptibly begun to differ. For him Kuruman was the creation, the source of achievement, the foundation on which much could now be built; for her it was the place from which she must, at all costs, free her children.

It was to be a year before she saw it again. Robert, finding too few compositors for the Government press at Cape Town, flung himself into the fresh challenge of learning the printing trade. In this he had as a companion Roger Edwards, an LMS missionary of the same age who had been at Bethelsdorp and was now to be transferred to Kuruman. Mary's health improved with the milder climate at the Cape and she found herself fully occupied laying in stores, preparing for the return to the interior, conducting mission business, much of which she had to attend to while Robert was preoccupied with the production of his translation.

In fact Robert worked himself so hard that his usually good health broke down and he suffered a severe attack of bilious fever and had to be carried aboard the ship when the time came to make the journey back to Algoa Bay en route to Kuruman. Mary, worn out by anxiety, the effort of nursing him and the need to oversee the loading of their goods, including the promised printing press, type, paper, ink, a finished edition of St Luke, the hymn book, a considerable amount of money towards the new church and a box of clothing materials sent by her friend Miss Lees, was exhausted when they arrived again at Bethelsdorp. Robert was weak and easily tired and she was nearing her time, but the goods had all to be unloaded again from the ship and packed into the waggons. On March 25th 1831 however, she produced 'a fine daughter whom we baptised Elizabeth, after my worthy friend Miss Lees'. She also had the great pleasure of visiting her two older daughters, finding them well and happy and altogether in much better spirits than when she had last seen them.

They came back to Kuruman—where Mr Hamilton and Mr Millen had looked after the station—quite a triumphal procession. As well as Mr and Mrs Edwards, with their two small children, they had also been joined by Mr and Mrs Baillie from Bethelsdorp. Robert had recovered and was full of his usual energy. The printing press was set up and proved a source of enormous astonishment to the local people who could not understand how a piece of paper went in white and came out covered with hieroglyphics. Although there had been a few backsliders, principally men returning to a polygamous wife, the work on the station had continued to grow.

For Mary this return brought one major and welcome change. The station now had a mission community, and with the arrival of new households, the increase of visiting families, her own work on the domestic side of the mission's economy grew in importance. Where she had been the only wife, struggling to keep her husband and family going, now she was mother to a whole community—and she enjoyed it. She had a good administrative brain and a talent for efficient management and was glad of the increased opportunity to use these gifts.

She immediately enlarged her own household to take in Mr Hamilton and Mr Millen, the former giving up his house to the Edwards and henceforth living in two rooms behind the Moffats' house and boarding with them. Mary was fond of them both. She had been brought up with brothers and liked and understood men perhaps better than she did women. In spite of hard work, ill health, an extreme climate and six children she had retained her looks, the bright blue eyes and fresh complexion of her youth.

For ten months of this year, also, two missionaries of the Paris Society, Samuel Rolland and Prosper Lemue, with their families, stayed with the Moffats while trying, with many difficulties, to establish a mission at Mosega to the north. They must have brought a breath of strangeness to the little community and Mary greatly enjoyed their company.

The sewing school was reopened and enlarged with the help of Mrs Edwards and Mrs Baillie, and in her own household Mary's arduous training of domestic help was beginning to bear fruit. One of her maids was Mamonyatsi, a young woman taken captive by the Matabele, whom Robert had brought back with him from the visit to Moselekatse. She was an intelligent woman who soon became interested in Mary's teaching and stayed with the Moffat household until she married and, shortly after, was baptised.

Suddenly the mission was alive and bustling and, with the growth of a more settled way of life and the increasing attraction of Kuruman as a resting place for travellers and a base for further operations into the interior, Mary found herself once more at the heart of the missionary work that had always been her first objective in Africa.

Life, however, continued to be harsh and lived in the shadow of disaster. It had been a dry season, with severe frosts, and smallpox raged in the north. Though the full force of the epidemic did not strike the Bechuana, the mission did not escape. Betsy, 'our beloved and interesting child', died of it in January 1832. She was ten months old and it was a painful death. She had apparently recovered from what her father called 'water in the head'. For twenty-four hours she lay moaning in great distress and then died, to be buried beside her baby brother in the Kuruman graveyard. Mary was torn between grief for a much-loved baby and a deep faith that Betsy's spirit had gone home to its Heavenly Father. But she was not to remain long uncomforted. In this same year James was born, named after his grandfather. Perhaps because he so soon replaced Betsy, this was the child who wound himself most closely round his mother's heart, although it would have been against her sense of fairness to have allowed anyone to perceive it.

The Baillies had not proved a success. It was becoming more and more plain that the school, for both adults and children, was of paramount importance. Now that there was literature in Sechuana, spelling books and lessons in addition to the Gospels, the people were beginning to see the value of being able to read. Robert Moffat realised that the harvest which lay at hand from the operation of translating and printing was beyond what even he had imagined. But the school remained a constant source of problems.

It had suffered, and still suffered, from being only one of a multiplicity of tasks that had to be undertaken by the hard-pressed missionaries. Building, planting, repairing and now translating and printing, were all apt to have a higher priority than teaching. They were basics, without which some of the mission's work could not go forward. The pupils too did not give precedence to schooling, and until recently had seen no necessity for learning any of the subjects taught. Now they recognised some value in the first R, but little in the second and none in the third, having their own method of calculating which bore no relation to the arithmetic that the Europeans tried to teach them. There were more important things than school. The boys had to spend long days bird-scaring when harvest drew near, there was hunting, working in the fields, household tasks—all more urgent than learning. It needed perseverance on the part of the teacher to overcome these obstacles and introduce some kind of continuity into the school. Mr Baillie was not such a man. Robert Moffat, who expected the highest standards from those who worked with him, thought him use-less. Robert himself, however, was very much against the training of local teachers. Though there were now one or two men in the church who might have fulfilled this function, he felt that it was impossible for them to have the profound grounding in the Christian faith that was essential for those who were to have the training of the young in their hands. The ultimate aim of the school was to introduce children to the Gospel and give them the means of reading it for themselves. In this view Robert

Moffat was a man of his time; a generation later his son was to criticise him for it.

With the arrival of the printing press which gave him the ability to produce as much printed Sechuana as he could translate, Robert's daily schedule of work reached outrageous proportions. His reserves of physical stamina were phenomenal but he came near to wearing them out. Mary worried about his health, but she made no effort to divert him from the tasks ahead. As long as he was engaged in the Lord's work she would support him to the utmost in it.

What had become plain to her, though, was that most of the planning and ordering of the family's life would be left to her. Quite apart from the fact that he was immersed in the affairs that were of paramount importance to him, she had what Robert had not—a good administrative brain. Capable, efficient, able to delegate responsibility, the days when she had wept in the face of her household chores and hoards of unwanted visitors were long gone. She had made herself mistress of the complicated skills needed to run a British household in primitive surroundings and, more important, she was able to communicate them to the women around her. Robert, instinctively untidy, kept her out of his study for fear of her equally instinctive need to create order.

She would not have considered it right or seemly to play a leading role in the affairs of the station, but she had little opinion of Mr Hamilton's management skills though she thought him 'an excellent and laborious man and his labours on the place are invaluable', and she knew her own Robert's all-consuming enthusiasms with their corresponding weaknesses. How much of the credit for the qualities which the mission at Kuruman developed and became famous for—warmth, hospitality, good management, productiveness, beauty—belonged to Mary Moffat will never be known. She would have preferred it that way. She did not believe in personal publicity.

It was three years since her two eldest children had gone to school in the Colony, and over two years since she had last seen them. After much thought Mary decided that she must undertake this arduous journey alone. She could not ask Robert to leave the station so soon, nor was it right that he should interrupt the work in which he was immersed for family concerns.

The preparations gave her some anxious thought. Not only was she facing a long waggon journey with three small children, Robert six, Helen four and Jamie just under a year, needing to give most careful consideration as to who should go with her as driver, assistant, nursemaid, general factotum; she was also leaving Robert alone for four or five months and must make as good arrangements as she could for his domestic comfort. Communication between Kuruman and the Colony was too infrequent not to make the fullest use of such a journey, so she was to bring back type and printing paper, and no doubt run many other errands for the station.

She left in April 1833 and was away five months. In the event the journey was 'exceedingly prosperous, nothing worthy of an accident having taken place'. She took with her five Bechuana men and one Hottentot, as well as a nurse girl. One of the men, Paul, a convert, proved a tower of strength. 'Not having my husband with me I had occasion to put the more confidence in him, and truely it was not misplaced.'

She found the children well, though she was rather guarded about their progress. It must, however, have been good enough for her to decide to leave Robert too this time. Mary was twelve now, and fleetingly her mother had 'been desirous of making [her] acquainted with the Infant School system before her return home; but she is still rather too young to leave school unless she could have been placed with a person who would have attended her education. . . .' It is not quite clear what she intended, but as there was talk of opening an infant school at Kuruman it is possible she was thinking of having her oldest daughter prepared to come back and take over as its teacher. The idea, if such it was, proved inappropriate and was abandoned.

Not only was this journey a success, she eventually arrived back to find that the maids whom she had trained and instructed to look after Robert had exceeded her expectations 'so that he had had very little to trouble him in that respect'. In view of the near disasters and frequent incompetence that attended so many mission journeys, it is tempting to speculate how much better some would have been managed had Mary Moffat been in charge!

She came back to the 'perpetual bustle' of the mission station. Robert was deeply immersed in the work of translation and 'the extreme anxiety of his mind to give everything as correctly as possible causes him incessant mental labour. Whatever he is doing or however engaged we are sure to find that his mind is occupied with some knotty passage of Scripture about which commentators and critics cannot agree.' Mr Edwards had to take his family to the Colony for some months because of the ill health of three-year-old Daniel. He was unhappy there, primarily it seems because he wanted to be regarded as an artisan rather than a missionary. He wrote, nostalgically, to the Directors that he had been very happy at Kuruman where the school and the printing kept him fully occupied and gave him a purpose to be getting on with. He was not a natural preacher and found it difficult to talk to people directly about spiritual matters. While he was away more cares than ever fell on Robert Moffat's shoulders.

It was a very hot summer, cattle died, milk was scarce. A youth was killed by lightning. Served by irrigation channels, Kuruman presented a startling contrast to the dessicated country surrounding it. The church services were packed. Hundreds waited on Sunday mornings for the doors to be opened. Of the first converts to be baptised very many were women, a comment both on Christianity's appeal to the underprivileged and on the influence of MaMary.

She was concerned about their financial affairs. Robert varied in his attitude to personal wealth, from a note to the Directors saying that he thought missionaries could do with less pay to an expression of thankfulness that the Society was now willing to be responsible for the board and education of children at school. No doubt it was Mary who persuaded him to suggest that the Directors alter their administration of the Society's affairs in regard to education, pointing out that there was no justice in the allocation of grants—one missionary allowed £60 yearly for two children, another £30 for two, another nothing. For himself, buying reference books for his translation work was now a heavy drain on his salary.

The Bechuana continued both to please and exasperate them. 'Dancing and other heathenish amusements are not allowed' on the station, Robert wrote. He also felt that shaving their heads in youth and exposing them to the sun might very well have an injurious effect on Bechuana brains! Their lack of curiosity he found sorely trying. They would not ask him questions—although when he spoke to them they showed a positive and welcome interest in what he was saying. Lying and pilfering were common, but they had a touching faith in the honesty and truthfulness of the missionaries and would give them their most precious possessions to keep when they went hunting or on a journey. All in all Kuruman had become an extended family, presided over by Robert and MaMary, with the affections, the respect and the tribulations that families engender.

But they were not a closed society. Strangers came to visit and the extension of the Gospel to those in the interior remained the Moffats' dearest wish. One day a Coranna chief of a distant village rode in on an ox accompanied by two or three attendants. He was well dressed, clean, unaggressive. He stopped at Mary Moffat's door and asked where he should sleep, saying that he had come to see Moffat. He gazed for a long time at Robert and his long black beard, looked at Mary and the children, came into the house and gravely regarded all the furniture. He said very little. When he retired for the night to an outhouse he refused the food Mary offered him, saying that he had brought plenty of his own. This was such an unusual occurrence that the missionaries were puzzled as to what exactly his object might be.

For two days Mosheu, the chief, stayed at Kuruman, carefully inspecting every aspect of the station's activities. He spoke Sechuana, so he could question the local people when he did not understand. Then he climbed back on to his ox and left, saying to Robert Moffat, 'I came to see you; my visit has given me pleasure; and now I return home.'

It was not however the last that they saw of him. Some time later he returned from his village, accompanied by a large retinue of brothers, wives, children and servants, and settled down to study the Christian doctrine, after which he again returned home to persuade his people to accept it.

Death was never far distant. Mr Millen, the mason, had gone into partnership with a trader, David Hume, and they had made one or two journeys to the north. In 1834 Millen set out alone on another journey to seek for ivory. He did not arrive back when expected and though they were anxious it was not unusual for waggons to be delayed, sometimes for weeks. At the same time waggons from Kuruman were going north to look for timber and hoped that they might meet him on the way— though in a country of no roads there was little guarantee that two waggons would take the same trail. In this case they passed each other unseen. Had they met it might just have been possible to bring help to Mr Millen's fatally stricken convoy. As it was, he was dead long before the news came to Kuruman.

Mary had been very fond of him. At the start of this particular journey she had been making him a baking of rusks and a roasting of coffee to take with him and they were not quite ready when he started. Distressed that he should be going off without them she had rushed into her room as he left, snatched a pillow off her bed and thrust it into his hands saying, 'There Millen, that at least may add to your comfort.' Now he was dead and a gap left in her household. She wrote to her father a description of what had happened.

'He had none but Bechuana attendants, and they, worn-out with fatigue with travelling night and day to bring him home, had slept while he breathed his last. They afterwards did their best to bring him to Motito for burial, but it was impossible, and they reluctantly committed his remains to the dust in the desert. . . . To the north of the Zulu country a bilious fever attacked several of his people, and he feelingly laments in his journal that he has no medicine to give them. Before they reached Moselekatse one of them died. The day they left Moselekatse's he himself sickened; two days after another man died, and, three or four days after, he himself. He said nothing in his illness, but one day told his people to drive on without regard to oxen or anything else, as he thought more of their number would die.' It was another of the many instances of remarkable African loyalty to the strangers in their midst.

Chapter 10

EIGHTEEN HUNDRED AND THIRTY-FIVE was to be a bad year. Mary had been in Africa now for fifteen years—years for the most part of unremitting effort, considerable ill health, five living and two dead children and growing family responsibilities. The possibility of a visit back to Britain had never been mentioned—or indeed thought of. The Society did not make itself liable for any home leave and, in financial terms, the Moffats were very poor. More important still, the time that would have been consumed by such a visit was unthinkable at this stage in the mission's development. The long journeys to the Colony were hazard enough.

The summer of 1834/35 was very warm with all the accompanying discomforts of excessive, thundery heat. Mary never grew accustomed to the hot weather and, unfortunately, the worst of the summer months coincided with the latter stages of many of her pregnancies. This time was no exception: she was again carrying a child. Nevertheless she had little time to spare for herself, for Robert, worn out by the exhaustion of continuous overwork, was prostrate with bilious fever.

The situation was saved by the arrival at Kuruman in January 1835 of an expedition from the Cape on its way to visit Matabele country and anxious to contact Robert Moffat and perhaps persuade him to accompany them. The Expedition for Exploring Central Africa, sponsored by the Governor and scientific elements at the Cape, was led by Dr Andrew Smith, later Director of British Army Medical Services in the Crimea, now stationed with the army in Cape Town. Dr Smith had undertaken several journeys before and was interested in the scientific exploration of the interior.

He arrived at Kuruman at a providential moment. It was the first time that the station had had the benefit of a qualified medical man, and but for his presence Mary Moffat might have died.

No sooner had Robert recovered than Mary, her weakness no
doubt exacerbated by the strain of nursing him, fell ill. The
baby—a fine strong boy named John Smith—was born on
March 10th, but Mary did not make the recovery that was
expected from the pattern of her other pregnancies. Doctor
Smith was optimistic and cheerful. She began slowly to
improve: then she had a relapse and he diagnosed dropsy and
an abscess on a lung, and warned Robert that he might be going
to lose her. It looked as though the fears which Mary had
expressed to her friend Mrs Wrigley in 1828 before the birth of
Helen were about to be fulfilled. '. . . there is indeed something
very painful in the prospect of leaving a beloved Partner with
3 or 4 small children in the midst of barbarity without one
civilised female who could render him assistance even for the
short time that he must of necessity remain here after such an
event. . . .' But her mind must have been a little eased by the
knowledge that times at Kuruman had changed in the inter-
vening seven years and that, thanks to her efforts and training,
there were now a number of women to care for Robert and the
children's material needs in the way that she would have
wanted.

Robert and Dr Smith took turns to watch at night. Mr and
Mrs Lemue, the French missionaries whose company Mary
had so much enjoyed when they stayed at Kuruman in 1831,
came to visit and remained to help. Gradually she began the
long climb back to health, but it was clear that her complete
recovery would be a slow business and probably almost impossible if she were in her own home at Kuruman where the
daily cares and responsibilities would inevitably make demands
on her which she would never refuse. Dr Smith strongly
advised a journey to the Colony.

Before that could happen, however, and while Mary was
still too weak to undertake much exertion, Dr Smith and his
expedition left for Moselekatse's country and Robert went with
them. He had invaluable knowledge, not only of the land and
peoples through which they would travel but also of the
tyrant, Moselekatse, himself, and Andrew Smith had pressed
him hard to accompany them. At first he had refused; but the
temptation of such a journey, which he also felt he could use to
open up opportunities for a group of American missionaries

who had written saying they wished to come and work among the Matabele, was too much. He told himself that he owed some return to Dr Smith for his skill in saving Mary's life.

Mary watched him go with mixed feelings. Had she permitted herself any indulgence in self-pity, the loss of Robert at a moment when she desperately needed support and comfort might have overwhelmed her. On the other hand Robert away on a journey which she knew he would enjoy, in the company of other men—one of them a good friend and a doctor—eased her mind of a perpetual anxiety. While he was away she might be concerned for his safety, but she did not need to worry about the enormous strain to which he subjected himself on the station or to watch anxiously the eroding of his iron constitution. On the whole she was glad to see him go.

Perhaps it was the twinge of conscience, as well as love, that made Robert Moffat on this journey start the journal letters to Mary that were to be a feature of his later travels. He wrote to her almost every day, collecting the letters together and sending them back by messenger when he could. He wrote everything: news of the expedition's progress, of the peoples whom they passed through, speculation about the possibilities for the work, observations on discoveries of interest, instructions and domestic details. Smallpox was raging among the Matabele, she and Mr Edwards, who had returned to Kuruman, should send for virus. He would send back a sewing school chest, a hamper and Parkhurst's Greek Lexicon, all found in a clear-out of the waggon. Mary must indeed have been weakly when he left her, for she would normally have supervised the cleaning and packing of the waggon herself. She was to kill a large black ox when beef was needed. Could she let him know the likely date of Mrs Edwards' confinement. (It was to be September 2nd.) He hoped the damp weather had not affected her. 'Remember me in your prayers.' Kiss the baby for him. He still sometimes heard him in the night and hoped he continued to be so good. He thought of James' pranks and sent his love to him and Helen. He hoped to bring the latter curious things if she behaved well and was obedient to her Mama. PS. If there had been no rain to water the orange trees behind the house. Compliments to all the domestics. Take care to keep his study shut and locked. He learned from Moselekatse that Helen, aged six, had sent him a message by one of the Bechuana to send her one milk cow and one for James who loved milk, and one for Johnny who was sucking. Mary had sent Moselekatse five blue basins and an embroidered cap. It was a measure of the relationship of the whole Moffat family with the Matabele chief, though only Robert ever met him, that he was delighted with Helen's message and sent the cows she asked for along with corn and cows for MaMary and a small calabash for Helen herself.

Not only did Robert write constantly to MaMary, keeping her informed of many things which would later be translated into reports for the Directors; he waited anxiously for any letters in return. He knew that she would calculate carefully their daily rate of travel so that when there was a chance of a man passing near their likely route she could send messages. He let her know how gladly they were received. 'I was running lustily, when I stumbled on two horsemen, and as soon as I heard the voice of Maganu my very heart seemed to leap into my mouth. I trembled to ask a question. I walked a few steps before I could open my mouth. At last I mustered as many words as made "How are they all at Kuruman? How is MaMary?" "All is well," he replied, "and MaMary is getting better daily." His reply made my tears flow and my heart as light as a feather.'

Robert had the stimulation and interest of travel, fresh company and a new opportunity to be grasped. For Mary, left at home, life moved more slowly. Though the stream of letters follows on from day to day, their despatch was an uncertain business. Weeks might go by before the chance came to send a bundle to Kuruman and for Mary the gaps seemed long and often weary. 'Another day far advanced, and we hear nothing of you. Shampan arrived this morning, and knows nothing. Once more I begin to feel that "hope deferred maketh the heart sick," ' she wrote on June 25th. All was well at Kuruman. The congregations were large; there had been some necessity for discipline. She had had a letter from Griqua Town about the American missionaries which she had discussed with Mr Edwards and Mr Hamilton and they had all agreed upon an answer. There were rumours—as always—about his progress. Some said that the expedition had arrived at the borders of

Moselekatse's territory and sent forward messengers to the king, but she did not know whether to believe this or not. 'My dear Robert, thus far I wrote on Thursday evening, fondly hoping to hear something of you before this. . . . I have now come to the conclusion to send Melomo and another with the little news we have, that you may no longer be kept in suspense, whatever we are. I continue to hope for the best, though I feel very impatient to hear in what circumstances you have been placed. I am aware that your situation is a critical one, and one of considerable responsibility. . . . For my own part I do not experience less support on this occasion than on former ones, believing that He who has hitherto been so gracious to us will yet be so. . . . I do, however, feel it necessary to prepare my heart for further trials, as I have always done under our separations, anticipating at times the most painful occurrences, and have frequently found that such anticipations are a means of deepening a sense of the Divine goodness when we are permitted to meet. . . .'

Towards the end of July she knew that Robert was safely on his way home. She packed her waggon, put Helen, Jamie and the baby John into it, and set off with her driver thirty-six miles towards the north, to Motito where the French missionaries were established. The children loved waggon journeys, when their mother, relieved of her daily cares, sat in the little rolling house and told them stories of her own childhood, the nursery garden at Dukinfield, the relatives they had never seen, the Moravian school of which she had fond memories. For Mary too a journey was a relaxation, the forced rest and inaction restored her stretched physical resources. For all of them there was the enormous pleasure and relief of the reunion at the end of it with Papa.

He had had another notable journey, the most remarkable aspect of which was his touching meeting with Moselekatse, who had greeted him with all the affection of a son meeting a loved father after a long absence, though the two men were about the same age. A free conduct in the king's Matabele territories had been procured for Dr Smith's expedition; permission was given to collect timber for the church at Kuruman from the wooded defiles in the king's country, and a way had been prepared for the American missionaries. Now that

Robert was back and Mary well enough to undertake a long journey herself, they began to plan again for her to go with the children to the Colony.

Now it was she who left him. She had made the journey once alone; this time there was David Hume, the trader, Mr Millen's partner, to escort her as far as Grahamstown. Reluctant as they both were to part again so soon, it was clearly Robert's duty to stay at Kuruman.

Her convoy of waggons left on November 19th. Robert rode beside them as far as the Vaal river, about a hundred miles, where the water was low and the waggons crossed easily. He parted with them with a heavy heart and watched the dust of their progress retreat slowly from him on the other side.

The easy passage of the Vaal had not prepared Mary for what she found at the Orange river, to which the borders of the Colony now stretched. The river was in flood and for a whole month her waggons were compelled to wait on the north bank, watching day after day as the tawny water, five hundred yards wide, flowed swiftly by, hoping every morning to find that it had gone down sufficiently to allow them to pass.

It was exposed flat desert country and, in the heat of mid-summer, Mary suffered severely. Several times she thought of giving up the journey and returning to Kuruman, but then her dislike of turning back from a task she had set herself made her wait yet a little longer in the hope of the water receding. Sometimes in the evenings the river did appear to fall and they would retire for the night confident of being able to make the crossing tomorrow. But always the next day there had been a fresh influx of water and the ford was impossible.

At last it became plain that unless they had recourse to some artificial means they were never going to get across. Upstream of them a party of Boers with their waggons had gathered in the same predicament. They had begun to make a raft and Mary with her little group joined them. There were altogether eighteen waggons and, with immense effort but without casualties of any sort, they managed to ferry them all across on a raft made of willow trees tied together with bark. It was pulled back and forward on a strong bullock hide rope by men standing on either bank of the eighty-yard stretch of river that they had chosen as affording the narrowest crossing and the best take-off and landing grounds. The waggons were emptied of all their contents and taken to pieces to be piled on to the raft, and had then to be laboriously put together again on the other side. It might all have been too much for Mary, but once again her spirits rose with the challenge of a practical task and the exercise of her talent for delegated organisation and 'it was gratifying to find that for all I had endured I was no worse but rather better'.

Nevertheless by the time they got to Grahamstown what strength she had recovered was exhausted. She picked up Mary, Ann and Robert from school and the whole family went to the coast to recuperate.

MaMary had decided to take the three older children away from Salem and send them to school at the Cape. It was a decision taken in faith and one which must have cost her many anxious hours' deliberation. There were frightening financial considerations—even with help from the Society, it was a great deal further away from Kuruman than Grahamstown, and she had no great opinion of the quality of life in Cape Town. But she valued education for her children and knew that she could not give it to them at home.

The arrangements, many of which had to be conducted at long distance, through uncertain communications, relying often on the goodwill of strangers, would have daunted a less re-doubtable spirit. There must have been in her a force of character and a strength of faith which gave her children from a very early age the resilience to meet every change of circumstance with courage.

In March they all travelled to Port Elizabeth to look for a ship which would take Mary, Ann and Robert, now fourteen, twelve and eight, the eleven days' journey to the Cape. A much longer delay than Mary had intended ensued because, although there were ships, all of them were 'destitute of female passengers who could take charge of them'. In the middle of April she was still waiting. A ship at last arrived in the bay with a suitable chaperon on board and Mary, thankfully, made arrangements for the children. Every day she expected to get news that the ship was ready for sailing and each day she was disappointed. Having made up her mind to the parting the interminable postponement fretted her terribly. Besides she was expected back at Kuruman and Robert would be impatient, perhaps worried, as the days went by and her return became overdue.

Then, at last, she was told that the following Friday was the definite sailing date. 'The Monday before I was getting terribly impatient, but suddenly got a check. Mary was taken very ill on Monday evening; her symptoms were so violent that she was twice bled, and had to take much medicine. You may in some degree conceive of my anxiety, expecting every hour to be called on board. During the whole of Tuesday I was harassed with messages that the ship was to sail. On Wednesday I was kept in the same state of agitation besides grief on Mary's account, want of sleep and excessive fatigue. The captain having assured me the day before that I should have timely warning I tried to keep myself easy, though some of my friends urged me to be off; but knowing the anxiety of the passengers, I viewed it all as report, foolishly trusting to the captain's promise, which he forgot. All the passengers were on board, when good old Mr Kemp came and assured me that the vessel was to sail before morning. The moon had now risen. Mary was altogether unfit to go, and I had no alternative but to pack up and get the others away without her. Mrs Atkinson and Mrs Chalmers, who were here, agreed to stop with Mary, and Mrs Robson and I went on board accompanied by the good old gentleman. I make no attempt to describe my feelings. The very evening, fine, still, clear, and a full moon beaming on the water; it was enough to procure a sentimental feeling, but I had little time for this. Deep perplexity and consideration of the mystery of this providence absorbed much of my thoughts. I left the two dear children in comfortable circumstances and in good company. . . . When we left the vessel they were speaking of drawing up the anchor, and just as the evening gun went off the captain passed us in the last boat.'

The ship was called the *Briton*. Several times in the night Mary got up and looked out her window to see if it had sailed, but in the darkness she could make nothing out. As soon as it was dawn she looked out again and saw that a ship was indeed standing out into the bay towards the cape at its entrance. Abandoning all thought of being able after all to get Mary on board she began to make alternative plans.

'About ten o'clock, however, Mr Robson came, out of

breath, to tell me the *Briton* was still in the bay, and the wind contrary. This was good news to me, as there was still a chance of getting Mary away should she be detained another night. Thursday evening I went down to Mr Kemp and begged him to order a boat to be in readiness tomorrow morning should there be any signs of the *Briton* sailing. As Mary continued to recover, I now began to hope; and after committing the matter to the Father of Mercies, laid me down quite composed, concluding that if the vessel were away before daylight it was for some gracious reason, and if not, I should certainly get her on board. As soon as day dawned I went to the window to see, but all was still. I lay down again, but was soon roused, hearing that Mr Chick wanted me. He told me the vessel would soon be off. I sent for Mrs Robson, and we soon got Mary up and a chair prepared for her. She walked part of the way, and was carried through the sand. The ship was now under weigh and we followed her about four or five miles. Mary bore it well. My mind was greatly relieved by finding Ann and Robert perfectly happy. The ship was out of sight by early afternoon. It is now stormy and I think much of Cape Lagulhas, but am enabled to hope in that mercy which has always attended us.'

She left immediately for Grahamstown, with Helen and the two boys, where there were things to be done in preparation for the long trek home. But she waited deliberately until the post arrived bringing the news that Mary, Ann and Robert, after 'rather a dangerous passage of eleven days', had arrived safely in Cape Town and were well and in good spirits. Then, with a sigh of relief, she set her face once again towards Kuruman.

Her progress was slow but uneventful. Along the way she bought livestock, sheep and cows, to make up the depleted herds at Kuruman. On June 15th 1836, at two o'clock in the afternoon, she arrived again on the banks of the Orange river. She had written to Robert telling him when she expected to be there, hoping that perhaps he might be able to come so far to meet them. There was no sign of him. About five o'clock in the evening, however, she saw a horseman approaching the other side. It was Robert! After seven months' separation, in a country where daily life was fraught with mortal hazards, their reunion seemed like a miracle.

Mary came home in better health, which during the next

two years gradually worsened as renewed exertions took their toll. She did not let it keep her, however, from full involvement in the affairs of the station.

Somehow, after the tremendous flowering of the last five years, the mission seemed to have entered a period of quiescence. The steady progress that the missionaries had hoped for did not materialise. There were backsliders, offenders, those who slipped again into the old ways of polygamy. Robert Moffat took a stern, patriarchal view of all sins. He separated members from the church for quite minor offences and was rigorous in the criteria required before admission for baptism. 'Were we to baptise all who desire it, we should have many members with many sorrows.' Both he and Mary felt that at this stage it was all important that those who stood before their fellows as full church members should be without blame. It was still too easy to bring the infant church into disrepute. Nevertheless the work of translating and printing, which continued unabated, brought with it an unexpected benefit. Of those who left the church a number could now read and prized this accomplishment, so that even though they removed from the mission station they insisted on taking their books with them and continuing to study the Gospel and teach it to others.

Robert was still irritated by the Bechuana's deplorable want of mental energy. Although he was a man of great kindness and patience, he saw no reason why other people should not possess the same powers as himself. He had taught himself everything he knew and he expected the same dedication from others. It upset him that the Africans would not ask questions. Mr Edwards, a man of much less remarkable gifts, saw more clearly that when the great concern was 'what they shall eat', there was a restricted amount of mental vigour left over for learning. Nevertheless, as Robert rather grudgingly admitted in a report to London, looking back over the years of struggle notable progress had been made.

The American missionaries, for whom Robert Moffat had opened the way with the Matabele, were not so fortunate. They had gone up to Mosega at the end of 1835, three men with their wives and two children, with a number of Kuruman Africans. With them also as nursemaid went Mary's adopted daughter, the Hottentot child Sarah Roby, now aged eleven. The party arrived at Mosega in February and were well received by Moselekatse's people. A year later the mission was broken up, the missionaries had retreated and one of the wives was dead.

The circumstances in which this mission failed were of great importance to the Moffats and Kuruman. For some time now there had been considerable pressure across the frontiers of the Colony by disaffected Boer farmers. As they pressed further and further north, seizing land where they could and destroying any tribes who opposed them, the missionaries became more and more concerned by the strains this put on their relationships with their own people. The Boers were white and Christian, yet they took a view of racial differences that was totally opposed to all that the missionaries stood for. For their part the Boers succeeded in getting the Colony government to ban the sale of guns and gunpowder to Africans outside the Colony border and accused the missionaries of breaking this law. Robert Moffat, while never dealing in gun smuggling, considered it a blatant injustice that the African tribes, who depended on hunting for their food, should be denied the weapons which were now becoming essential for this exercise because of the growing scarcity of game due to the activities of armed Boer hunters and European traders. Although as yet there had been no direct conflict between the encroaching Boer trekkers and the mission, apprehensions had grown steadily over the months.

Now a mission had become directly enmeshed in the clash between white and black. The Boers, raiding far to the north-west, entered Matabele territory. What then happened is not absolutely clear. The Matabele attacked any who came armed into their country, the Boers retaliated killing many and driving off six thousand head of cattle. Moselekatse eventually retreated back beyond the Limpopo, taking all his people with him. Mary wrote to her father a description of what had occurred at the station itself. An epidemic of fever had struck the mission from which young Mrs Wilson had just died. '... the Boers came upon them quite unexpectedly one morning early. The Zulus were entirely off their guard, knowing nothing till the bullets were flying about them in every direction. The Boers brutally commenced hostilities at the mission station and one ball fell at the foot of the bed on which Mr Venables lay sick. The outhouse in which their servants slept was literally shot to pieces. Two of our poor people who were with them, one of them a lad we brought up, have disappeared, and it is not known whether they were killed or fled. One of those who has come back narrowly escaped several times. What induced the missionaries to go with the Boers we do not yet know. . . . These pillaged the house before their eyes. . . .'

The damaging part was that the American missionaries had not stood in the middle, as Robert Moffat in other conflicts had so often done, refusing to desert their people. They had withdrawn with the Boers, which must in Matabele eyes accuse them of complicity. Robert Moffat felt this the more because it was through his friendship with Moselekatse that the mission had been permitted to be established. And indeed it was to be many more years before the king would again agree to accept missionaries in any territory which he controlled. '. . . The interior is now effectually closed,' Mary wrote, 'and if Government will wink at the proceedings of these Boers they will annihilate the aborigines, as we hear they intend seating themselves in the Baharutse country.'

The French mission too, at Motito, was in trouble, though not of such a serious kind. Mrs Lemue, of whom Mary was very fond, was extremely ill. Leaving the two small boys, Jamie and Johnny, aged three and six, with their father and taking the nine-year-old Helen with her, Mary hastened to Motito to return the help that she herself had received in similar circumstances in 1835. Her own household was by now so well organised that she was free to look to the larger concerns of the mission and to building up Kuruman as a base, always able and ready to provide practical help and assistance.

She was now beginning to have thoughts about the possibility of a visit home to England. She had been in Africa very nearly twenty years, and it especially concerned her that her girls had never been back to their parents' homeland. Mary was seventeen, Ann fifteen. She wanted them to have some experience of their own country. Robert's health also worried her. He was on the last stages of translating the New Testament and the tremendous effort had taken its toll. He could hardly sleep at nights, tossing and turning, his brain churning with the mental stimulation of his day's work. Yet she did not see how she was going to get him to leave—and this journey she had no intention of undertaking alone.

In November 1838 the great stone church, which had taken so many years and so much labour to build, was finished. It stood in the middle of the station, a landmark for miles around. At the same time Robert's New Testament was also completed. It was too great a work to undertake on the Kuruman printing press and, with how much subtle pressure from Mary is not known, the whole Moffat family decided to set out for Cape Town to find a professional printer and to give them all a chance to recover some semblance of good health.

KURUMAN CHURCH

Chapter 11

THEY SET OFF in December. They were both forty-three and their family consisted of three girls and three boys. It was high summer and Mary was pregnant again. She took this condition and its attendant discomforts for granted; in any case there were other problems to concern her.

Both she and Robert accepted that their children would follow them into service with the mission. Kuruman was, in the real sense, the young Moffats' home and, certainly at this stage, the children acquiesced in this view of their future. Perhaps only nine-year-old Helen felt stirrings of well-concealed rebellion.

However, in their attitudes to preparation for that future the Moffat parents were very different. A firmly based faith and a good home seem to have been Robert's criteria. Once again, as with the Bechuana, his own experience led him to believe that a person could make and educate himself if he really wished to. Anyway he was seized by the total preoccupation of a man who finds himself engaged in work that he loves and is profoundly fitted for; he trusted Mary to do what was best, which meant in effect letting her get on with it.

Mary, on the contrary, took this responsibility very seriously. Herself a trainer of some talent, she wished her children to have the benefit of the best training that they could, in the circumstances, get. It was not easy to know what this was, and any decisions she made were essentially lonely ones, for although Robert listened to her this was a burden he did not want to share.

She was determined, though she did not see how, that the children would go to England; and she had confidence in the working out of providence. So it probably did not surprise her when the way was quite suddenly, and unexpectedly, opened, and no doubt she was sufficiently alert and prepared to see the opportunity and help make the decision.

On arrival at Cape Town, carrying his precious manuscripts with him, Robert Moffat discovered that there was no printer in the town able to set up and carry out the printing of the whole New Testament in Sechuana. Neither the skilled manpower nor the necessary founts were available. Where he would never have gone to England for the purposes of his children's education, Mary found it possible to persuade him to do so in order to get his books printed.

It was a decision which also brought tragedy. There was an epidemic of measles raging at the Cape. Many had died. The Moffat family and their Bechuana and Hottentot servants were not immune. Once they had decided to go Robert took passages on the first ship available. It happened to be a small troopship coming round the Cape from China and conditions on it were appalling. On board also measles was rife.

They embarked, six children, one African, John Mokoteri, and Mary very near her time. The children were all ill, as was Robert. The worst was Jamie, the apple of his mother's eye. In desperate circumstances, in a cramped, packed troopship reeking of human misery which had already been many months at sea, Mary nursed her family to within a few hours of her own confinement. They were all sea-sick in the rolling swell of Table Bay. The baby, a second Elizabeth Lees, was born small and delicate and it seemed impossible that she should survive. Jamie, who was the worst of the invalids, was brought in and laid on the bunk beside his mother. Mary, watching in anguish while this beloved child drew closer and closer to death, saw no sin in praying that, if she had to suffer a loss, it should be the puny baby that might be taken. But the prayer was not answered. The baby lived and two days after her birth Jamie died and was buried in Table Bay. The next day, in a terrible storm, they sailed for home.

It took three months till they were beating up the English Channel towards the Isle of Wight. For the children the voyage, their first really long one with all the excitement of a mythical homeland at the end, must soon have wiped out the sorrows and terrors of that terrible embarkation. For Mary it cannot have been so easy. Though she grew to love Betsy, as she loved all her children, she deeply mourned her bonny and gifted Jamie. She must often have been reminded of the voyage out in 1819, with its hopes and fears and visions. This was the reality of the decisions she had taken at that time—an enduring partnership with the man whom then she had hardly known, six children living, three dead, a mission established after tribulation, suffering, endurance, happiness, the full measure of which only she would ever know.

As once before she had journeyed in a limbo from one destiny to another, now again she was conscious of a shifting perspective. The nearer the ship drew to the shores of England, the more conscious she was that Africa was her home. It was a strange country to which she was returning: much had happened in twenty years to both private and public life to make her feel that she no longer belonged. Her mother was dead; as was also her brother William; James had gone to America, John was in Madras. Mr Smith, old and indigent, had retired to a cottage at Flixton. She feared that similar news might await her of the families of many of her former friends. George IV was dead and William IV; a queen now reigned; the London–Bath–Bristol railway had been built and opened; the Reform Act, Poor Law Act, Chartism, riots and unrest, were all contributing to changing social conditions. To point the difference, and to the great excitement of the children, their ship ran aground on a sandbank in the channel and was pulled off by a passing steamship, one of the very earliest afloat and certainly the first the Moffat family had ever seen.

They arrived off Cowes on June 6th 1839. The Bogues in Gosport, who had been the last friends to see Mary twenty years before, were still alive and she went ashore to be welcomed by them. What a strange and emotional reunion that must have been. They returned to the ship, to make a leisurely passage round to the Thames and up to London, the latter part in tow to a steam tug. They must have made an outlandish little group, the tall man with his small wife, five children and a tiny baby, weather-beaten, dressed in unfashionable clothes, drawing together for mutual support in their uncertainty of what awaited them, flanked by John Mokoteri, who was to prove a great trial to them.

It was to be a leave unlike any that she had imagined. She had worried about educational decisions that must be made, with all that they entailed of passing over the responsibility for

123

her children to other people. She was concerned about Robert's health, the family's financial situation, her own father's declining prosperity and increasing age. Perhaps she schemed and planned ways of getting Robert to stay for a little longer than he intended, so as to give her more time to make adequate arrangements—for Robert hoped to get straight on with the printing as soon as he had found a suitable printer and thought of being back in Africa in a few months, before the winter set in.

In the event it was to be over four years before they saw Kuruman again and Mary was to find the leave, which she had thought of as a time of recuperation, as demanding in its own way on all her resources of courage and endurance as ever Africa had been. The one thing she had made no preparation for was fame.

Robert Moffat did not expect to find himself known and in demand either. He was preoccupied with the production of his translation and had given little thought as to the kind of reception he might meet. He had always written well, with an immediacy and a gift for vivid description and human detail which had made his reports back to the Directors of the Society valuable publicity documents. Portions of them were reprinted in the Society's magazine and found their way into local publications. Copies of his and Mary's letters to friends in Manchester and the surrounding area had been circulated to all the congregations. At a time when an interest in the work of missions overseas was beginning to grow and the first response to the fascination of African exploration to be heard, Robert Moffat's stirring accounts of life and work among the Bechuana, with all its difficulties, dangers and small hard-won triumphs, caught the Christian imagination. He had gone out an unknown, ill-equipped, gardener turned preacher; he came back to find himself lionised. As soon as he stepped off the ship in London he was deluged with invitations to speak, and as he began to fulfil them his fame and reputation grew. Characteristically he accepted the challenge unhesitatingly—so much so that he overstrained his voice and after some months had to be forbidden to speak. He became rather ill and had to go to Brighton to recuperate.

Robert was not averse to celebrity and all that it brought

with it, large enthusiastic audiences, public acclaim, gifts both personal and for the mission. He had a message for the times, and a fire for the cause of the Lord in Africa, and was prepared to expend himself to the utmost to spread the Gospel. Mary was not so certain. It was not only that she worried ceaselessly about the pressures to which her husband was subjected, or deplored the frequent absences which left her, once again, with all the vital family decisions to make alone; she distrusted the glare of publicity and the effect on men of too much public admiration.

Essentially Mary was a private person. Her desire was not for recognition but for assistance. The work was all important. When she castigated the Directors for neglect of the mission at Kuruman it was not with failure to recognise Robert's merits that she charged them but with omitting to support the work adequately. She feared the subtle distortion of motives that could creep in when frail human nature became tempted to credit success to personal virtues rather than the overriding power of the Almighty God. With her husband she was made more anxious by the strain on his physical strength rather than the subversion of his moral nature; with the son-in-law she was shortly to acquire she was never absolutely sure that he had not succumbed to the temptations of worldly acclaim.

One of the places where Robert Moffat often went to speak was Mrs Sewell's boarding house in Aldergate Street, London, where the new missionaries who were waiting to go overseas lived. Among them in 1839/40 was a young Scotsman whose ultimate destination was China, David Livingstone. He became fascinated by the older missionary's stirring account of life among the Bechuana and caught up in his vision of expansion into the interior of Africa, and decided to abandon China and volunteer for Kuruman. There seems to have been little difficulty in getting the Society to agree to this change of plan, and it was arranged that late in 1840 David Livingstone would sail for Cape Town in the company of another young missionary.

Mary Moffat was delighted at the acquisition, at long last, of such valuable reinforcements. She had a soft spot for young men, and in these two she particularly approved of their sensible, plain, down-to-earth manners. They came from the same kind of simple, hard-working background as her Robert.

Mr Livingstone was not married—and indeed showed no signs of being interested in such a proposition. He reminded Mary at times of the young Robert, full of vision and enthusiasm, with a fluctuating, sometimes moody, temperament and a disregard for the more practical domestic details of life. She did her best to persuade him to find himself a wife to partner and support him in the hardships ahead. He appreciated her concern, but made no effort to take her advice.

She had one other, quite unexpected piece of good fortune. Her brother John, who in 1828 had so bitterly disappointed her by accepting a posting to Madras, arrived in England on leave. He had last seen her twenty years before, young, pretty, determined, anxious, setting out to marry a man she hardly knew. It was to her and all that she had then represented to him that he owed his subsequent career. He returned to find a matriarch surrounded by her family, still determined, still anxious, but with a force and sweetness of character developed through many tribulations which made her the mainstay of her dedicated, indefatigable husband, the rock around which her large family revolved, the secure centre of an ever-increasing missionary connection.

There was, however, one major cross to be borne. For the whole of their time in Britain the conduct of John Mokoteri was a source of pain and scandal, causing much trouble and worry to the Moffat family and injuring the reputation of the mission.

This young man had been known to the Moffats from childhood, Robert Moffat having been responsible for redeeming him from slavery after one of the many tribal wars. He had been taught Dutch and to write Sechuana by Robert, and through his influence had remained at the school. After some years with his parents, who did not live at Kuruman, he returned to the station with a chest complaint which made an invalid of him. Robert interested him in the printing business and tried to make him a compositor. He took him to the Cape to act as a proof-reader for the translation of the New Testament and, when printing facilities failed at the Cape, John Mokoteri travelled to England with the family. It was intended that he should take much of the burden of proof-reading off Robert Moffat's shoulders.

They had been absent for twenty years and no doubt thought of English society treating John in much the same way as happened in the Colony—as a servant who was made rather too much of by the missionary family with whom he lived. They had reckoned without the interest and excitement which his black face roused in a country where Africans were not so frequently seen and where the abolition of the slave trade was still a recent memory.

From the moment they landed John Mokoteri was an object of fascination and patronage. Hardly surprisingly he lost his head. Robert took him aside and solemnly warned him of the results of his extravagant conduct. It had been a promise that John would be baptised in England and Robert wished to postpone this ceremony until he showed himself more worthy. Mary took a different view, hoping that the very act of taking his vows at baptism would have a good effect on the boy. She persuaded her husband to agree.

It was no good. He became unbearable to live with, giving himself airs and refusing to give Mary or the girls any help. In fact when asked he became abusive and insulting. Meanwhile he was the recipient of numerous invitations which they could not stop him accepting. He was taken to platforms and schools to be admired, invited to picnics and evening parties, taken by the arm and led into dazzling drawing-rooms, became the toy of young ladies—'and some old ones too'—was asked the favour of locks from his hair and mementoes from his pen. In other words John Mokoteri was a lion, and he had not the character or common sense—or indeed the loyalty—to withstand such concentrated flattery.

He still did a certain amount of work on the proofs of the New Testament, but all the time he and Robert Moffat studied together John was on tenterhooks, expecting invitations to arrive for him or a carriage to draw up at the door to collect him. All remonstrance made him very angry. He turned against MaMary, who treated him with the same discipline and kindness that she treated her own children, and called her now his enemy.

It became plain that they could no longer have him in the same lodgings. With great difficulty they got him boarded out—only to be pestered to remove him again. He went round saying that missionary work was a humbug and a lie, which must have been a sore trial to Mary, jealous for the good name not only of the mission and her husband, but also for her 'sable children'. The Moffats would have liked to have sent John back home, but it was not possible, so throughout the whole of their stay in Britain he was a constant source of worry, especially for Mary who had to remain at home with the family.

Even had she wished to accompany her husband on his many speaking engagements about the country—usually by stage-coach but sometimes by the newly-opened railways—it would have been impossible for her to do so. She had her own pressing commitments, to an aged father, to her children and the arrangements that needed to be made for their education and welfare, and to a new baby, the last of the family, Jane, born in her grandfather's cottage at Flixton in August 1840.

Perhaps if she had been able to go with him she would have resented and feared less the demands that public life made upon her husband. Robert was incapable of refusing any invitation that would seem to further the cause to which he was devoted. Nor did he neglect the work which had originally brought him to Britain, seeing his Sechuana New Testament through all the stages of its printing. To this commitment he presently added another—the translation of the Psalms—and then, by popular request, he started to write a book about his experiences in Southern Africa, to be called *Missionary Labours*. Mary, who from the hardships of Kuruman had so often thought with longing of the comfort and ease of England, yearned for Africa which now she finally recognised as her real home.

In November, when the baby [Jeanie] was three months old, she wrote to Robert Hamilton who was holding the fort at Kuruman:

'Since my baby was born he [Robert] has never been with us except for a few hours at a time, and since the 8th of October I have not seen him, as he is in Scotland, interesting his country-men with African details. . . . I am sure you will greatly enjoy the company of the two missionaries [William Ross and David Livingstone, who were to sail for Africa in December] both being Scotchmen and plain in their manners. I do hope they will be a blessing to the country. They must of course look to our garden for their present supplies. Anything about the premises they can make use of. You must not from this infer that we are not to return. No! If Moffat lives we shall return, but it cannot be immediately. The Psalms have to be finished, the Selection reprinted, and perhaps hymns too, and besides all this the public is determined to have a book. You will smile and so do I, for I have felt opposed to it till very lately, but I see it is of no use to refuse. It must be so. I fear this will detain us very long. Our present plan is to leave this time next year, but I doubt very much; it will require another winter. Mr Moffat says not, but I fear he will again be sent to different parts of the country. . . . I long to get home. I fear I shall forget what I knew of the language. I long to see the spot again where we have so long toiled and suffered, to see our beloved companions . . . and to behold our swarthy brethren and sisters again; and I long for my own home, for though loaded with the kindness of friends and welcome everywhere, still home is homely!

'We have, however, much that is painful to anticipate: the parting with some of our children, and my aged father . . . Moffat's parents have also to be left . . . in fact, long as our visit to England is, it is a state of constant excitement, bustle and anxiety. We are seldom together as a family. I should have accompanied Mr Moffat on many of his journeys, but the Lord has given me other work to do. I have two lovely little girls whom you have never seen, and they are sweet little ties. I enjoy good health: one reason may be that I am exposed to no hardships; everywhere taken care of as a hothouse plant. . . .

'My husband is terribly worked, but keeps well thus far in the season. How his head stands it I know not. Our dear children are doing well according to their capacity. I have done what I could to persuade Livingstone to marry, but he seems to decline it.'

It did require another winter, and she continued to live in an unsettled state, which must often have tried her orderly spirit. Arrangements had to be made for the children which would remain valid whether their parents stayed or left. An old friend, Miss Eisdall of Walworth agreed to be responsible for them. Mary and Ann were young ladies now of nineteen and seventeen respectively, but Robert, Helen and John were all destined to remain in England for their education. Robert, aged thirteen, had been fortunate in finding a family, Mr and Mrs Jacob Unwin, who took a great interest in him. It had warmed Mary's heart to 'notice your labour of love towards our dear boy and ourselves, the kind and maternal interest you took in his being comfortably fixed, to fit himself for the arduous work in which he is anxious to be engaged, and your personal endeavours to further the object we have in view . . . for it was evident to me that it was your intention to be as a mother to him when his own was far removed.' Mrs Unwin was dying of a malignant illness when Mary wrote this letter to her and both women knew it. The young Robert, already oppressed by the responsibility of his father's fame, was to lose a foster mother at a critical time.

John, Mary's youngest son, started at a small kindergarten in Walworth and was then transferred to the school for the sons of missionaries at Walthamstow. He became ill with bronchitis and was for many weeks an invalid so that, when the time came for the family to return to Africa, it was thought prudent that John should not be left in England but go back with them.

Missionary Labours was published in 1842. It was dedicated to Prince Albert and had an immediate success. Robert Moffat found himself not only famous but for the first time in his life the possessor of a small private income. It had taken considerable toll of his health, however.

'We have great reason to be thankful for the completion of the book,' Mary wrote to his parents, 'for many a time I trembled lest he should become poorly before it was finished and have to lay it aside and disappoint the public. He has found it an arduous task. I always dreaded it and often wished he would not do it, but had I known how formidable a work it would be I should have felt more opposed to it. I can assure you his head is thoroughly tired and he ought to have at least a fortnight's relaxation; but this was out of the question. He has had some engagements for the middle and later end of this month, standing over for six months, and these he could not break; and not being able to finish so soon as he had hoped, he has consequently been sadly hurried. He was some days in Buckinghamshire last week; and yesterday morning, after sitting up till two o'clock to correct, he had to depart at seven for Cambridgeshire, there to labour very hard indeed as the printed bills testify. I am anxious to hear how he gets on, for he was quite unfit; he said he was so fatigued that his head felt empty. If all be well I expect him here tomorrow evening, when, if possible, I hope we shall go down to Brighton for two days at least, as, by what I consider a merciful providence, some mistake has occurred, so as to leave next Sabbath vacant. . . .'

Towards the end of 1842 it became plain that most of Robert's commitments had been fulfilled. He still lived in a whirl of speaking engagements, but there was no longer any major work preventing his return to Kuruman. They made arrangements to sail at the beginning of the new year, and began to collect together the various machines and instruments, some of them presents, which they were taking with them. These included a magic lantern and a gun. Mary was also receiving a good many parcels from well-wishers for the use of the mission. They varied considerably in quality. She was especially grateful when a letter arrived out of the blue offering to make clothes for little boys and suggesting that most gifts were for girls. Such perception was rare. Mary wrote back, '. . . this is exactly what you conjecture and it is really very kind of you to be an exception. Often have suggested the thing, but it has very seldom been responded to. The striped jackets of dark colour will be very much liked, and waistcoats too—and I have often thought that a kind of *blouse* made of coarse striped or blue cotton would be very much liked and be a very suitable dress to introduce because loose and cool. Brown Holland is not so suitable for them, because when once washed it so soon becomes dirty again. But the strongest blue cotton you could get, I mean simple *calico* would do very nicely: I acknowledge, on account of the dye coming off on to the hands of the ladies, a little more self-denial would have to be exercised in the making of them. But it would be doing a real service to the dear boys and if distributed as prizes in the school, would be a strong inducement to many *little heathens* to come to school. . . .'

Did she, when writing this, remember those days at Dukinfield when her sewing thread had become blue with the dye from the nervous fingers of the young cotton manufacturer who had hoped to supplant Robert Moffat in her affections? If she

131

did, it did not soften her in her opinion of the ladies who disliked dirtying their hands.

The round of farewell meetings began to gather momentum. In late November she accompanied Robert to a tea party in the New Corn Exchange, Manchester, where nine hundred people were present, and they were given a purse of one hundred and thirty-five gold sovereigns. She said a sorrowful last farewell to her father. By the time they embarked on the sailing ship *Fortitude* with their own five children, John Mokoteri and two other missionary families in January 1843 their baggage weighed fifty tons. It was to be twenty-seven years before Mary saw her daughter Helen again.

PART II

MATRIARCH

Chapter 12

THE JOURNEY TOOK seventy-three days. The weather was bad, and John Mokoteri was a cross. He took offence at not being seated at the captain's table, made the worst elements in the crew his boon companions and told them he intended to be 'a tyrant among the natives' when he got back to Africa. At the same time he spread stories everywhere of Robert Moffat's robbery, tyranny and deceit. In the confined, hot-house atmosphere of the ship his behaviour mortified Mary almost beyond bearing. He became known as the 'black liar' and one day was waylaid by the officers who dipped him in an empty flour bag and sent him up on deck to be what he desired—a 'white' man. From the poop Robert watched this scene with indescribable feelings.

On arrival at the Cape John lived like a lord, in the Moffat's lodgings and at their expense; going to wine shops and horse-racing, until in despair Robert called the whole missionary community to discipline him. For a while this had some effect, but John Mokoteri never returned to Kuruman, and Robert Moffat was a sadder man for the experience.

A long delay now took place waiting for the baggage to arrive. At last, after three months delay, the *Aggripina* made a landfall and all their goods were safely landed. New oxen had to be bought; waggons made ready and packed. On October 10th 1844 they set off for Kuruman. Though Mary did not know it till some months later, her favourite brother John had been drowned in the Bay of Bengal in May. When the news did arrive it brought her much pain.

She returned to a different life. Perhaps for the very first time she truly came home to Kuruman. Henceforth it was England that was the strange land and Africa was where her heart and her family ties, as well as her life work, lay. They had been away nearly five years and few of the Bechuanas ever expected to see them come back. When the news filtered through that Moffat

135

and MaMary were on the way home their journey became a royal progress. Old and young, even the little children, wanted to shake hands with them; some gave way to 'heathen wildness', others silent floods of tears. In the arduous years when they had wrestled with, chastised and fought for their people they had not realised how much they had come to be loved and respected.

For two weeks the station was all bustle. At one time no fewer than twenty waggons, filled with Bechuana visitors from far and near, were outspanned around Kuruman. The royal family came; Mothibi, who had been baptised in their absence, stooping with age, accompanied by his wife, Mahuto, who had never set foot in Kuruman since the day that her eldest son Peclu died there. 'It was to us an affecting sight to witness this ageing couple alight from their waggon and with their sons and daughters enter our house and testify with an ecstasy of feeling their thanks to God for having brought us back,' Robert Moffat wrote. There were closer ties and memories too. It was Mahuto who, twenty-two years before when Mary had arrived at Lattakoo with her first-born, had snatched the baby out of her arms to press it to her breast and kiss it.

That Sabbath the chapel was filled to overflowing and four hundred sat down to communion.

They had been met on the road back by a young man on horseback, wearing a home-made suit. David Livingstone had ridden hard from a journey of exploration through the territory north of Kuruman to greet the man who had inspired him in London. He was already critical of much that he had seen, but for Robert Moffat he retained, as he was always to retain, a warm affection. MaMary he regarded with more detachment. 'Mrs Moffat is a good motherly woman. She takes a kind interest not only in her own family . . .' he wrote to his parents shortly after that meeting. He underestimated both the strength of her character and the quality of her concern.

Kuruman had now become the centre of a growing missionary community. Robert Hamilton, that good and humble man whose responsibility it had always been to keep the mission going through vicissitudes and absences, was still there as were the Edwards. David Livingstone was temporarily based in Kuruman, and two new young missionaries, one of them William Ashton, with their wives, had come up from the Cape to join the station. Suddenly Mary Moffat, at forty-eight, found herself MaMary to a whole new generation.

It was not at all an easy position to fill. These were young men of strong individuality, all of them with quirks and eccentricities and ideas of their own, coming into a sphere of operations which Robert Moffat, himself a man of uncompromising character, had pioneered over twenty arduous years. Young men like Livingstone were not content to work on a station where settled values and habits were already establishing a pattern. For him the north called, the unknown, mysterious lands where millions had never heard the message. Others could not come to terms with the older missionaries and wished only to be on a station of their own. There were disagreements and upheavals, some stimulating and creative, others—exacerbated by the isolation and the mission and its overriding preoccupation with the rigours of the daily task—unpleasant and damaging. Like particles subject to a centrifugal force, the younger missionaries revolved round Robert Moffat, flying off in the attempt to escape his influence, yet always drawn back by the sheer magnetism of his personality. In the still centre of the turmoil Mary Moffat talked, wrote, argued; trying to convince, convert, cement differences for the sake of Robert and the work.

David Livingstone, along with the Edwards, set off two hundred miles to the north in January 1844, to establish a new station at Mabotsa. It was here, very soon after his arrival that he was attacked by a lion which badly mauled his left arm. Another station was also established at Taung, a hundred miles east of Kuruman. These outposts depended for physical substance in no small part on Mary Moffat's superb housekeeping and provisioning services. The domestic talents learnt with such pain by the girl who had wept as she lit a smoking fire, were now being handed on to an increasing number of young missionary families.

Her personal household had changed. For the first time she had grown-up daughters to support her. Young women with whom she could laugh and talk and share burdens. Mary took charge of the infant school, a work for which her mother had long destined her; Ann, trained as were all MaMary's daughters in the arts of home management, helped to run the Moffat home and look after Robert Moffat.

Mary herself had multiple preoccupations. There were two babies to be cared for, Betsy nearly five and Jeanie three-and-a-half, and there was John's education.

John was close on nine. Except for his breakdown in health he should have been at school in England. As it was he had missed a great deal of schooling and there was nowhere in Kuruman to cater for his needs. Robert, immersed in the work of translating, doctoring, gardening, smithing, preaching, had no time or thought to spare for the education of his son—except in so far as the small boy worked the bellows in the smithy, or guided the irrigation water to the vegetables, or sat silently beside his father when itinerating. It was Mary who undertook the main burden of his lessons. While all his life John Moffat remained conscious of the gaps in his education, he never failed to be grateful to his mother for the devotion and ability with which she taught him during these four years at Kuruman.

A month or two after his encounter with the lion David Livingstone came down to Kuruman for a visit, to recuperate among the comparative comforts of life on that station. To the astonishment of the Moffats, who had long ago accepted that he was not a man to marry, he proposed to their daughter Mary. 'Mr Livingstone's marriage was to us a most unexpected event. We, indeed everybody, set him down as a stereotyped bachelor, nor did the idea ever enter our minds till he came here after recovering from the bite of the lion,' Robert Moffat wrote.

David Livingstone himself took a rather pragmatic view of the step he had decided on when he wrote to the Directors of the Society. 'Various considerations connected with this new sphere of labour and which to you need not be specified in detail having led me to the conclusion that it was my duty to enter into the marriage relation, I have made the necessary arrangements for union with Mary, the eldest daughter of Mr Moffat, in the beginning of Jan. 1845. It was not without much serious consideration and earnest prayer I came to the above decision and if I have not deceived myself I was in some measure guided by a desire that the Divine glory might be promoted in my increased usefulness.' He hoped that this might be considered sufficient notification and did not regret having come out single.

To his fiancée he had written in rather more jaunty terms

some weeks before. '. . . you must put him [Robert Moffat] in remembrance about writing to Colesburg about the licence. If he forgets then we shall make it legal ourselves. What right or portion has the state church in me? None whatever. If they don't grant it willingly let them keep their licence. We shall licence ourselves.'

They were married at Kuruman on January 9th 1845.

By this marriage Robert Moffat gained a son-in-law after his own heart. David Livingstone had the qualities he admired in a young man: self-sufficiency, energy, adventurousness, humour, robust individuality—the very qualities that his own temperament and prestige inhibited in the Moffat sons. His son-in-law returned in full the affection and admiration of the older man. They would not have found it easy to work together, but for both the bond of kinship was one that they truly valued.

The relationship between Mary Moffat and her first son-in-law was much more complex. No doubt she approved of him marrying—she had herself urged him to it after all—and was glad to see her daughter make a match which would keep her in the mission field and in close touch with her parents. Many things she admired in David Livingstone, but not all. She thought him wild, unpredictable—which he was. She was never sure of the purity of his motives when the urge to uproot came upon him. Although he loved and needed his wife and family, he retained the instincts of a bachelor and she did not hesitate to rebuke him when she considered him neglectful of his duty to his family or his mission. Robert Moffat and his son-in-law liked to joke with each other: Mary had little humour and may unconsciously have resented the strong bond of affection between Livingstone and Robert.

She came to regard her daughter's husband with the irritable love of a mother towards a wilful child who is constantly determined to cross her. He, for his part, treated her with wary caution, making light of her rebukes while at the same time showing that he was conscious of occasionally meriting them.

Mary Livingstone was a placid, good-natured young woman, with neither her mother's looks nor her force of character. She had always considered Africa as her home and had been brought up to look forward to a life in the mission field. She was well trained in the arts of housekeeping and inherited her

139

father's talent for gardening. She married a man whose consuming passion was to bring her much unhappiness.

David and Mary Livingstone reached Matbotsa, twelve days from Kuruman by ox-waggon, towards the end of March. Already Mr Livingstone's eyes were turned further north. Robert's public success in Britain had roused some jealousy and his new son-in-law was regarded with mixed feelings by his colleagues.

Mary had causes for anxiety of a more serious nature with both the children whom she had left at home. Robert, destined to follow his father, was beginning to feel himself unable to do so. Letters indicated that he was uneasy and dissatisfied in his studies. His heart was in the right place, but in this difficult time the best that his parents could do at long distance was to encourage him to persevere. Robert Moffat consulted his new son-in-law, who strongly urged that 'nothing is like the preaching of the word'. But the preaching of the word was just what Robert junior was beginning to feel himself incapable of undertaking.

Helen had taken an altogether more radical step. She was sixteen and had received the addresses of a young man. He had spoken to her before her parents were aware of his intentions— an action which the Livingstones upheld: 'we think the young man did right in speaking to Helen first. . . . I would not have come to you first for the world,' David wrote to his father-in-law. Mary's anguish, separated from her child by six thousand miles of ocean with letters taking many months, can be imagined. She was, however, a woman who later showed herself to have sympathy and understanding with the problems of young people and, whatever decisions were taken at this time, two years later Helen married her silk merchant, James Vavasseur.

Mary Livingstone became pregnant early in the first year of her marriage. Ann went up to Mabotsa to stay with her sister while David Livingstone moved to set up a fresh mission station yet further north at Chonwane. When the house was built and he was ready to receive his wife, her sister returned home to Kuruman.

Robert Moffat Livingstone, Mary's first grandchild, was born on his mother's wedding anniversary, January 9th 1846.

The baby, delivered by his father, was healthy and welcome. Though life on the northern mission stations remained precarious, not only because of disease and isolation but also fresh uneasiness caused by the northwards trek of the Boer farmers, the family unit—husband, wife and children—was still of major importance in pioneer missionary expansion.

MaMary's pleasure in the safe arrival of the baby was dimmed by a serious accident at Kuruman. Robert Moffat caught his arm in the cog wheels of a new corn mill and was disabled for many weeks. Fortunately it was his left arm, so that he was still capable of writing and note-taking, but the shock of the disaster and the huge gaping wound left by it took a long time to heal. It was September before Mary felt able to undertake the long journey to Chonwane to see her daughter and the new grandson. She took with her the three younger children, John, Betsy and Jeanie.

It was the first time she had travelled so far to the north and she was fortunate to have as escort a large African hunting party. For her as well as for the children the journey was a relaxation and a pleasure. Away from the cares and anxieties of Kuruman, released for a while even from the connubial tensions of life with Robert, she found herself excited and exhilarated by all she saw. She was an efficient and sensible woman in charge of an ox-waggon and its crew, bringing to her daughter and son-in-law the comfort of her presence and the products of her housewifely skills, a mother with time to entertain her young children with games and tales, yet this journey still roused in her something of the romantic expectations of her youth, the eager enjoyment of her earliest encounter with Africa.

'I was perfectly enråptured,' she wrote to her husband, 'on entering the first valley of the Bakhatla; and it being necessary for me to get out of the waggon on account of the rugged path, I could examine the shrubs to my great delight . . . we still had to go through a small and romantic kloof, forming a passage between two valleys, and we had to cross the stream two or three times.'

It was not entirely pleasure, however. In that same stream their escort's waggon stuck fast 'and all efforts to extricate it were in vain'. The man whose waggon it was sent her a message to go on without them. This Mary resolutely refused to do. 'He had behaved politely to me all the way; besides the conviction that our people ought to do their best to help our fellow travellers, who had broken their disselboom.'

She was stirred, elated, nervy. As always at moments when she was expected to succumb to womanly weakness, she rose to the challenge. 'I had had a long walk up and down the hill, and was greatly excited by everything about me, and felt terribly nervous and weak and was glad to lay down my head to rest in that beautiful kloof. Had I not been so tired I would have sat till midnight, that the moon might send additional beauty on the scenery.

'As soon as the moon rose the men returned to their work . . . unloading, pulling it out, and mending the boom. We had a good breakfast, a fine eland steak shot the day before. . . .'

She had a habit of giving the meat two taps with her knife before she started to eat it, 'by way of making it more digestible' her son-in-law said. No doubt she tapped the eland steak.

While she was enjoying her journey they were a good deal more nervous at Chonwane, both for her safety and perhaps because it was her first visit to their matrimonial home—she had high standards and an observant eye. 'We are daily in expectation of the arrival of your better half,' David Livingstone wrote to Robert Moffat, adding that they wished heartily that she would come and relieve them of suspense. He would have preferred a visit from his father-in-law.

MaMary too had her reservations. The baby was ailing—a few days after she left in October he was acutely ill—her daughter was again pregnant and already regarding the lot of the missionary wife as that of 'domestic drudge'. Her son-in-law, vocationally unfulfilled, had his gaze fixed still further north. She comforted, admonished, trained, taught, put in order, and then hurried back to her own responsibilities.

Immersed again in the endless daily grind the hopeful mood of the homecoming had dissipated and the future was clouded with anxieties. The Livingstone baby was frequently ill and MaMary was concerned for her daughter. Robert junior in Glasgow was still uncertain about what he was going to do. Mary herself was in indifferent health, suffering from the headaches which had dogged her all her life, and beginning to see her husband's constitution gradually deteriorate.

But most painful of all was the knowledge that she would soon have to part with her babies, Betsy and Jeanie. She would have given anything to avoid the need for a decision about their education. To be bereft of the last of her children was unthinkable. John too, who was so happy at home and had been so sick at school, how could she let him go? She could not face the ending of a time of family happiness that this parting would mean.

This time it was Robert who at last persuaded her that the two little girls must go to school in England. 'My heart rebelled for some time, and I felt the thing impossible,' she wrote sadly. Once she had conceded the necessity she began, as always, to look at the practical advantages. They could go to the school for missionaries' children now set up; there were many kind friends to look after them; John must go anyway and it would not be possible to make two long expensive journeys to the Cape. Besides, she was conscious that her own uncertain health and busy life prevented her from providing them with an adequate education. 'I saw that, should I be called to leave them, my deathbed would be embittered by the consideration that they might have been placed in circumstances more favourable to a proper training for usefulness in the Church and in the world, but for the victory my feelings had got over my judgement.'

It was with a sad heart that she began to make preparations for the protracted journey to the Cape. Though she had made up her mind to the separation, it was a long time before she was reconciled to it.

Chapter 13

PLANNING FOR SUCH an undertaking was not completed quickly. Ann, who would remain behind to run the infants' school and look after her father, had to be meticulously instructed in domestic management, including also being responsible for maintaining the supplies which brought additional comforts to out-station wives and transient strangers. Oxen had to be found and waggons prepared. The innumerable commissions required of any traveller going to the Cape had to be sorted out. There were preparations for the children, spiritual as well as material.

Nor did life stop making its usual demands while all this went on. Mary Livingstone's daughter was born in May 1847. Her small brother had suffered badly while teething, the family was by no means settled at Chonwane and Mary Livingstone was harried and overburdened. They were persuaded to travel south for a period of rest and recuperation. 'The Livingstones came out . . . half withered away with fatigue and privation. I laboured hard to fetch up their strength and sent Mary back with her children like roses' MaMary wrote to her father. But in doing so she felt guilty of some neglect of her own small children and determined to make it up to them on the journey.

At last, in August 1847, Mary, with John, Betsy, Jeanie and an adequate number of men to look after the oxen, climbed into the waggon and set off on the two months' journey to the Cape. She was happier this time to be leaving Robert in the capable hands of a daughter, but all the same it was a sad parting, the end of an era. There would be no more small children of her own running in and out of the home at Kuruman. She felt as though her life was nearly over, although she was only fifty. As always, however, she cast her faith upon the Lord and went forward confident that He would guide her for the best. The thought of her two small lambs undertaking the arduous journey to England in the company of strangers was much in her mind. She knew from experience what it could be like and dreaded it for them. When she parted from Robert 'it was with this understanding distinctly, that if I met with favourable protection for them for the voyage they should go; if not I was to bring them back again. This was to be the finger of God pointing the way. . . .'

She was to have need of her faith.

The journey went well, for the children an immensely enjoyable experience, for Mary one of great responsibility as, once outside their own country, her Bechuana Africans were often bewildered and uncertain when meeting new conditions and unexpected difficulties.

She arrived in Cape Town to bad news. Her son Robert had finally had a breakdown in health and was returning at once to Southern Africa without having finished his course of study. His mother was flung into a turmoil of anxiety, in which concern about his health was mingled with deep disappointment at his failure to fulfil the hopes which she and his father had for so long cherished. The news pitched her into an agony of uncertainty as to what she should now do for the best with regard to John, his younger brother. It seemed to her that John should not be asked to face the difficulties and damp weather which had proved too much for his brother. Robert, after all, had always been physically strong. No one recognised that the stresses were more likely to have been caused by the boy's striving to follow a career for which he was not really suited than by the climate of Glasgow.

She wrote immediately to her husband to ask his advice, knowing it would not be possible to get an answer for many weeks, if at all, and that in the meantime a good opportunity to send the children home might arise and she would then have to make the difficult decision alone. Uncertain when he was supposed to have left Britain, she expected her oldest son hourly, wondering how best she could help him. Though her personal disappointment at his failure to follow in his father's footsteps was profound, her concern was to comfort and not to blame him.

Meanwhile she was constantly searching for a suitable couple taking ship for England who would be willing to take charge of the little girls. Without her faith in the goodness of God and her strongly practical nature she would have been lost during the four months that went by before a minister and his wife, travelling home with a young family, offered to take Betsy and Jeanie. They would have taken John too, and for a moment Mary wondered if she was doing right to refuse. There was still no word from Robert and, remembering his insistence on her parting with the girls, she wondered if he would blame her for keeping John in Cape Town.

At a moment when she was in great perplexity a Cape Town friend offered to take John back to England with his own family a month or two later. With relief she made the decision to put him into a private boarding school in Cape Town, a decision which was endorsed by Robert Moffat three days before the ship taking the girls away sailed.

Betsy and Jeanie embarked on February 10th 1848. Mary spent the night on board and Betsy never forgot the picture of her mother in the small boat which carried her away from them shorewards after the parting, 'her hands lifted up to us, her eyes streaming with tears'. She was not to see either of them for another seven years.

Had she but known it at the time the chaperons who had appeared so ideal were to prove very negligent of their duties, but so affected by Mary's grief was the mate of the ship, 'a great sunburnt seaman', that he offered to care for her children. 'O Mam! don't take on so! I'll be a friend to your little ones.'

And so he was. He rigged up an enclosure on the deck where they could have baths: in the evenings he told them stories: he allowed no one to tease them—although himself subject to much ribald comment by the crew. When the second mate stole Betsy's doll and stuck it in the rigging where it began to melt, she very soon had it back by an appeal to her champion. Mary's faith in the Lord had not been misplaced—though the instrument through which He worked was very different from what she had imagined.

The two little girls arrived safely in England where they were met by their sister Helen, who had offered to be responsible for their education. Some months after their arrival a kind, rugged seaman turned up at the girls' school and took them out for the day—their old friend the mate! Hearing that he was still in touch with her 'lambkins', Mary wrote to Helen and asked her to give him a copy of Robert's book, *Missionary Labours,* as a token of gratitude for his kindness. Alas, he was never seen again.

Back in Cape Town Mary, desolate, faced a long solitary journey, every step of which would remind her of past happiness with her children, and at the end of it a return 'to my husband and home childless'.

Her son Robert had arrived in Cape Town on January 2nd 1848 and found a government appointment as a surveyor. There is no record that he and his mother met at this time, and it is possible that he did not even know she was in the Colony. Equally possible is the conclusion that he avoided seeing her. If so it must have been an added sorrow to Mary. Hardly surprisingly her health deteriorated rapidly.

She had been five months in Cape Town when she left on March 6th 1848 to return to Kuruman. It had been a time of great stress. 'I have never had the powers of mind and body more taxed as a mother than during the last two years,' she wrote to her father. She had headaches and less easily identified pains and the thought of her own death was never very far from her mind; nevertheless she attended to the many arduous, practical arrangements for the seven-hundred-and-fifty-mile journey by ox-waggon with her usual efficiency. Robert's letter in January, giving permission for John to stay in Cape Town, had also brought good news of the station. 'Ann earning a splendid reputation as a housekeeper and infant-school-mistress combined.' The Prophecies of Isaiah and Bunyan's *Pilgrim's Progress* had both been printed in Sechuana since she left. Even at this moment of personal distress the work of the mission still came first with her. 'This is some consolation to me that though I have had to pass through so much alone, something so important has been done, which could not have been done had my husband come himself.'

John went with her for the first forty miles. They parted under the shadow of the Groote Drakenstein. He was thirteen, and was to be twenty-three and a married man before she saw him again. Alone with her African servants she turned her face towards the north, cutting the last ties with her family's childhood.

147

As she travelled, however, the slow cumbersome journeying soothed her. She rose to the challenge of 'a broken axle, heavy thunderstorms, and much rain . . . and consequently oxen with sore feet and sore necks; quagmires in abundance; sometimes we stuck in them for three or four hours; one night we slept in one.' By the time she reached the banks of the Orange river on April 20th, almost within reach of Robert and her 'beloved home', she felt that all that was needed to complete her happiness was the knowledge that everything was well with them both. Her last news had been three-and-a-half months before, and she knew with what devastating suddenness disaster could strike.

She had hoped that Robert might come to meet her, and her heart sank at the sight of the swollen angry water with no possibility of crossing and no sign of a welcoming party on the other side. 'We arrived here last night in a heavy thunderstorm, after having spanned out at midday because we could get no further; the waggon having stuck fast in a sandbank, and there, with the front to the wind, I was some hours in showers of sand.'

For four days they waited on the river bank watching the turgid water hurrying by, impatient, but no longer anxious, for a swimmer had made the crossing and brought a budget of letters from Griqua Town. He also brought advice to go up the river to Read's ford where swimmers would meet them.

At Read's ford however the water was still too high, so they continued to the junction of the Black river and the Vaal, where there was known to be a boat. 'On Saturday night we arrived, not at the place, but not far from it, and when dressing in the morning the maid told me papa was on the other side! You may be sure I lost no time in letting him know where I was, and on Tuesday evening we had the happiness of saluting across the beautiful expanse of water at the junction. The boat had not arrived, and papa, having a severe cold, dared not to swim.'

So they had to spend yet another night encamped, separated by the river. Next day the boat was brought and they soon had a 'joyful and sorrowful meeting'. 'Yes, it was trying for papa to see me alone, with not one little prattler . . .' Mary wrote to one of the 'lambkins'.

Chapter 14

THE NEXT FEW years, though full of problems, both political and domestic, were without the dramatic alarms which had distinguished the early times at Kuruman. They were bad years for drought and the harvests failed. The station itself flourished and had now the outward appearance of a long-established settlement with well-built houses, full-grown trees, irrigation, handsome crops, yet it had never quite fulfilled Robert Moffat's dreams. For one thing there were too few people. The really large populations lay to the north and, as Livingstone was constantly reminding his father-in-law, it was here that the active, evangelising missionary should be. Somehow, even among the smaller tribes of the Bechuana, now familiar for twenty years with the preaching of the Gospel, there was still a tiresome streak of obstinacy, of refusal to question and search, of un-hallowed conduct which should long ago have been renounced. Immersed in each day's struggles the Moffats were more conscious of failures and lapses than of progress and success.

Only occasionally, when writing the yearly report, did it become plain that progress there was. Many of the people could now read and the distribution of the works that came off the printing press was very wide. There were over a hundred children in the schools and large congregations in the church. A number of smaller stations had been established acknowledging Kuruman as the centre.

But there was a cloud on the horizon: the increasing encroachment on African territory by Boer farmers, pushed further and further to the north by the expanding boundaries of the Colony, casting greedy eyes on any fertile land and implacably hostile to the missionary presence with its championship of African rights.

News of what was happening all around them varied, depending on the messenger and how long it had been on the road. In January 1849 Mary sent a letter to one of her children.

'When I wrote to Mr Mathew I told him that our fears about the Boers in the interior were given to the wind, that they were quite tamed, acknowledged the superior power of the English, and were all at once become very civil and quiet with the natives. This was our latest news. . . . But alas! It appears they were only pausing to consider what they would do. Yesterday a letter came from Joseph Arend. . . . He found the people at Sitagole all in commotion about the Boers, who, they say, are forcibly taking possession of all the fountains and fine lands of the Bahurutse and Bakhatla. . . . The report runs that they first met opposition with stroking of the hand; but now they have recourse to their guns, so the natives are in despair. It is said that the Bakhatla country was all in an uproar. . . . We have many fears for our missions, and more for the poor natives.'

In March she added further news. 'Now I have some sad news to tell you. The Boers in the interior have written to the Committee of our missions here insisting on Mr Livingstone's being immediately removed to the Colony, and that for ever! . . . Their chief reason of requiring this to be done is that though he knew that they had issued laws that no coloured person should possess a gun or a horse, he had failed to give them information of Sechele's (chief of the Bakwena) having made large purchases in this way. . . . The Bakwena seem to be inclined to fight for it. They say they must die at all events, for they know they must do so or give up their arms, which they have struggled hard to procure, and which are now essential to their subsistence, for it is impossible for them to get game by the spear in a country overrun by well-armed Boers with abundance of powder. . . . It is quite plain that this ill-will against Sechele arises from the conviction that he is a superior man, who by his attainments threatens them in the rear, and this is intolerable in a black man, a Kaffir. Sechele is marked out for destruction, the first convert to Christianity in those regions.'

Sechele, chief of the Bakwena, the tribe among whom the Livingstones had settled at Chonwane, was a versatile, able, devious man, determined to resist the encroachment of the Boers. His relations with the church were to be stormy and intermittent during the years ahead, but he had a genuine friendship for Livingstone, and when Livingstone and his family moved further north yet again, to Kolobeng, Sechele took his people with them. From here, still nearer to the tantalising mysteries of the interior, Mr Livingstone, rather cruelly, diagnosed his mother-in-law's state of health, while she for her part showed no great confidence in his ability to look after his harassed wife.

Her travels and all the accompanying anxieties had, not surprisingly, resulted in physical collapse when Mary got home. 'Am sorry to hear Mrs M has been so much reduced by her journey, thought her made of a piece of clay that would not wear out in a hurry,' her son-in-law wrote with unsympathetic jauntiness to Robert Moffat. He had little understanding of the anguish and disorientation she felt at being bereft at a single stroke of her three youngest children, not to speak of worry over her oldest son, and briskly suggested that now she had got rid of them it was time to be thinking of a new mission somewhere else. He recommended bleeding and had no reason to fear apoplexy, adding unkindly, 'she might do better than read medical text books and think on her sensations.' He then noted that she should stop thinking about dying and get on with living to some purpose—an unforgivable remark from a young, as yet untried, missionary about one so much his senior in trials and endeavour as well as age. 'I might add if she intends to leave us anything to send it by Paul for we shall assuredly be more grateful for it now than we shall ever be at any future time. The only thing we shall care about receiving will be her blessing after she is gone.'

Mary would have read this letter, indeed there is no reason to believe that he thought she would not. She would not have been amused by it. It may very well have coloured her own view of his consideration for her daughter's feelings.

For Mary Livingstone was pregnant yet again, the third time in as many years, and she was tired, harried and much troubled by pains. Her mother sent her up a present of herrings which she felt greatly the better of; vegetables were non-existent at Kolobeng, food scarce and lacking in variety. They ate locusts and found them very good. But still, early in March, a strong healthy boy was born.

Almost as soon as she was able to travel Livingstone packed Mary and the children into the waggon and sent them off to Kuruman to the ministrations of grandmamma Moffat. Torn between the comfort and support of her old home, which at this moment seemed to her a haven, and anxiety about the fate of her husband left behind to the tender mercies of the Boers if they attacked Kolobeng, Mary Livingstone left in tears. 'My poor lady is away out crying all the road in the full belief that I shall not be seen by her again,' David Livingstone wrote. He was genuinely devoted to his wife and growing children and, at this moment, he still accepted the concept of the pioneer missionary family facing the risks and hazards of a harsh life as a unit; but even while Mary was disappearing down the trail to the south he was already planning his most adventurous journey so far, to try to reach Lake Ngami to the north-west, and he was not altogether sorry to see her go.

It must have been a joy for MaMary to have the grand-children again at Kuruman. Robert was just three, talking fluent Sechuana but very little English, an obstinate, slender little boy with a mind of his own, who liked to imitate his father by doctoring any African who would let him. His sister was 'all fun and frolic' and wound herself very quickly round her grand-father's heart. The baby was fair, sturdy and good. She missed her own lambkins very much.

Mary Moffat's one real friend among the missionary wives was Anne Helmore, whose husband was in charge of the station at Lekhatlong. In such a tiny society, full of the frictions and jealousies that are engendered between highly individual, dedi-cated men living close to the limits of physical endurance with a common aim which yet seems to each one to be peculiarily his own, the wives passionately espoused their husbands' causes and lived, of necessity, isolated lives. Robert Moffat's fame, his translating skills, his age and experience all made him the target—and sometimes the scapegoat—for his younger col-leagues' frustrations. Mary, who all her life loathed mission gossip, held herself aloof from quarrels and intrigues—though she was not afraid of engaging in personal battles on her husband's behalf—and in doing so was by some considered distant, formidable, even frightening. Ann Helmore too was a woman of dignity and decent reticence; her husband Holloway Helmore was a man who did not take sides in petty quarrels. Mary became very attached to them both.

Mary Livingstone and the children went back home to

Kolobeng after four months at Kuruman. They expected to meet David there in August, but on the first of that month he had just arrived at Lake Ngami. When, two months later, he returned to Kolobeng it was to find that the whole family had been ill and much of MaMary's good work undone.

Robert junior was also in trouble. He was a young man with considerable gifts and it seems to have been his misfortune that his natural inclinations were at variance with the opportunities that his background opened up for him. He had inherited from his father a strong physique, a real talent for friendship with African peoples and an interest in their welfare, and great linguistic ability. The one thing he had not inherited was a driving compulsion to preach and teach. In March 1850 he came on a visit to Kuruman. Whatever estrangement there had been with his parents was completely healed. He was not, however, settled. In October 1850 he resigned his job as a land surveyor and was for a time at a loose end.

He had engaged himself to a Miss Walton of Newcastle. As the months went on strains appeared in this relationship. The young lady began to write suggesting that Robert might come home to settle in England, where she was of the opinion that he would be more useful than in Africa. Mary bristled at the suggestion. Robert sent her the letter, seeking advice. She suspected that his fiancée was changing her mind, and was greatly concerned lest her impetuous son should take some hasty action which might prejudice his future. In due course Robert went to the Cape to meet his bride. Probably to his mother's great relief, though no doubt she was also indignant at the slight to her son, Miss Walton did not come.

Meanwhile, accompanying family friends, her younger son John sailed for England on March 21st 1850 without seeing his parents again. He had reached his fifteenth birthday and, in spite of two years schooling in Cape Town, was largely self-educated.

Mary worried about them all. She worried about her husband's health and the headaches that he now had; she worried about the state of the missions and the situation with regard to the Boers. She was always a worrier. Her own health fluctuated. She learnt to administer her time as carefully and efficiently as she managed her household. Waggon loads of vegetables, apples and other good things went up to Kolobeng for the family there. 'I'm sure we all sincerely thank Mrs M for the trouble she put herself to in her weak state. It may however have contributed to her restoration . . .' her son-in-law wrote in thanks. He touched on a truth. She was always better when she needed to be active meeting a crisis.

David Livingstone was determined to go back to Lake Ngami as a prelude to still further exploration. This time he was going to take his family with him. Mary Livingstone was pregnant again and her mother thought it madness for her to go on such a hard dangerous journey. She knew that her daughter was constantly poorly and that, unlike her mother, she disliked waggon travel. There was always the possibility of a miscarriage. Mary distrusted her son-in-law's desire to penetrate ever further into the interior. Where he maintained that the only place for a true missionary was on the frontiers with the Gospel, pressing forward to bring it to more and more of the multitudes beyond its range, she suspected that his primary interest might well be the worldly one of exploration. Her own instinct was to settle, put down roots and engage in the long, slow battle of conversion. For this purpose she would gladly have relinquished any of her children, to live in any circumstances however dangerous; but in Mary's case she saw little evidence of it.

She did not protest openly, but when they had been away some six weeks she wrote to Mrs Helmore, 'We are still in deep anxiety about the Livingstones; we have not heard a word about them since they left—and if dear Mary is right in her calculations she is to be confined next month. It was an ill-managed affair for her to go with him and if experience does not teach them that, then I shall say they are dull scholars.'

Experience taught them a good deal—but not the one lesson that MaMary hoped they would learn. The trip was dogged by fever, there was little choice of food—meat, bread, milk—and the one accident that Mary Livingstone had always dreaded happened, the waggon overturned. Fortunately there was no great damage done, but they all arrived back at Kolobeng exhausted and debilitated in early August 1850. Seven days later Mary Livingstone had a tiny baby daughter, 'about the size of MaMary's middle finger'.

At first all went well, then Mrs Livingstone complained of

earache and shortly after she had a stroke which paralysed the right side of her face and head and affected her right leg. At the same time the baby Elizabeth died.

The parents were desolated. 'It is wonderful how soon the affections twine round a little stranger. . . . She was very beautiful, had very fine blue eyes and was very strong,' her father wrote. Her mother recovered slowly, getting back the movement in her facial muscles but continuing for a long time to suffer considerable pain. On October 1st MaMary girded herself and left for Kolobeng with comforts and supplies, to set the family to rights. They were all extremely glad to see her, even David, for whom she had no doubt a few tart words. He was suffering from a bad throat, overwork and the semi-starvation that afflicted them all. There had been a heavy hail-storm which had broken windows on the station and he had not got round to replacing them. 'MaMary was not pleased.'

She bundled them all into the waggons and brought them straight back to Kuruman, probably as much for her own sake as for theirs for she was once again alone in the house, Mr Hamilton was bedridden and she had no one she could trust to look after Robert. In September 1850 Ann had married one of the missionaries from the Paris Mission, Jean Fredoux, and gone to live at Motito.

Relations with the Paris Mission had always been very good. Jean Fredoux and Ann Moffat were the same age, twenty-seven. The service was conducted by Robert Moffat at Kuru-man and they left the following day 'as happy as I suppose they could well be'.

In the unsettled state of the country to the north-east, where 'missionaries are forbidden to go eastward, and edicts are issued by the Boers to the different native chiefs commanding them to prevent all English travellers and traders from penetrating beyond them, while they, if they refuse, will be accounted enemies of the Boers', Jean Fredoux had thought that he might be able to travel freely. He was mistaken. 'Mr Fredoux . . . started in March to go north-east to visit an interesting people in that quarter who have three times sent messengers to my husband seeking friendship,' Mary wrote to a Manchester friend. 'Mr F thought as he was not an Englishman he would meet with no opposition, but he has come home thoroughly convinced that it is not Englishmen, but friends of the aborigines, who are to be expelled the country. He was allowed to travel among the Boers a fortnight, and was after all surrounded on a Sabbath morning by a host of Boers on foot and thirteen horsemen, all armed, demanding to know from whence he was, whither going, and what to do? On telling them his object he was strictly ordered to go no further. . . .

'. . . The natives are confounded. They have always been led to believe that the English nation is not only powerful, but benevolent and generous, and that they should now drive away their rebels to destroy them is a puzzle. It is calculated to produce a degree of scepticism as regards missionaries, especially as it has been judged proper and prudent for the latter, as men seeking the welfare of all mankind, to be conciliatory towards the Boers, hoping thus to prevent hostility. This is difficult for the poor barbarians to understand. . . . If some measures are not speedily adopted by our Government it seems likely that every mission in those regions will soon be broken up. We have had no darker prospects for twenty years than we have now.'

Chapter 15

ONCE AGAIN THEY were embattled, though this time they were not alone as had been the case in earlier days. Robert Moffat, immersed in translation, the aim of which had now become the whole of the Bible in Sechuana, but unable to relinquish his multifarious other duties, was beginning to suffer from a continuous buzzing in his head. The periodic fits of depression, during which in the early days of their marriage he had looked to Mary for relief, had never left him. They may even have been aggravated by the constant urgings of his son-in-law that Kuruman was now a settled backwater and it behoved all true missionaries to press on into the unknown.

Mary's instincts were not against the unknown—but they were strongly against the unknown for its own sake. She recognised the value of Robert's work of translation—which Livingstone had once rather light-heartedly suggested might end up in being totally wasted and Sechuana an extinct language—and she would have fought any intention to persuade her husband to abandon it. For her too the network of commitments which had grown up over the years was strong and demanding. She was the centre on whom they all relied and, though she often found the weight of their unthinking acceptance of her strength and support almost more than her physical stamina could bear, her spirit never flinched.

Robert Hamilton was slowly and quietly dying, 'like a candle going out', having to be nursed night and day. The Livingstone family stayed four months, from October 1850 to February 1851, a joy to have but yet another responsibility for MaMary. Her daughter's recovery was still not complete and she was again pregnant. Due to drought and a severe hail-storm it was the worst fruit season that the station had ever had and the grandchildren ate everything that ripened.

Ann Fredoux, whom her mother greatly missed, was also pregnant. News of the Chartist demonstrations in Britain, particularly affecting the Manchester area, had just penetrated to Kuruman and Mary's anxiety was heightened by worry over her 'lambkins'. In the Colony the Hottentot rebellion had struck a blow at the missionary cause. The web of life and the cares of her extended family engulfed Mary Moffat.

Then her son-in-law announced that he was preparing once again for a journey north, up to the lake and past it, to the country of the Makololo; and that Mary and the children were going with him.

He had been talking about it for weeks, but there had been an unwritten agreement, so MaMary understood, that he would leave his wife and family behind if Mrs Livingstone were pregnant. She was—but still they were going.

It was not a decision taken lightly by Livingstone. Indeed it was in a sense his last effort to make the pattern of the missionary family as a pioneering unit fit his own compulsive way of life. He knew what it might entail. 'I feel much when I think of the children dying, but who will go if we don't?' Mary Livingstone, submissive, 'a dejected Christian' her husband once described her, does not seem to have protested. She loved her husband and all her life had been aware of the dilemma of missionary wives. If she did not go she faced loneliness, possibly even total separation.

Mary Moffat, however, had no hesitation in taking action on her daughter's behalf. She had seen the state of the family on their arrival back from Lake Ngami in 1850. She attributed Mary's stroke and the death of the baby directly to this journey. She too believed in the pioneer missionary family— but only if the head of the family were genuinely engaged in the work of the Gospel. She wrote one of her rare letters to her son-in-law:

'My dear Livingstone. Before you left the Kuruman I did all I dared do to broach the subject of your intended journey, and thus bring on a candid discussion, more especially with regard to Mary's accompanying you with those dear children. But seeing how averse both you and Father were to speak about it, and the hope that you would never be guilty of such temerity (after the dangers they escaped last year), I too timidly shrank from what I ought to have had the courage to do. Mary had all along told me that should she be pregnant you would not take her, but let her come here after you were fairly off. Though I suspected at the end that she began to falter in this resolution, still I hoped it would never take place, i.e. *her going with you*, and looked and longed for things transpiring to prevent it. But to my dismay I now get a letter, in which she writes, "I must again wend my weary way to the far interior, perhaps to be confined in the field." O Livingstone, what do you mean? Was it not enough that you lost one lovely babe, and scarcely saved the others, while the mother came home threatened with paralysis. And will you again expose her and them in those sickly regions on an *exploring* expedition? All the world will condemn the cruelty of the thing to say nothing of the indecorousness of it. A pregnant woman with three little children trailing about in the company of the other sex, through the wilds of Africa, among savage men and beasts! Had you *found a place* to which you wished to go and commence missionary operations, the case would be altered. Not one word would I *say*, were it to the mountains of the moon. But to go with an exploring party, the thing is preposterous. I remain yours in great perturbation, M. Moffat.'

She did not alter her son-in-law's mind. But at least she had told him what she thought, she had made her protest in the strongest terms and redeemed her own earlier cowardice. Her husband's reluctance to discuss the issue with her and the indications that he was not wholly on her side must have made her more than ever lonely in the loss of Ann.

The Livingstones left on April 26th 1851, and the news that she dreaded did not come. Mary Livingstone was delivered of a fine boy on the banks of the River Zouga.

But in spite of the successful end to her pregnancy the journey was one of constant hardship for Mary and the children. They suffered badly from fever. They were all stung by bees; the children were bitten by the tse-tse fly; there was a shortage of water. 'As is always the case the children drank more than usual as the water became less, and their mother sat crying over them as she saw the precious fluid drawing to the bottom of the bottle. It was no wonder. We did not know for certain that the man would return with water, and the very idea of the little ones perishing before ones eyes for thirst is dreadful,' wrote their father. The man did return, but this journey finally decided Mr Livingstone to send his family to Britain and leave himself free to answer the call that burned in his blood. It was also to have another, more disastrous, consequence some years later, through Livingstone's report that Sebituane, chief of the Makololo, had expressed his appreciation of the fact that the missionary had shown sufficient confidence to bring his wife and children with him.

Robert Hamilton's candle had at last gone out. He died very quietly on July 11th 1851, while Mary and her husband sat beside his bed. Some months before his mind had failed and he had required continuous nursing, but it was twenty years since he had come to live with the Moffats and they loved him. After he was gone Mary felt very lonely.

Yet there was little time for repining. The Livingstones came back from the north and stopped at Kuruman on their way to the Cape. Half-humourously, half-seriously David Livingstone had written to his father-in-law, 'From the way Mrs M has written to us for some time past I expect to be obliged to pull down as soon as we reach Kuruman and get my bottom warmed with the "taws".' He had not seen her since she wrote in anger about Mary and the children.

But Mary did not bear grudges—and she was only too glad to have got them all safely back. While saddened at the thought of her eldest daughter and grandchildren leaving Africa for Britain, she was doubtless greatly relieved to have them beyond her unpredictable son-in-law's power to drag them off again into the unknown. Livingstone was surprised at the change in her attitude to him once they were gone; in fact he quite missed her tart reproofs. 'MaMary has not given me a "touching up" since I came back here. Hope she ain't dead,' he wrote a month or two later. She was not. In her own way she loved him, and perhaps understood him better than he gave her credit for. Once on his own she followed his explorations with genuine interest and affection.

Robert junior had come to stay at Kuruman for some months. He was considering becoming a trader. To his parents' great pleasure he had finally found a girl who loved him, and in December 1851 he married Ellen Platt of Natal and brought her back to Kuruman.

Once again Mary was in the thick of a busy life, with little time to write to her ageing father when the day's chores were done. 'In this country if the mistress of a house abstracts herself from domestic affairs, all hands seem to hold up—they seem as if they could not go on without propelling.' Robert too found that his involvement and encouragement were constantly needed if things were to progress on the station. He was the kind of man whose creative energy unconsciously overshadowed the contribution of other men. William Ashton, who had taken over the whole work of the printing press and the training of African staff, felt himself undervalued. He admired Mr Moffat but found it difficult to work with him.

The Livingstones with their four children left for the Cape in January 1852, to find a ship to take Mary and the family back to Britain. Her husband, having small opinion of Scottish education, would have liked to have sent his children to the United States. He felt no great affection for his own country and feared that the climate might be too severe for them. He was planning an immense journey for himself as soon as they had gone, and the knowledge that her husband was about to undertake an expedition full of dangers cannot have made the parting any easier for Mary Livingstone.

They sailed on April 23rd, on board the *Trafalgar*—a large ship with a good company of Indian officers and their wives on board. The children all had bad colds, caught through getting their hair cut two days earlier, their father explained. They had also had measles—and the whole family had been baffled by the staircases in the Cape houses and felt like turning round and coming down backwards.

No sooner were they away than David Livingstone had an operation for a dropped uvula which had been giving him great trouble for some time. Twelve days after she left he wrote to Mary assuring her of his great affection. '. . . I can say truly, my dearest, that I loved you when I married you and the longer I lived with you I loved you the better. . . .' She was to have little comfort except this message to carry her through the long dark years ahead.

While he was away in the south the Boers attacked Kolobeng and wrecked Livingstone's house. The Bakwena's town was reduced to ashes and Sechele, the chief, and those of his people who survived were driven off into the mountains. Sechele, a man of strong character, made the long journey to Cape Town to ask the Government for assistance in this calamity. He was coldly received and given no satisfaction.

Before this disaster overtook the Bakwena, however, Sechele had decided to send his older children to Kuruman to be educated. Robert Moffat was at first reluctant to accept this charge. Sechele was a past master at living in two worlds and Robert felt entitled to ask that he abandon some of his old practices in return for the privilege of placing his children in Mrs Moffat's care. Before this piece of moral bargaining was complete Sechele put his son, three daughters and a niece into a waggon, with a retinue of twenty-four attendants, and sent them off the two-hundred-and-fifty miles to Kuruman.

MaMary took them into her own house, giving the girls Mr Hamilton's old room and the boy, Sebele, a room in an out-house. The children, aged between nine and thirteen, accepted the change easily. Only, when twenty-three of the attendants returned home, leaving one man behind, did the little boy Sebele weep bitterly at parting with his nurse. Mary took him in her arms and comforted him. Sechele had written to Robert Moffat, 'I know that you are kind hearted and gentle among the people of the land.' It was true of Mary Moffat also.

When catastrophe struck Sechele's town and he decided to take his case to the Cape, he brought with him on his way south the mother of his son, MaSebele, and his remaining small children to leave them and their retinue at Kuruman. Mary now had a large number of Bakwena, both adults and children, living in her compound and dependent on her for supplies.

The association with Sechele's family was to continue over the next few years with varying success. Mary took the children gladly. Though they added to her cares, they also filled a portion of the gap left by her own departed family. She took special pains with the girls, teaching them to sew and cut out clothes, supervising their reading and writing lessons when they came home from school.

The little boy Sebele was lonely, having no companion from his own people to play with, so Robert sent to his father to ask for another Bakwena boy to come and join him. This request Sechele promptly acceded to and a second youngster arrived in the Moffat compound. The two boys shared a room. Sebele was a nervous child, though a good-natured little boy who laughed a great deal. He was very naughty. The three elder daughters, all by discarded wives, were of quite different temperaments: Ope, handsome, clever, courteous but resenting correction; Kereboletswe, less polite; Kwantheng, of lower rank than the other two because she was the daughter of a concubine, comely and sweet tempered. She was Mary's favourite.

By the time Sechele came back from his abortive journey to pick up his wife and the children, MaSebele could already read and make her own and all the children's clothes, and all was sweetness and light. Mary wanted to keep two of the youngest children with her, Sebele and Bantshang, but Sechele insisted on taking them all home. A year later he asked Robert Moffat to take Sebele and Bantshang back to Kuruman and Mary agreed to have them. At first they were obedient and happy and made good progress, but it did not last. Over the next months there were rows and disagreements. The children accused MaMary of starving them—possibly because the food she provided was so different from that which their own mothers cooked; Bantshang stole things; MaMary's high standards irked them. Robert regretted having taken them back. Nevertheless Bantshang and Sebele became for a time part of the Moffat family—though a troublesome and worrying part.

Towards the end of 1852 David Livingstone disappeared into the interior on the great journey which was eventually to take him across the width of Africa. For the next three years news of him was to reach his family only at long intervals, and it was to be four years—instead of the expected one—before his wife saw him again. She had not anticipated such a prolonged separation and the months without communication, when her experience of her native land must often have told her that he was as likely to be dead as alive, required sometimes more fortitude and stamina and faith than she possessed. Some of Livingstone's early letters to her, before he travelled too far from even the most primitive of postal arrangements, had a patronising quality which can only have added to her misery. 'I am thankful that you are where you are, and if you improve your opportunities you may have cause for gratitude through life. Hope you give much of your time to the children. You will

be sorry for it if you don't. Give my love and kisses to them all.'
MaMary would have had something to say about that.

In 1853 the British Government prepared to hand over to its settlers, mainly Boer, the Orange River Sovereignty, the vast tract of land between the Orange and Vaal rivers which the Governor of the Cape had annexed five years before in order to try and control the continuing expansion of the Boer farmers. Now British policy had changed. Attempts to administer the enormous sovereignty had proved a failure and Sir George Clerk was sent out from England to persuade—or bully if need be—the emigrant farmers, both Boer and British, into taking over their own independent state.

The missions were greatly alarmed at this abdication of responsibility by the British Government, having little confidence in the future of missionary interests or native rights within an independent Orange Republic. Kuruman did not lie inside the proposed jurisdiction of the new state, but Robert Moffat nevertheless rode to Bloemfontein in August 1853 to present a memorial drawn up by a meeting of all the northern missionaries. It had no effect, either on Sir George Clerk or on the terms under which the Orange Free State ultimately came into being, and an atmosphere of apprehension and gloom pervaded the missions. War and confusion surrounded Kuruman. The interior stations were broken up, the missionaries ordered out by the Boers, and the work had to be left to native teachers.

Towards the end of this year Mary's father died, at the ripe old age of ninety. She had retained with him the strong links of her youth, although their separation had been so long and so final. She had never regretted the decision made with so much pain thirty-four years before, and she knew he had come to accept it as the will of God. Alone of all his immediate family her son John, now studying for the ministry, stood at the graveside when his grandfather was laid to rest.

Both Robert and Mary were suffering increasingly from ill-health. The Directors suggested to Robert that he might go to England, or to the Colony. He refused. His headpains were worse, a source of continual discomfort to him and anxiety to Mary. He was white bearded now and had lost all his teeth—at fifty-nine a patriarch, widely respected and deeply loved. One of those who loved him, and had done so for twenty-four years, though he had not seen him since 1835, was Moselekatse, chief of the Matabele.

Now established in new lands in the very far north, in country just south of the Zambesi, Moselekatse had retained a strange and genuine affection for his friend Moffat. In 1853 messages filtered through to Kuruman that he would like to see Moshete again. Robert, for whom the north always held a fascination, had no thought at that time of undertaking such a journey. He was too preoccupied with translation to be able to contemplate leaving Kuruman. In mid-1854, however, a set of circumstances suddenly made such an expedition seem not only possible but desirable. Letters had arrived from Livingstone in February saying that he was hoping to find a road to the west coast and that he was unlikely to come back through Kuruman. Since then news had been scanty. He had been away seventeen months and it was not known exactly where he was—except that the Zambesi had been one of his objectives. He would need stores, as well as news, if these could be got to him. Also the mission would increasingly have to look to the north for any expansion of its activities. Moselekatse's evidence of continuing friendship might prove an important opening.

At the moment when he was contemplating all these arguments, two young trader-travellers came through Kuruman bound for Matabele country and urged Robert to go with them. Mary, seeing a chance to distract him from the study which was damaging his health, added her encouragement. He could take supplies for Livingstone. She was sure that Moselekatse, when he heard that the son-in-law of MaMary and the husband of his friend's daughter needed help, would not hesitate to take what steps he could to discover him and send the goods on. She sent a blue waistcoat, white shirts, woollen socks, quince jam, lemon juice, tea, coffee, and everything else that her experience and skill could suggest. She also sent a note which for once contained nothing but affection and the assurance of her prayers for him.

In the end the decision to go was taken quite suddenly and, in a very few days, Robert was off with the two young men. Mary, though content to see him go, was fussed at being given so little time to make preparations for his comfort and for the

165

presents she would send to Moselekatse. She packed raisin loaf, home-cured ox-tongue—which Robert later complained was too hard for his toothless gums—rusks, and *Uncle Tom's Cabin* for him to read as she refused to allow him to take any work with him. At the very last moment she put in two of a litter of kittens to give him company and amusement.

MARY MOFFAT'S HOME

Chapter 16

THEY LEFT KURUMAN on May 22nd 1854, Mary going with
the party as far as Motito, where she paid a visit to Ann and her
family. The baby Samuel was ill, Ann was again pregnant and
there was three-year-old Theophile to look after. MaMary set
them all to rights and then returned to Kuruman to prepare
for a journey of her own. She was going to Colesburg to visit
her daughter-in-law Ellen, and try to regain some of her
strength. There was also a possibility that Mary Livingstone
might be coming back.

Balked of his work, Robert Moffat kept a journal from the
moment he left Mary at Motito. He was light-hearted, full of
pleasure at being once again on the move, travelling as he had
first done when he came to Africa to unknown and adventurous
places. Whenever there was a chance he sent instalments back
by passing travellers. For a long time now he and Mary had
been preoccupied by their own concerns, harried by daily
cares, plagued by ageing bodies. The partnership on which all
their work was based had been taken for granted; the love they
bore each other largely unexpressed.

Now, released temporarily from his worries, Robert missed
her. He thought of her starting out alone for Colesburg. 'Tar or
smear in the buckets for greasing waggon hubs—if not get more
made. Spare whips hanging in our back room at Kuruman.
Yoke slings (spare) perhaps in the packhouse and spare yoke
somewhere. If the forewheel is weak get it mended temporarily
at Campbell. . . . Take care of the waggon tumbling, and when
you pass into civilised society do not forget me.' He supposed
that at 9 p.m. she was remembering him while preparing for
bed. Her gingerbread things were prime companions on the
road. The Matabele females walked about totally naked—yet
he had to admit he had never seen the sensuous looks he saw in
civilised society—'NB. Dear Mary, this is for *your* information
only.'

Mary was in Colesburg when Ellen Moffat had a second son in July. They called him Hamilton, after his grandfather's fellow missionary. While there '. . . important intelligence reached me that, though Mrs Livingstone was not coming, my younger daughter Bessie was. Just when all was ready for my journey home I heard this, and at once started for Port Elizabeth.'

Bessie. Whom she had last seen on the deck of a ship in Table Bay in 1848, aged nine: now a young lady of fifteen-and-a-half. The expectation, the tension, the excitement were almost too much for her. The next day she had a violent headache.

Bessie was already in Port Elizabeth when Mary arrived on September 30th, so Mary had no time to worry about the hazards of this dangerous shore 'where there is no jetty and the surf sometimes runs high for weeks together'. Ten days before, the *Charlotte*, bound from Queenstown to Calcutta, had been totally wrecked in Algoa Bay and sixty-two soldiers, eleven women and twenty-six children perished.

But Bessie had had a good voyage, this time with a chaperon who earned Mary's gratitude for her motherly concern. Mother and daughter greeted each other rapturously, Bessie thinking how pretty her mother still looked, with her blue eyes and bright complexion; Mary overjoyed at once again having a child with her.

Bessie, whose luggage had not yet come ashore, had no dress for church except what she stood up in. Mary Moffat was not going to show off her newly found lambkin to the congregation in a soiled gown. She brought out one of her own dresses, which she was delighted to find fitted Bessie exactly. They were both very small. Bessie, just back from England, where fashions had changed in the last few years, regarded it as a 'quaint old satin gown' and was naturally reluctant to wear it. Mary was oblivious to her daughter's discomfort and Bessie, not yet certain enough of her new relationship with her mother to protest, put it on. Mary proudly draped a silk shawl about her shoulders and off they went.

This slight disagreement did not last long enough to cloud their happiness in being together again. Only one thing marred Mary's pleasure—the fear that she would not now be home in time to greet Robert on his return from Matabele land. She could not bear the thought of his arriving back to an empty house.

While waiting for Bessie's luggage to come ashore, Mary bought and supervised the packing of stores for Kuruman, enough to last them for the years that might go by before such an opportunity recurred. Bessie was delighted to see the old waggon in which as a child she had spent so many happy weeks. She explored it from top to bottom, the commodious bed with side sacks all round and curtains in front and behind, the leather-cushioned seat at the end of the bed where they sat during the day, the forechest in front of that where Cornelius drove the oxen, the space at the back portioned off for the girl.

Mary, nervy at the delays, her mind increasingly back home at Kuruman and on the road with Robert, was further tried by constant questions about her husband's journeyings and enquiries as to what her son-in-law thought he was doing wandering about in the wilds. 'With the few more intelligent I have to expiate on the probable results of your journey, and Livingstone's reasons for adopting the course he has done.' She found it all tiring and trying, and her nerves were often frayed by the lack of understanding of what it was really like to be an interior missionary.

Above all it was Robert that she missed and whose comfort most concerned her. 'I feel very unhappy at the thought of not being at home as soon as you, and all is so dark about you; your last date which came to hand is July 13th,' she wrote in early October. 'We commenced this sort of suffering at Dukinfield Nursery, and it looks as if we should continue much in such feelings to the end of our lives. The last six months have been very trying in this respect—all things dark and obscure, my mind like a bow at full stretch—you and Livingstone at one end, Mary and Bessie at the other. I felt sometimes as if the string was too tight but was wonderfully sustained.'

Nevertheless she was happy and optimistic, 'taking as I do the most cheerful view of things'—so much so that she felt rather apologetic about it and hoped that Robert would not think her unprepared for future trials.

At last the day came when they could leave. They climbed on to the waggon, Cornelius and the leader spurred on the oxen with tremendous noise and shouting. Mary and her daughter settled down for the long haul home, Mary telling endless stories of her childhood, Bessie reading aloud from the books that she had brought back with her.

For once Mary was impatient with the slowness of waggon travel. She had chosen Cornelius because he was careful and cautious, now, in changed circumstances, she felt him to be too much so. He was afraid of the waggon upsetting, as indeed was Bessie, and resisted his mistress' urgings to press on at greater speed.

One evening, towards dark, with the threat of rain in the sky, they came to a drift. There was a lot of water in the stream and the approach to the ford was of heavy wet mud full of holes. Cornelius became agitated and at a critical moment the waggon lurched, one of its wheels tipping over into a hole. Thrashing, yelling, struggling, men and oxen floundered about in the dusk, the oxen becoming wilder and more stupid, the waggon settling deeper into the mud. Perched up on the seat Mary and Bessie watched helplessly, while the frightened girl peered out behind.

At last it was clear that there was no hope except to disentangle waggon and oxen and start afresh. Slowly and laboriously Cornelius and the leader began to unload at the back all the baggage so painstakingly packed on at Port Elizabeth. It was a heart-breaking task, made no easier by the darkness and the drizzling rain. Taking off Bessie's small chest of drawers, which had come with her all the way from England, some of the drawers slipped and many of her treasured possessions were spilled into the mud. The three women, their long skirts bedraggled about them, gathered up these things and took them to a little knoll where they lit a fire and tried to dry them out. Mary was almost despairing. Below them the men and the oxen struggled hopelessly, no nearer freeing the waggon than they had been an hour earlier. She said aloud to Bessie, 'This is the Slough of Despond. O for help!'

Not long after they heard the creak and rumble of another waggon—a most unusual sound on a trail where waggons met but rarely. When it drew closer the team stopped and the owner of the waggon jumped down to find out what was happening. Immediately he outspanned his own oxen, joined them to Mary's and, taking charge of the operation, succeeded in pulling the Moffat waggon out of its hole and across the ford.

There had been no chance to ask who he was or where he came from. In the hurly-burly of righting the waggon Mary was content to call him the 'messenger of the Lord'. When everything was straight he came over to speak to her and it was then that Mary discovered, to her great pleasure, that her rescuer was a Moravian missionary, the first she had ever met in Africa. It added a peculiar flavour to this providential encounter that the man who had come out of the dark should belong to the group whom she had so much admired in the far off schooldays that she had so recently been recalling to her daughter.

They boiled up a cup of coffee on the smoky fire, then he left in haste and she never saw him again.

They were still a long way from home. Towards the end of November they reached the Orange river, only to find it impassable. After three weeks they eventually got across—then to be kept a month at the Vaal. There they were joined by Robert junior and his family also *en route* for Kuruman, where Robert junior had decided to set up a trading post.

At least the agony of waiting was mitigated by news. Robert sent oxen to meet them on the far side of the river—and with the oxen letters. He was safely back, in improved health: Livingstone had reached the west coast—'a wonder to the world' his mother-in-law added; she did not approve of the world's adulation. Robert was experiencing a reaction from his journey, finding it difficult to settle, so he asked Mary to write on his behalf to the Society reporting his news. She did not altogether relish this, telling them she was not herself in much better shape!

It was very hot on the banks of the Vaal. There was no shelter for the numerous waggons which had collected there to wait for the subsiding of the water. Robert Moffat arrived on the opposite side and he and Mary gazed at each other across the river. After consultation it was decided to attempt a crossing. The water was still high and the rush of the current under the waggons formidable. Deeper and deeper they sank till the foremost stuck in mid-stream and not all the shrieks and yells, whips and bullying of the drivers could make the demented oxen move it one inch further.

Night was coming on, so it was arranged to carry the women and children over on the shoulders of the men and abandon the waggons till morning. Mary was carried ashore between Robert Moffat and another man. For the first time her daughter, seeing her mother struggling to maintain this perilous perch, thought of her as old and infirm. She was close on sixty.

A huge bonfire was lit on the bank and bedding disposed around it. Bessie slept the sleep of the young and exhausted, untroubled by fears. Her father and mother lay awake, giving thanks for being together again and for news of Livingstone, listening anxiously to the sound of the river in case it rose and swept the waggons away.

The next day the waggons were all pulled back to the far side and a fresh ford sought. They arrived at Kuruman in January 1855. As they neared the station crowds came out of the villages to surround the waggons and greet them. The oxen smelt home and quickened their pace. The oasis that was their home rose out of the barren country surrounding it, a lovely vision of crystal clear water behind the dam and in the irrigation ditches, weeping willows, flowering and fruiting trees, fields of corn and maize; the rows of stone mission houses along the broad grassy street, the fine church, the compounds scattered round the periphery. For each Moffat it was a return full of emotion. 'My dear husband had travelled seven hundred miles north-east of this, through savage beasts and savage men, and had been brought back again in perfect safety and improved health. . . . My journey too had been attended with difficulties and dangers, out of all of which the Lord had delivered us,' Mary wrote; and for Bessie, 'brought safely over the stormy ocean after nearly seven years absence', and Robert junior it was finally coming home.

The mission station was in the charge of an African teacher. Three months before, William Ashton had decided that he could no longer postpone taking his wife to the Cape for her health. Robert Moffat was agreeably surprised with the way the work of the station had continued in the absence of the missionaries. The school had good numbers of pupils, services were held regularly with crowded congregations. In spite of war and confusion in the surrounding country—or perhaps because of it, for as a result Kuruman had a bigger population than usual—the Christian community flourished.

There was another scourge over the country, lung sickness—a disease fatal to cattle. For the Bechuana this was a disaster. Cattle were their wealth, and hundreds of families were reduced to poverty by the death of their beasts.

Mary Moffat set out immediately to teach Bessie the arts of household management in Africa that she had certainly not acquired in the comparatively affluent surroundings of her sister's English home. It was trying for them both. Bessie was a small lean girl, quiet and seemingly easily overridden, but under her meek exterior she had a mind of her own and had developed a number of views which ran counter to those of her parents. Her mother deplored her 'heterodox' opinions and spoke severely when she voiced them. It was the beginning of a gradual realisation by Mary Moffat that her children had grown up into a changing world.

It was a shock for Bessie to find that she was much less skilled in the essential tasks of keeping a community going than her mother's African pupils and servants. Mary was a splendid trainer, with a 'sense of ease' about her teaching, but she was also a perfectionist and could be tart about work badly done. Her anger, however, was short-lived and her patience in showing an anxious learner how to get something exactly right was infinite.

Bessie began on half-a-dozen calico shirts for her father. This task was chosen because shirts had every kind of seam, hem and tuck on them. Slowly and painfully, only too aware of her own deficiences, Bessie sewed, unpicked, redid and eventually finished, the shirts. Then she progressed to a set of fine muslin caps for her mother, with narrow hems, whipping and long rolls of bordering. That done she learnt how to starch and iron and launder. Mary might live in a remote, uncivilised outpost, but she did not intend to lower her standards. When the rudiments of fine sewing were mastered Bessie accompanied her mother to the sewing school, where girls of all ages made everything from dusters to garments. Later she took over this school. Her pupils were rough and very noisy—and she hated it.

Twice a week, in the large brick oven, fourteen loaves, of coarse meal kneaded in an immense bowl, were baked. Bessie started on Mary's special brown bread of fine wholemeal ground in a patent mill. She was shown how to make pastry and churn butter. The five servants, all home-trained, watched in surprise this grown-up daughter of MaMary who did not know how to cook in the black three-legged pots, or roast coffee in the large flat pan. They saw MaMary, who had fought a long and successful battle for immaculate organisation in her kitchen and storerooms, make on Bessie the same meticulous demands that she made on all her pupils. Anything left lying about was known as 'a nest egg for others' and had to be tidied up and put away. It was a lesson MaMary had learned early in her life at Lattakoo.

On week-days Mary and her daughter drove out in a small phaeton, drawn by two oxen, to the neighbouring villages to visit the old women who could no longer come in to Mary's Bible class. Her shrewd eye took in the state of their homes and she gave help and advice freely. She always carried a workbag with sewing materials and patches from the missionary boxes that came out from Manchester. Patchwork dresses were the current fashion in Kuruman.

It was a peaceful happy interlude. Major worries were unresolved: the political situation remained uneasy, the tribes harried each other; there was no news from Livingstone. But Robert was better and, because of Mr Ashton's absence, there was no printing being done so that the pressure on him was relaxed. Mary had a daughter with her once again, and her son and his family close at hand. John was doing well at College and proposing to follow his father into the Society.

Ann and her rapidly growing family were settled near enough to call on MaMary in an emergency. Mary Livingstone was in the unhappy situation of not knowing where her husband was or how he did—but at least she and the children were safe in Britain, as were Jeanie and Helen with all her brood. It was thirteen years since they had seen Helen and she had just had her fourth child. When posts arrived Mary cleared everything out of the way, then sat down in her armchair with her feet on a footstool, or lay on the sofa that Robert and Mr Hamilton had once made for her, and read to her heart's content. The news might be four months out of date, and she was always conscious that much might have happened since they had been written, but this was the moment that joined her to the outside world, that restored the links with those whom she loved.

She had entered her sixties. Looking back, which now happened more and more frequently, she had to admit that there had been work well done. She had put her confidence in the Lord and it had not been misplaced. She was prepared for a serene old age. It was as well that she could not see what the next ten years would bring.

Early in 1856 her links were restored with her son-in-law. David Livingstone, having reached Loanda on the west coast in 1854, retraced his steps back across the whole width of Africa, finding *en route* at Linyanti the goods that his mother-in-law had sent up for his comfort a year before. Neither the Matabele nor the Makololo had touched a single item.

He wrote a rather snippy letter of thanks to MaMary. He had not forgotten, even if she had, her distrust of his judgement in spiritual affairs, and he brushed aside her concern for his health and safety.

On May 20th 1856 he arrived at Quelimane on the east coast, four years almost to the day since he had left Cape Town. He sailed for Britain by a rather roundabout route, taking him to Mauritius, Ceylon, Alexandria, Marseilles, where impatient with the slowness of the journey he left the ship and proceeded overland. 'I have been seven times in peril of my life, not from choice certainly. What do you say MaMary . . . though you had four parishes to pick out of you would not get a pluckier son-in-law though your spectacles were on the search. There's no going about the bush in that is there?' he wrote in a letter to Robert Moffat. By mischance the first person to greet him in England was not his wife, who had gone down to Southampton to meet the ship, but John Moffat, now twenty-one, his devoted admirer.

Mary's friend Anne Helmore was also on leave in Britain at this time with her husband and family. Mary had written a warm letter to a dear friend giving them a personal introduction. Bessie, when she returned home from Britain with fresh eyes, had been greatly struck by the slowness of missionary work, the need to be constantly engaged in keeping body and soul together, and had felt how little this was understood back in England where the glamour and adventure of Africa distorted reality. Mary had seen many young couples come out; some had survived, others had not. Holloway Helmore had arrived a very handsome, gay, brilliant young man, whose life had so far come easily to him. She had feared for him. She had watched him face the realities and accept the discipline of an interior mission station. She admired him for it. She was only just beginning to recognise that her son-in-law perceived the challenge of the Gospel in other terms; to realise that he marched to a different drummer in the service of the same Lord.

KURUMAN STREET

Chapter 17

EIGHTEEN HUNDRED AND FIFTY SEVEN came in on a less agreeable note. William Ashton reached Kuruman in August 1855, after almost a year at the Cape. He did not find the return easy. Though there had been financial and other anxieties in Cape Town, it had also been a time of liberation. The family was treated with great kindness and the respect due to those who worked on the mission frontiers, and William Ashton had been in demand as a preacher, to take services for colleagues. He had approached this task with some diffidence, especially because it was many years since he had preached a sermon in English and his tongue at first felt clumsy in this language. But he was a success; people liked him for himself and on his merits. He was not a vain man or one who overestimated his own gifts, but he enjoyed being free of the shadow of a colleague whom he acknowledged to be greater than himself—Robert Moffat.

Unsettled by this experience the return to Kuruman was a shock. All his previous resentments were suddenly magnified by comparison with his stay in different and more openly appreciative surroundings. It was not that the Moffats did not value his work, but they had themselves come through a hard schooling, where every man did what needed to be done and expected little thanks for it, and they took it for granted that any interior missionary worth his salt understood this to be his lot. Like many men carried along by the obsessions of their own genius—and with the satisfactions that exercise of that genius of itself brings to them—Robert Moffat was apt to forget that his more ordinary colleagues had human failings. William Ashton's was a very natural one. He wanted to be given public credit for the work to which he had, at great cost to himself and his family, devoted the last ten years of his life. He did not want to quarrel openly with Mr Moffat, so he asked for a transfer.

The news that Mr Ashton actually wished to leave Kuruman was a shock to the Moffats. Relations had been uneasy for some time, but that he would ask to go had not crossed their minds. Indeed it was difficult to see how he could be dispensed with. Since Robert Hamilton's death he had been the only other missionary permanently on the station and this was no moment, when they were both beginning to feel the effects of age, for the Moffats to have to take up the entire burden alone.

It all added up to an unhappy state of affairs. Neither man any longer felt at ease with the other. For Mary, often attempting to act as peacemaker and go-between, hating quarrels, it was a disagreeable time. Necessarily, in the last push to get the Sechuana Bible completed, they had to work closely together.

While Mr Ashton supervised the sheets going through the press, Robert with Mary beside him sat in the room next door. There Robert set out the translation, tested it with a Bechuana assistant, while Mary read out the English slowly and distinctly to see that nothing was left out. The page then went to Mr Ashton, who again read out the English while Robert followed the Sechuana. Only then was the translation handed to a compositor and put through the press, when a reverse process of reading and correcting proofs had to be followed. It was demanding, detailed, exhausting work, not calculated to assuage tempers or relationships already strained.

Nevertheless the great work, a triumph both of translating and printing, was finished early in 1857. The Bible in Sechuana, after thirty-two years of hard work, was an accomplished fact.

With the end in sight and with Mr Ashton's desire to leave, another consideration had begun to assume great importance. The Moffats were sixty-two now and the question of a successor was unresolved. John was at the end of his studies. He had offered himself to the Society. His parents had never brought any pressure on him as to which mission field he should choose, but now Robert wrote to the Directors suggesting, somewhat diffidently, that they might consider appointing his son to Kuruman with a view to his taking over from his father.

The letter that came from London, however, contained quite a different proposition and flung the station into confusion.

Back in England the London Missionary Society had been greatly excited both by Livingstone's epic journey and by Robert Moffat's own Matabele journals. Suddenly it seemed vast tracts of Africa were being opened up by their missionaries;

opportunities, the like of which had not come their way for very many years, were there for the grasping. They wrote to Mr Moffat announcing their intention of starting two new missions, to the Makololo, with whom Livingstone had formed strong links, and to the Matabele, with the assent of Moselekatse, Robert Moffat's friend. Would Mr Moffat take a year off and accompany the mission to the Matabele to ensure its friendly reception by the king? Mr Ashton would take charge at Kuruman.

At this time the Makololo were settled in unhealthy country south of the Zambesi, but Livingstone, who had taken some of the carriers for his journey across Africa from this tribe, had persuaded the chief, Sebituane, that it would be advantageous to move his town across the river to higher ground on the north bank. Now the suggestion was that, with Livingstone's help, the removal of the Makololo to new lands might coincide with setting up a mission station among them.

It was a heady prospect; a gigantic leap one thousand miles to the north of Kuruman, with no supporting mission stations in between. With two men whose names were now a by-word both in Britain and Africa to carry the Gospel outward what triumphs might not lie in wait if the Society were courageous enough to accept the challenge?

Robert Moffat, who knew the realities, was much less sure of the wisdom of what was proposed. He too responded to the vision of expansion to the shores of the remote Zambesi, but a lifetime of frontier living had taught him that visions only succeeded when allied with hard practicality. About one thing he had no illusions. Moselekatse, his friend who loved him, had nevertheless resisted all his persuasions to become Christian. So far he had refused to consider the idea of a mission on his lands and it would be fatal for any party to arrive taking his acquiescence for granted. Only Robert Moffat himself would be able to get consent for the missionaries to settle among the Matabele. If the mission was to have any chance of success he must go at once to Moselekatse to prepare the way.

Mary agreed that he should go, and perhaps was not displeased that he should take yet again a journey which, for all its exhaustion and danger, he had done before with considerable benefit to his health. He was suffering severely from head pains and was troubled about his heart. He kept those ailments to himself—for fear that Mary would lock him out of his study, but she knew that he was unwell.

Mary too had seen a vision when the letter came from London and, for the moment, she saw that here, at last, was the work which would settle her restless son-in-law and make it possible for his wife and family to join him; and the mission to the Matabele would be the ideal opening for her son John. This relationship between the two missions, and of both with Robert Moffat, would heal the enmity which existed between the Matabele and the Makololo. 'Only think,' she exclaimed to Bessie, 'my daughter there on one side of the river—and my son on the other—amid that fearfully savage people! What an honour.' And, indicating her absolute belief in the gentlemanly qualities of the awesome tyrant of those very people, she sent a message up to Moselekatse by Robert, 'Leave my daughter's people alone.' Robert agreed to deliver it, remarking teasingly that as Moselekatse had a great respect for MaMary (whom he had never seen) he was sure that her wishes would be obeyed!

Preparations for Robert's journey were made hurriedly, with the chaos and 'stir' that Mary so much disliked. It was already late in the travelling season and both heat and rain could be hazards. William Ashton had agreed that it was his duty to stay while Robert was away, but all the same Robert had some doubts about the burdens which would fall on Mary during his absence. It was Bessie's presence which finally influenced his decision to go. At least she could take many of the domestic duties off her mother's shoulders and look after her if she fell ill.

Mary herself, agitated, fussed by the fact that in the rush to finish the translation of the Bible and get Robert's waggon packed much of her regular domestic routine had had to be left undone, nevertheless accepted the separation as a fact of life and faced it calmly. She wrote to John, 'The poor heart will ache in anticipation of all these separations, and the life of privation and hardship which seems destined for so many loved members of my family, as well as your father at his advanced age. . . . What I would have faced courageously (when once convinced of my duty) seems now very formidable to me. I can however call to mind how we have been sustained and strengthened for the last forty years and our lives preserved. . . .'

John Moffat had been told to hold himself in readiness to leave for Africa. His parents had asked the Society to make arrangements for Jeanie to travel with him. On July 28th 1857 Robert Moffat left Kuruman for his fourth visit to Moselekatse with the knowledge that he could offer him his son as missionary to the Matabele.

During the seven months that Robert was away Mary held the fort at Kuruman, strengthened by a constant stream of letters sent back by the traveller whenever possible. On several occasions he even sent his washing home. Without him Kuruman seemed flat and dull. He sent back instructions about accounts, sowing seed, planting vegetables, what to do about guns for repairs and return. He confessed that his heart troubled him but was now better. It was a relief to have the translation finished. 'I do not feel willing to forget the emotion I felt when the last galley was read, nor the just indignation I feel at being locked out of my study, towards which I felt a kind of sacred awe.' It was a sore point, a fundamental difference between them which all their long years together had not resolved. He was disorderly by temperament, she was orderly and every now and again his untidiness became too much for her. She swept through his working room and put his 'pigsty' in apple pie order. Then his mind came to a standstill and he found it impossible to work again until he had recreated chaos around him. He needed the piles of papers, the books left open, the random notes, his 'memory stimulants' to fuel his creative imagination. The nightmare of her interference in this vital sphere haunted him. Two months later he came back to it. '. . . I feel it is impossible to forget your trying, your actually locking me out of my study—the thing rises before me sometimes like a spectre.'

He wrote of all the other large and small, trivial and important, items of their daily life together: the difficulties of either of them 'taking it easy'; the wildness of the Fredoux children 'by grandparents' standards'; not certain whether he disapproved of Livingstone getting a public testimonial—he would defer to her judgement. He was knocked down by one of his own oxen and badly bruised; it was all tremendously hard work, but he was infinitely better in health than when he left; he felt very cold at Moselekatse's town and was wearing two pairs of woollen stockings, a comforter and a green handkerchief round his neck. 'You will say, "It is because you are getting old that you feel the cold." True, but the fireplace tells that young as well as old feel the cold, and damp too.' And, when Moselekatse had poured out a torrent of thanks for the gifts MaMary had sent him—including a red flowered tablecloth—'I was rather tickled to hear a tyrant of some hundred wives, some sitting beside him, expatiating most eloquently on the mementoes of MaMary, the only wife of a teacher. I only wished he had seen you, or rather that you had seen him.'

In October the news from the north was cheering. While Robert was still on the road they heard that Moselekatse 'had laid his spears in the water, and was expecting Moffat and was longing very much to see him again. . . . This intelligence was most seasonable to me,' Mary Moffat wrote to the Directors, 'for up to that time I had *when in low mood* had some misgivings about the new project, so suddenly resolved upon. I feared that people or rather the tyrant king, was not prepared for such an event. . . .'

By November Robert Moffat had promised Moselekatse, in return for his safe conduct for a mission, that it would be led by John Moffat. He knew very well that Moselekatse was intelligent enough, and wily enough, to recognise the dangers to his own absolute authority if he countenanced the spread of Christianity among his people. Robert Moffat had never believed that the Gospel should progress through political pressure, but by the spirit of God working through the word and example of the missionary. Though he abhorred the tyranny by which Moselekatse ruled, he had never attempted to subvert his people or interfere in Matabele justice. There were many ways in which he admired, even loved, the old king—as the old king loved Moffat. They were both men of strong character and dominating personality—the one devious, wily, implacable; the other open, sincere, persistent. Over the enormous gulf of nation, culture, belief, which separated them each yet saw in the other the lineaments of a friend. Robert Moffat won a promise from Moselekatse that he would receive the mission to the Matabele: but he was not deceived into thinking that more than a precarious foothold had been gained.

No one, either at Kuruman or with the Matabele, had news

of the Livingstone family or knew where they were. Robert imagined that already they were on the way up the Zambesi, having come round by sea. Mary was glad enough to find scraps about them in newspapers. She complained that no one told them any news because it was taken for granted that the Kuruman family already knew everything. Nor was she any wiser as to the plans of John and Jeanie. In fact all three were still in England.

Robert Moffat's return home in February 1858 coincided with a number of painful occurrences. In the middle of January Sarah Ashton was confined. Worn out by ill-health, heat and constant exhaustion she had a difficult labour. Not long after it was born the baby died. William Ashton and Mary, differences forgotten, worked unremittingly to save the life of the mother. They succeeded, but the struggle cast an ominous shadow on Mrs Ashton's future. Four months later she was pregnant again.

Robert was only just back when news arrived from London that the Livingstone party would be in Table Bay about March 20th and the rest of the Matabele missionaries shortly after. Immediately the Moffats decided to set out for the Cape to meet them. Robert felt it important that he should be concerned with the new missionaries from the moment that they landed in Africa. But that was not the only reason for the sudden decision to undertake another long journey so soon. Both her parents felt a strong premonition that this might be their last chance to see their eldest daughter, Mary. They took it for granted that she would go with her husband and the rest of the Makololo mission round by sea to the mouth of the Zambesi and up river from there. It seemed to the Moffats that they would be unlikely to survive the number of years that must elapse before the mission was again able to make contact with southern civilisation.

On the way news, both good and bad, reached them. John was engaged to Emily Unwin, daughter of J. S. Unwin, a tea merchant of Brighton; and David Livingstone had left the London Missionary Society and accepted the job of H.M. Consul at Quelimane, which gave him a considerably increased salary and some official backing for an expedition up the Zambesi. The Moffats were dumbfounded by the latter news. For Robert it was a blow both 'confounding and painful'. He had himself been critical of the Society in the past; he knew its faults and felt, as does every man who works in the field for a remote headquarters, often impatient with its lack of understanding. He had been accustomed to protesting—or better still ignoring—decisions and advice with which he did not agree. But for forty-two years he had given his loyalty to the Directors and served the Society gladly.

He was torn now between anguish for what seemed like treachery to the cause on Livingstone's part and his own essential fairness of mind which made it possible to perceive justification for this step.

For Mary this may have been the realisation of long held doubts, though none the less painful for that. She had always suspected Livingstone's priorities were not hers: when fame came to him she had not been absolutely sure of his firmness of purpose in the face of the temptations which it brought. For an instant the phrase 'I knew it' may have flashed across her mind. If it did she repressed it instantly. Livingstone and Mary were going with the mission to the Makololo and for her that was the important fact.

The real blow came in another letter from John which reached them at Cape Town. In this they learned 'with surprise and grief' that John too had dissolved his connection with the Society and that he had been enabled to do this because his brother-in-law, generously making it possible for him to marry Emily Unwin, had offered to give him £500 and a waggon, plus £150 per year so long as Livingstone was alive.

The confusion which this news brought to his parents was total: confusion and deep sorrow. What was to happen now? If David Livingstone had offered to support John so as to fill the gap left by his own departure from the mission, would he expect him to go north with the Zambesi expedition? But he had been promised by his father to Moselekatse and the Matabele—and the whole success of the Matabele mission depended upon the honouring of that promise.

There were personal griefs too—but these they did not mention. Robert, whom they had hoped to see follow his father in the mission, had not felt able to take over the burden of this exacting vocation. He had made himself an honourable career in trading. They had long ago accepted his choice. But with

184

John it had seemed that there might be a second chance to fulfil the dream of a Moffat succession. Now that possibility was once again snatched from them. In the meanwhile there were a multitude of practical problems requiring attention. Robert had to try to resolve the many contradictions in the plans so far put forward for the new missions—which he frankly admitted 'bewildered his brains'.

He had now heard that though Livingstone was going on an expedition up the Zambesi which was to open up a path for the mission to the Makololo, that mission, led by Holloway Helmore, was expected to travel overland from Cape Town. This news appalled Robert Moffat. In his view the land journey would be infinitely longer in time and more expensive than going round by sea and up the river. It was through difficult country, as yet unexplored except by individual traders and hunters, with the added problem of tsetse infestation which might make it impossible to get oxen through.

In late April 1858 the steamer *Paarl* came into Table Bay with David and Mary Livingstone aboard. The journey, which in her mother's day had taken three months under sail, had lasted just six weeks. For Mary Livingstone it had been a very bad one. She was in the early stages of pregnancy and ever since the ship left Sierre Leone on the west coast had been continuously and devastatingly sick. The decision was taken to leave her at Cape Town. 'She would only be a hindrance instead of a help as we anticipated,' her husband wrote to John.

It was with considerable relief then, as well as with surprise, that the Livingstones found the grandparents waiting to greet them on the quay. It tempered somewhat Mary Livingstone's immense disappointment at once again being separated from her husband. She was wretched and depressed. 'We sail in one hour. Mary remains. Be kind to her,' David Livingstone wrote to his brother-in-law, whom he had already warned that if he left Emily at Kuruman 'your wife would be thoroughly put through her facings by MaMary'. David himself was in Cape Town only a short while, then sailed for Quelimane. He had not resolved his father-in-law's doubts about the tasks that lay before him.

John and Emily, accompanied by Jeanie, arrived a month later. It was ten years since the Moffat children had last seen their parents, John had been thirteen and Jeanie eight. Now John was twenty-three and a married man; Jeanie a grown-up young lady of eighteen. They had been nervous of this reunion after so long a time, and had talked on board of the possibility of failing to recognise the old people, but in the shock of meeting all that was forgotten. Mary, seeing again these beloved faces, and receiving her newest daughter-in-law, was overwhelmed with joyful agitation, but it was not long before it became very clear to her that the new generation did not see things as had the old pioneers. She did not bemoan this state of affairs, but she clearly recognised it and there were moments when she and Robert, in the privacy of their room, faced the fact that the young people had little knowledge of what it had cost their predecessors to make the progress that had been made, and even less of what was going to be demanded of themselves in the days that lay ahead.

John Moffat, the small boy with the odd ears whom Mary had parted with on the road out of Cape Town, came back a man of resolute character and unyielding temperament. For him life was black or white; he detested any softening of the naked truth. He had inherited his mother's suspicion of any form of public relations or uncomprehending social approval, and as yet he had not developed her compensating understanding of the frailties of human nature. He was a young man of absolute integrity, lacking the charm and lightness of touch which made his father so attractive, and, like many such young men down the ages, he found it difficult to understand and impossible to condone the compromises of his elders.

Emily Moffat, a young woman of good education and considerable intelligence, had lived all her life in the sophisticated atmosphere of Brighton. The extent of her travelling, until she sailed for Africa, had been in the London to Brighton train. Though she had heard John talk about his youth at Kuruman and had grown familiar with the mental pictures of life there that he drew, the reality of setting foot in the Colony was a profound shock.

Life in Britain had moved on since MaMary's time. The pace had quickened. In spite of the disasters of the Crimea and the shock of the Indian Mutiny, the last seven years had ushered in an age of prosperity with increasing population, Free Trade, expanding production and, above all, speed. Railway trains, steamers, horse-drawn omnibuses, the stimulus of the Great Exhibition in 1851, all these had enlarged the gap between England and Africa. It was the pace of living that first struck Emily as intolerably frustrating. Far from going immediately into their chosen sphere of action, she had to endure months of painfully slow, to her often wasteful and unnecessary, preparation and negotiation for the job ahead. She was, however, a courageous young woman and she set herself to bear what could not be helped. She had been miserably ill on the ship and was already pregnant. 'The young people have very much to learn and the *fastgoing* propensities of the present age will be severely tried,' Mary remarked—with truth.

On July 13th 1858 the *Athens* sailed into Table Bay carrying three more young missionary couples, including John Mackenzie and his wife Ellen, and Roger and Isabella Price. Mary Moffat, standing on the pier to greet them looked 'still hale and cheerful' despite her worries and was indeed immensely uplifted at the sight of all these new reinforcements for the work that she loved.

The provisioning of the two new missions was not made easier by disagreements among the missionary group and disturbing news from Kuruman. Expense was a point of friction. To Emily and John the preparations Robert was making seemed enormously extravagant. They were very conscious of being dependent on Livingstone's bounty and naturally anxious not to be thought profligate. They were constantly reminding Robert and Mary that *they* had managed when they began with very much less than the pile of stores, tools, utensils, seeds, crockery, etc. that now seemed to be accumulating and all had to be paid for. The Moffats did not need to be told that they had started off with very little. Mary remembered her early struggles all too vividly. It was for that very reason, and armed now with experience, that they were determined that so far as possible these missions should go into the interior well provided for. Robert Moffat had been to Matabeleland, which no one else had; he knew the rigours of the journey, the uncertainties of the welcome, the two or three years which would go by before any further opportunity occurred of replenishing their supplies.

He was still beset by fears for the mission to the Makololo, particularly Livingstone's part in it. Would David Livingstone reach the tribe and get the necessary surveying done in time? The Makololo would only make the removal, a hundred miles to higher ground, if Livingstone was there; and if they did not remove the mission might be gravely endangered by fever.

Meanwhile the news from Kuruman was ominous. There was trouble between Boers and natives in the new republics of Transvaal and Orange Free State, and threats to Kuruman itself. The mission not only stood across the road to the north, which the Transvaal Boers hoped to dominate; the missionaries were on the side of the African and were suspected of gun-running to enable the tribes to resist the encroachment of the farmers. The charge of gun-running had been a constant, and unsubstantiated one, for many years. Unfortunately at this moment Robert junior brought 600lbs of powder and a great quantity of lead to his trading post at Kuruman and stored it in his father's garden. William Ashton, who discovered this, was appalled, forseeing the far-reaching scandal that would result if it became known that Robert Moffat's back garden was a cache for ammunition. With considerable difficulty, for he was a young man of quick temper, Mr Ashton persuaded Robert junior to remove the offending materials one dark night and store them elsewhere. Nevertheless, the very fact that his son was trading in gunpowder gave ammunition of another kind to the gossips—of whom there were always plenty around the station—and this news greatly upset Robert and Mary when they heard it.

Altogether by the middle of August, when the Helmores arrived back from leave, Robert Moffat was almost worried out of his mind. In the worst possible conditions, with rain pouring down and oxen which, because of lung sickness and consequent scarcity and expense, were inferior to the usual teams, the waggons at last drew slowly out of a suburb of Cape Town and across the Cape Flats on August 20th 1858. It was the start of the most calamitous journey that the senior Moffats had ever experienced. It took three months, at first in persistent, mud-oozing rain, later, across the Karoo, in blazing heat. From the very beginning the oxen died like flies or were so lethargic that they had to be mercilessly whipped on. Jeanie was travelling in a light gentleman's waggon which Robert had bought for Moselekatse. It was drawn by mules two of whom absconded and returned to their farms; the donkeys, which Robert was taking back in an endeavour to form a permanent postal link, behaved with maximum obstinacy and wickedness. Emily and Mary Livingstone were both pregnant and the latter constantly poorly. There was a shortage of water; Emily's dog was lost. Unremitting, back-breaking, exhausting toil was required from every man to get the waggons along a trail equipped with the maximum of hazards. 'If Africa is destined to be Christianised and civilised at bullock-waggon pace,' Emily remarked, 'the end of the world cannot be so near as some believe.'

Out of forty-three oxen, twenty-six died before they reached Beaufort West on October 17th. Here John and Emily decided to stay until the baby was born. Mary would have liked them to push on, but Emily had had enough and she had little difficulty convincing her father-in-law. 'Mr M quite saw the reasonableness of our stay here, and I think Mrs M's judgement agreed to it, when her *feelings* were opposed.'

The separation was no doubt a blessing to both sides. Robert must have been painfully aware that the young people blamed him for much of the journey's unpleasantness. The parting enabled both sides to regain their equilibrium, and Mary to concentrate her whole attention on her older daughter whose state of health was causing considerable alarm. They pushed on to Hope Town on the Orange river where they found strong rumours that the Boers were attacking Kuruman. When they got to Griqua Town, Robert rode forward to find out what the situation really was. As he suspected the rumours of an actual attack proved to be unfounded. On November 10th, after the most appalling journey of their lives, they arrived home. Mary was ill; they found Bessie recovering from scarlatina and Robert junior very poorly. Six days later Mary Livingstone gave birth to a little girl.

Chapter 18

IN 1859 KURUMAN was full of babies and children. Practically all Mary's family was gathered within reach again: Mary Livingstone, with her daughter Anna; Robert and Ellen, with two boys and a baby girl; John and Emily with baby Unwin; Bessie and Jeanie; and at Motito Ann with her husband and five offspring. Once, when his little son had picked up a shell on the banks of Lake Ngami and said that he would give it to grandma, David Livingstone had written to his father-in-law, '. . . . When her seven children are increased to about 49 and all of them trying to do something for Granny she will become so buoyant. I can fancy her about 1870 snapping her fingers and dancing for joy.'

But the happiness of being surrounded by her children was now amply counter-balanced by the problems and tensions which arose out of the influx of fresh young blood. Kuruman was crammed; the three new families as well as all the young Moffats. One couple slept in the Ashtons' spare room, another in the infant school, another in the room adjoining the church. The new missionaries ate with the Ashtons, and every morning William Ashton ran a class to teach them Sechuana. The wives helped Sarah Ashton, now nearing her time and aware of her danger, in the kitchen. Isabella Price was pregnant and poorly, and her husband Roger had a bad accident, getting his big toe caught in a waggon wheel and being dragged for some distance with the result that his nail was torn off and his knee and leg badly cut and bruised. Both the other wives were also pregnant and no doubt nervous at the thought of having their first babies so far from any proper medical attention.

They were all anxious about the political situation with the Boers, for whom Robert Moffat was a particular target of opprobrium. Threats of an attack on the station were still circling ominously around. Robert, with long experience of similar threats, remained calm. He was recommended to leave, 'but if I should flee who is there who will stay?' '. . . in this Mrs M is of one heart and mind.'

The new young missionaries, with apprehensive, inexperienced wives, were much more jumpy and uncertain. Robert Moffat received a letter signed by three Transvaal officials, saying that they had heard of his proposed journey to Moselekatse and demanding that he obtain an order from His Honour the President otherwise they would forbid him passage. He forwarded this letter to the Governor of the Colony, asking him to make it plain that the Boers had no jurisdiction over the movements of British subjects in this way. The whole fate of the northern missions seemed in jeopardy.

There were domestic as well as political problems for Mary Moffat. Mary Livingstone, her intention of joining her husband overland through Makololo country looking daily more impracticable, was edgy and uneasy. The return of another beloved daughter, Jeanie, had brought home to MaMary how much the life that she had once known outside Africa had changed and how great the age-gap was between sixty-four and eighteen. Jeanie and Bessie had greeted each other with joy. In the last four years, when she had been alone with her parents, Bessie had taught in the school, learned how to run a home, and conformed to the family pattern. But she did not really like teaching and, underneath a quiet exterior, hid unorthodox views. With the arrival of her younger sister and the change in atmosphere brought about by the influx of her own generation, Bessie began to show signs of rebellion. She and Jeanie joined forces and it was plain to MaMary that a spirit of resistence to much that she cherished was beginning to grow in them.

Mrs Ashton was near her time. There had been talk among the young wives about pregnancy and childbirth and, as always on such occasions, the horror stories took pride of place. They all knew that Mrs Livingstone had lost a child after her journey north and suffered an attack of paralysis. Poor Isabella Price, in Robert Moffat's view a rather hysterical young woman— perhaps with reason—was filled with gloom, which was not lightened by the knowledge that Robert had grave doubts about the whole Makololo expedition.

William Ashton, only too conscious of the history of his wife's pregnancies, had asked Robert to be present at her confinement this time and, as always, MaMary acted as assistant and midwife. The baby, a little girl, was born very quickly at 4 a.m. on February 8th 1859, but even so Sarah Ashton could not rally from the effort involved. An hour or two later she was dead and by 5 p.m. the same day lay in the little graveyard. She was forty-one and 'thought very humbly of herself'.

The small missionary community at Kuruman had had few adult deaths, and none since Robert Hamilton faded away in old age in 1851. It cast a gloom over the station and must have sent an ominous shiver down the spines of the young wives. Everyone was nervous about the continuing possibilities of a Boer attack; and there had still been no word from the Governor.

Holloway Helmore, who was to lead the new Makololo mission, came to Kuruman from Lekhatlong for a meeting to discuss the situation. Besides the sheer difficulty of getting to Sekeletu's town there were other problems. It was not known whether Livingstone had arrived, and if so whether he had managed to persuade the chief to move at least some of his people across the river.

The suggestion was put forward that the men should go alone to explore the ground. Roger Price supported it. Holloway Helmore, who felt that there were strong reasons for taking the women and children as an earnest of good faith—remembering the late chief, Sebituane's, remark to David Livingstone—said that he must return and consult his wife Anne on this issue. Robert Moffat offered no opinion, feeling it a matter for the mission itself to decide, but there is little doubt that Mary would have considered it important that the wives accompany their husbands in any endeavour to set up a new station.

In the event 'Mrs Helmore refused absolutely to let her husband go without herself and the four children, out of their family of seven, who were with them—and this was also Mr Helmore's inclination. The younger missionaries bowed to his experience, which was in fact very slight in so far as an extended journey was concerned, and it was decided that the families would travel together.

In the middle of March John and Emily, with the baby Unwin, arrived from Beaufort West. Emily, a rather prim young woman, had been shocked by much of the free and easy life that she had seen in the colonial homes which had provided hospitality on the road from the Cape. She had her pride and it had 'been nettled more than once'. John's arrival home already married removed from his mother any opportunity to re-establish the warm relationship broken by their ten-year parting. She did not find her new daughter-in-law easy, and Emily resisted—passively—MaMary's efforts to instruct her. Differences of opinion became apparent. John and Emily, young and high-minded, thought the old people had settled down in too much comfort and ease. David Livingstone's philosophy, as well as his views on MaMary, unconsciously coloured the young couple's first impressions. MaMary, who had given directions to Emily as to what she would need in the way of provisions and stores and requested her to keep minute lists of everything, was put out to find that her instructions were not adhered to and considered by the young people unnecessarily extravagant. One generation's essentials were another's luxuries.

Temperamentally father and son were poles apart, the one warm, extrovert, adaptable, with charm and panache, who had made himself—whether he wished it or not—a figure of note in all Southern Africa; the other austere, introverted, humourless, earnest, distrustful of public esteem, unwilling under any circumstances to compromise. Each man recognised the other's qualities, neither would openly have wounded the other, but their personal relations were not easy. Although his inclinations would have taken him north with the mission to the Makololo, and hopefully a meeting with Livingstone, John agreed to honour his father's promise to Moselekatse and the Matabele.

Robert Moffat was himself pulled in different directions. In spite of his doubts he was ready and eager to be off to the north again. At the thought of climbing into his waggon and setting out to face the challenge of bringing the Gospel to thousands who had never heard it, his heart forgot its uncertain pulsations and beat strongly with the thrill of anticipation. All this time he had been sending careful messages to the chiefs up-country to prepare the way for the mission when they should at last set out. Emily was rather shocked to see him so eager to go—'poor grandmama'. But Mary, though every time he now left her she committed him to God uncertain whether she would ever see him again, had no doubts about the rightness of his decision.

Then news came that the Governor had told the Boers not to touch British subjects, and there were rumours that Livingstone had arrived at Linyanti. The season was getting on. If a start was to be made it should be while winter still offered reasonably easy travelling. After discussion a decision was taken that the missions should leave for the north in May and immediately Kuruman was in a flurry of preparations. Mary began to look for a girl who would go with Emily. For the moment the threatening noises of a Boer attack were ignored.

But they did not go away. Indeed they became rather more specific. On April 15th, after a bout of influenza, Emily's baby died. She accepted the loss stoically. Africa had set its mark on her.

A kind of panic began to run through the mission. On May 4th a meeting was held at Kuruman for prayer and deliberation about the future and a resolution was put forward 'that in consequence of the disturbed state of the country and the advanced period of the season, it is exceedingly improbable that the Makololo, or even the Matabele mission will be able to proceed this year.'

A Boer attack seemed to be imminent. Mary Livingstone decided to return to England and her brother John escorted her as far as Hope Town. It was the last time that her mother saw her. The younger missionaries took their wives to safety in Griqua Town and Fauresmith. Robert and Mary 'would not leave the people and further undermine their confidence in the British as a nation'.

At the beginning of June the Boer attack was definitely off, and the start of the two interior missions on. It was decided that the Helmores and the Prices would make up the first Makololo party and the Mackenzies would stay to look after Kuruman while Robert Moffat was away and go up to the Makololo in a year's time. It seemed a satisfactory arrangement all round.

On the 8th of July 1859 the waggons of the Helmores and the Prices pulled out of Kuruman, set at last for the long journey to the Zambesi. Isabella, pregnant and always a prey to gloomy fears, drove out bravely. Mary watched her friend Anne Helmore and her four young children go with pride, commending them to the care of the Lord and sending her love to her 'poor dear Livingstone'. On July 14th John and Emily left for

Matabele land, Bessie and Jeanie going part of the first day's travelling with them. At the last moment Mary had been able to persuade the parents of Mokalahara, the girl who had accompanied her to the Cape, to allow her to go with Emily in the 'Pavilion'—her waggon nostalgically christened after far-off days in Brighton. On August 1st Robert Moffat followed them.

Both Robert and Mary were exhausted by the turmoil of the previous months and agitated by underlying fears and tensions. Always close to each other, the frictions with the young generation had drawn them even closer. Mary assured Robert he was always uppermost in her mind; he replied that he was thankful for sympathy from any quarter. Nevertheless he looked forward to the journey with some of his old excitement; and she, in her contentment at sending out her son in the company of his father, to start a new and important mission, was even glad to see him go.

KURUMAN SCHOOL

Chapter 19

MARY WENT BACK into her house to face a difficult year. As always at the start of a journey Robert bombarded her with notes, instructions, memos of things forgotten. Bessie and Jeanie were taking over the school. But here there was trouble. Bessie had infected Jeanie with her dislike of teaching; Jeanie made Bessie restless with her talk of England—neither was able to explain to their mother why they should so much resent what was plainly their duty.

The last time Mary had had two young daughters with her was fifteen years before. Then she herself had been forty-nine, Mary Livingstone, a placid, easy-going young woman who had quickly married, Ann 'mild, amicable and diligent'. Now things were very different. Mary was sixty-four. Forty years in Africa and the experience and authority of a hazardous life stubbornly overcome had turned her into a formidable woman. She liked to think of herself as constantly on the point of dissolution and, as was not unnatural in a situation where physical ailments could, and did, so easily prove destructive, she spoke much of her bodily infirmities. Humour, lightness of touch and imagination had never been her strong points; her son John's stern sense of duty was inherited from her. But she had lived a lifetime in harmony and partnership with a husband who had full measure of these attributes. When with him she saw life less rigorously, just as he found support in her constant faith and unyielding optimism. Now she was alone, facing her daughters, aged twenty and nineteen, after a parting of ten years. For Bessie and Jeanie she was an old woman, demanding of them a lifestyle which, for all their fortitude and family solidarity, they could not find it in themselves to accept.

In England Jeanie had grown accustomed to a society no less devout but wider, not so claustrophobic as Kuruman. She suffered severely from the shock of transplantation—and she infected Bessie. Bessie had her own problems. She was twenty and looked forward to marriage. All her older brothers and sisters were married and she was next in line—but where were the young men? Suddenly Kuruman was empty. The fuss and bustle of young life had departed leaving Bessie stuck for ever in uncongenial employment in an African backwater. Mary, the stern trials of her own youth in mind, would have recommended self-discipline and put the future in the hands of the Lord. Bessie rebelled against such a supine solution.

It was an unhappy time for all of them, made the more so because they loved each other. Mary wrote to Anne Helmore, the one friend in whom she could confide, in what was for her an unusual mood of despair, fearing that even before Robert returned she would be forced to take the girls to the Colony, perhaps even to agree to their returning to England.

In September John and Ellen Mackenzie came back to Kuruman from Fauresmith. It was a relief to have them. John Mackenzie was happy to go to Mary for information about the people and their spiritual condition. Jeanie and Bessie grew very fond of Ellen Mackenzie and were glad to have someone to talk to who was not a Moffat.

News from the northern expedition trickled in slowly. Mary found the long silences one of the most difficult things to bear: the knowledge that letters had been lost, or simply mislaid by messengers, the uncertainty, the lack of contact. She knew that the Matabele mission had had many accidents, drought, heat, waggon breakdown. 'My poor old husband being the only one possessing mechanical skill had had much fatigue,' Mary reported to the Rev. Mr Thompson in Cape Town.

More disturbing, however, was the dissension between generations. Robert did not want to worry Mary with this, not knowing that she too was having similar difficulties, but it was easy to read between the lines. On arrival at Inyati Moselekatse had vacillated about redeeming his promise given the year before to provide the new mission with a grant of land. This was 'especially painful to him [Robert] who was expected by his influence to have ensured them a more cordial reception'. There was a tendency to blame the old man for everything that went wrong.

The Makololo party were reported as having reached the Zouga with all going well. Isabella Price had her baby in the waggon under a very fine thorn tree. In January 1860 in a letter to the Foreign Secretary of the LMS to report progress, Mary gave a glimpse of her own problems. 'My debility is just now so great that I cannot enter into any particular, but may have to do so at some future time. Just this much I will say, that my two daughters who have been carrying on the school most efficiently, are not likely to do so very long, and it will have to be placed again in the hands of the native schoolmaster. This, my dear Sir, is strictly in confidence as I should not like them to hear of it in England and we do not know what change of mind will take place. Thus I am in deep trouble—having put up with very much, that the school might be well attended to.'

This was the lowest point of her despair. Her faith and prayers were not misplaced and she was openly and generously grateful to the agent of change, Ellen Mackenzie. In May she wrote again to Anne Helmore, who although Mary did not know it was already dead, 'In January I wrote a very sad letter —despairing of being able to keep my two youngest daughters here, even till their father's return. They then seemed quite unlikely to settle down for usefulness here. But blessed be God, I have better news—an entire change of mind has taken place. . . .'

It had indeed. In June Jeanie was writing 'Bessie and I take the school and enjoy our work. The dear children get on nicely and it is our delight to teach them. They are so bonny that they have chased away our horror of teaching.'

In mid-April the Mackenzies set off to reinforce the new mission on the Zambesi. Mary was sorry to see them go, though she had no desire to keep them from their duty. She prepared presents and stores for Anne Helmore, corn, raisins, a pot of pickles packed in dried apples to prevent the pot rolling about. Walnuts sent for the children, a bag of fine ground meal, millet, pumpkin and melon seeds. A box for each of the two wives with home parcels in them. Children's shoes: newspapers. A duplicate case for Isabella Price—everything marked in black paint. With all this she sent a letter with Kuruman news and, as always, 'Love to my poor Livingstone, he is never forgotten.' She had last heard from Mrs Helmore in a letter dated October 10th 1859.

As much as it had ever been, the lack of news, aggravated by rumour, was the great trial. There was no chain of mission stations between Kuruman and the new missions to facilitate post by reasonable stages. It had to be by courtesy of hunters or travellers, or by relay from one tribal group to another with endless possibilities of delay or loss. In June disturbing whispers were circulating of possible disaster. Jeanie wrote to Olive, the eldest Helmore daughter in England, to warn her that all might not be well. The week before a man from a northern region had arrived at Kuruman with a tale that the mission waggons had wandered into a waterless area and suffered fearfully from thirst. He had not actually seen the Helmores and on his one attempt to get in touch had had no reply. Jeanie did not hesitate to tell Olive the truth and spell out the possible consequences. She too had been in England separated from her family and had always felt that she would rather know the worst.

The weeks went by. Robert Moffat arrived back at Kuruman on August 21st. Moselekatse had at last relented and provided the mission with a fine piece of land beside good water.

Early in November, when their last written news from the Makololo mission was over a year old, a hunting party stopped at Kuruman. They said that Livingstone had reached Linyanti and the Helmores and Prices were also there and all was well. The monthly post to England carried this good news. Almost immediately different, more fearful, tidings arrived.

It was a catastrophic story—and still they did not know the whole of it. The party had had a disastrous journey, suffering from fever, tse-tse, drought, taking seven months during the hottest season to reach their destination on February 14th 1860. Livingstone had been delayed on the Zambesi and had not arrived, nor was there any news of him. The chief, Sekeletu, was hostile and suspicious. Four years before, Livingstone had taken a number of his men on the journey to Loanda and none had yet come back. The mission party were already enfeebled by their terrible experiences. It was impossible to persuade Sekeletu to move his people to the higher ground across the river—only someone he knew and trusted could have done this.

On the 2nd of March the Price's Bechuana driver died of fever; on the 7th the youngest Helmore child died. On March 9th, while she was looking after a desperately sick husband, Isabella Price's baby died. On the 11th Selina Helmore and the

African deacon died. On the 12th Anne Helmore died. There remained Roger and Isabella Price, Holloway Helmore and his two remaining children, Lizzie and Willie, all weakened by fever and harrowed by tragedy. 'They were all scattered about, white people and black, those in their tents and these on the ground outside, like logs of wood, unable to help themselves.' They struggled on for another three or four weeks, with most of their African servants dead. On April 22nd, Holloway Helmore died.

The chief, probably fearing that he would be blamed, then told the Prices that they must leave. He drove them out with the maximum inhumanity, demanding as tribute before they left all the possessions of the dead Helmores and everything he fancied belonging to the Prices. He then provided them with men to lead their oxen who, deliberately, took them into tse-tse country and abandoned them. On the 4th of July Isabella Price died and was buried by her husband under a tree. Later he heard that her corpse had been dug up and the head cut off and taken to Sekeletu. Roger Price and the two children, Lizzie and Willie, wandered on until they were taken in by a friendly chief, cared for and looked after until, quite by chance, John Mackenzie, travelling north to join the mission, found them on September 6th.

It was a tremendous blow to Robert and Mary Moffat. In all their forty years no such major disaster had befallen the mission, and in the Helmores they had lost real friends. For Mary, Anne Helmore had been one of the few people in whom she had been able to confide. But they had always been aware that death was possible, they lived too close to it to deceive themselves, and they had no doubts that their fellow workers had all known and accepted the price that might have to be paid to take the Gospel north. For all of them, and for Robert and Mary Moffat, the cause was infinitely greater and the love of God immeasurably more profound than any earthly trial. They had done what seemed necessary; the future lay, as always, in the hands of the Lord. Almost immediately the possibility of a return to the Makololo was being discussed. Though Roger Price was at first convinced that poisoning had been involved in the deaths, he was nevertheless ready to go back.

There was no recrimination by Robert Moffat—no doubting

of the ultimate purpose of the mission. The Moffats understood the combinations of adverse circumstances and unpredictable events, indeed the nature of man, which could result in tragic consequences. Nor did these shake their faith. The Lord moved in mysterious ways and his wisdom was often only dimly perceived by men. 'My husband preached yesterday,' Mary wrote on the Sunday after the fearful news had arrived at Kuruman, 'from the words "What thou knowest not now, thou shalt know hereafter." '

Exactly a year to the day after the ill-fated party had reached Linyanti the survivors arrived back at Kuruman. Only then did Mary hear all the heart-rending details of the disaster. It must have been a sad and emotional moment when the waggons drew up before MaMary's door with all that remained of the party that she had seen off with so much pride and hope eighteen months before. She took them in, to feed and fuss over the children and help to give them the inspiration and courage to go on which were basic to her own philosophy. For the time being her own weaknesses were laid aside and, as always, she rose to the challenge of being needed.

Ellen Mackenzie had had a second son while she and her husband were *en route* to the north. Not surprisingly she returned to Kuruman exhausted and ill, and in need of more professional medical care than Robert could provide. The Mackenzies set out for the Colony, taking Bessie with them to look after the children.

Robert junior offered to escort Roger Price and Lizzie and Willie Helmore to Port Elizabeth, there to get a boat for the Cape and then England. Robert and Mary were alone again at Kuruman, with Jeanie—a lively and energetic young woman running the school with great efficiency, as though she had never rebelled against doing any such thing. 'An active life is best for me,' Robert wrote, 'and as long as I have the aid of my beloved, but ageing, I might nearly say worn out, partner, who has been my solace and counsellor in many trials, I trust thro' Grace to get on.' Mary would have agreed with his estimate of her physical resources, but all the same she was not yet ready to abandon the struggle.

Chapter 20

LIFE HAD TO go on all the same. The school and the large congregation had to be looked after. In so far as possible Mary visited her old women, taught her Bible class, oversaw her household, dispersed and gave thanks for the stores and presents that came in from supporting groups overseas, kept in touch with the young people struggling for a foothold in Matabele land and took an interest in news from Britain and the rest of the world. Emily's health had suffered sadly in the past months and John had been very ill. The country was swept by scourges, drought, lung sickness, smallpox, measles.

Mary was sixty-six. She had expected to be dead and laid to rest in the graveyard at Kuruman long ago. Many of her contemporaries in her home country were already gone, others old ladies long retired from any kind of an active life. But, whatever her body felt like, in the midst of her continuing commitment to Africa and to the increasing family, her spirit could not rest. She wondered constantly about Livingstone, always hoping that he might, even yet, be brought back to the pattern of real mission settlement. 'Poor dear Livingstone,' she wrote to her daughter-in-law, 'we hold him with a loose hand, thinking it quite likely we shall hear of his death as of his coming out alive.'

Roger Price was in Cape Town seeing the Helmore children off to England, and there he met Mary Livingstone 'in excellent spirits' back to join her husband at the mouth of the Zambesi. Mr Price had decided not to go home, perhaps because he had had the chance to get to know Bessie Moffat better. On October 23rd they were married quietly in the Kuruman church and Bessie prepared to go north with him again.

All the children were married now except Jeanie; settled and off her hands, but it did not stop Mary worrying about them. indeed her anxiety range was greatly widened by the inclusion of many grandchildren—the Livingstone five parentless in England; the wild young Fredoux at Motito; Helen's brood whom she had never seen; Robert's four little ones; John's son in the dangerous health conditions of Matabele country and the new baby that Emily was expecting; and now Bessie, who would shortly be facing the trials of pregnancy and mother-hood. It was not only because she was turning out to be an excellent teacher and administrator that Robert Moffat said, 'I hope no one will run away with the present schoolmistress for some time to come.' They had come to a period when they both felt the need of one child to comfort and care for them, whom they could cherish without responsibility or anxious fears.

It was not a quiet life. Robert complained that their house was like a caravanserai, with constant coming and going, visitors, messengers, travellers, questioners, from all over this part of Africa, arriving, staying a few days—or weeks—then moving on. He had become a prophet; he and MaMary legends in their own lifetime. They had to take on two extra servants to cope. No doubt Mary paid as much meticulous attention to their training as she had in days gone by.

Robert still went out itinerating, away for several weeks at a time in his waggon, talking, discussing, teaching, preaching. Once these waggon journeys had been a joy to Mary, now they were too much for her—though she still retained an affection for this form of travel. Robert suffered continuously from heart tremors, which worried him, but her own health seemed to have stabilised in these last years except for the increasing weakness of age. Robert had lost touch with the world outside Kuruman—and did not care. Heart-rent by the American Civil War, alarmed by news of the state of things in Europe, he felt that even if they had a steam conveyance from Kuruman he would not be tempted to use it—much as he might enjoy seeing the wonders of the world: the work he was doing was still too important to leave.

John and Emily, for the sake of Emily's health, were forced to make a journey south. On July 31st 1862 they arrived at Kuruman, taking the parents by surprise. A week later Robert junior set off to fetch his family from Natal. He was not well and had exhausted himself constructing buildings. His mother pressed him to delay the journey for a few days while he rested and recovered, but he was an impulsive young man and he insisted on starting. He had a strong constitution and Mary hoped that the waggon journey, which had always been one of her remedies for run-down bodies, would restore him.

Six hours from Kuruman, on the 6th of August 1862, he became desperately ill with 'inflammation of the stomach and lungs' and was dead before help could reach him. He was thirty-five.

His body came back home in the waggon in which such a short time before he had set out on the long journey to the south. William Ashton made the coffin and held the burial service in the little cemetery. A great number of people came to pay their respects.

For Mary it was an agonising blow. It had taken her a long time to become reconciled to the fact that her oldest son was a trader rather than a missionary, indeed she still felt some additional pain that his early death had not been for the cause. But he was a generous, upright, warm, loving man, who had been concerned to show that a trader could also be honourable and a Christian. She loved him dearly and had come to rely on his presence near her. At a time when she thought to live peacefully beside him, it was anguish to have him taken from her.

Worse was to come. Very shortly after Robert's funeral some traders came into Kuruman bringing news that Mary Livingstone, their first-born, had died of fever at Shupanga on the Zambesi.

She died on April 27th, having been little more than three months with her husband, owing to setbacks and delays on her way to him. Though Livingstone had still not resolved in his own mind the question of family commitment or solitary journeying, he was delighted to have her back with him and she was very content to have a husband to look after again. 'Livingstone is very well, not much altered. The Zambesi is a fine river, rather rapid. Shall write when time allows. L's clothes want looking over' and remaking. My hands are full.' she had written to her brother John in February. She had taken out to Livingstone the boat in which he hoped to sail up the river, the *Lady Nyassa*. Because *Lady Nyassa*'s engines had been sadly neglected they failed to get away from the Delta as quickly as had been expected. Instead of three or four days,

Mary Livingstone had three months in the low-lying heat. 'She was so strong and well, and I had got so into the habit of feeling her to be a part of myself I did not fear but that she would hold out,' David Livingstone wrote to John. But she did not.

For Livingstone it was the most shattering blow of his life. Until the moment that Mary died he had always viewed the future as a challenge, all difficulties were there to be overcome. But this loss seemed 'to take the spirit out of me and to blacken all my horizon'.

He wrote to his mother-in-law two days later—a letter that did not reach her for many months, as hers to him did not arrive till his wife had been long buried. For both of them a measure of bitterness was added to their grief by the lack of communication. Although she had always expected that she might one day have bad news of her eldest daughter, to hear in this way, by word of mouth brought in casually by travellers, compounded the shock.

Her son-in-law's letter, when it did reach Kuruman in September, gave her the details of her daughter's death, though she found it lacking in feeling. She accepted, however, that in this matter their temperaments were very different, hers tending towards open, even exaggerated, expressions of grief and spiritual comfort. Could she have seen his journal she would not have accused him of coldness.

'My dear mother,' he wrote. 'With a sore heart I give you the sad news that my dear Mary died here on the 27th. This unlooked for bereavement quite crushes and takes the heart out of me. Everything else that happened in my career only made the mind rise to overcome it. But this takes away all my strength. If you know how I loved and trusted her you may realise my loss. . . . There are regrets which will follow me to my dying day. If I had done so and so—etc. etc.' Mary had had a little fever, but got over it so quickly they were not alarmed. 'But on the 20th she had spasms in the stomach and then bilious colic but moved about not much worse. It was relieved by a mustard poultice on the stomach, then vomiting ensued which nothing could stop . . . on the 25th I had to lift her up when she wanted anything. I tended her night and day myself, and she expressed herself pleased with my services. . . . On the morning of the 27th she began to moan and said "I am not in pain but cannot help moaning from a feeling of distressing weakness." She thought the room hot and I opened the window about 3 a.m. A Portuguese had sent up four melons the day before, and she being fond of them I had fed her with the heart of one during the night and it seemed to stop the vomiting. When day broke I began to fear the worst and soon after on lifting her up to drink she had lost the power of drinking except from a spoon as she lay. I burst into tears and said. "My dearie, my dearie you are going to leave me. Are you resting on Jesus?" I had to speak loud to make her hear as her ears were affected by the quinine.'

She was quite sensible and not in pain, and she answered his kisses till within half-an-hour of dying. To a friend her husband wrote, 'On 27th I had to part with my good and faithful companion of eighteen years whom I married for love and the longer I had her I loved her the more.'

The two tragedies, coming so close together, further diminished Mary's already receding physical strength. Though she was no stranger to anticipation of death, for herself or those she loved, the finality of the reality was a hammer blow from which even her still strong spirit found recovery difficult. It was Robert's death which continued to trouble her, long after she had reconciled herself to accept her daughter's as one more sacrifice in the cause which she had so long served. But Robert, the oldest son of whom she had once so fondly hoped great things in his father's footsteps. Perhaps, secretly, she had always felt that he might some day be brought to missionary work even yet, and now that hope was annihilated, the potential of his spirit unfulfilled.

Despite his sixty-seven years, trouble with his heart and a life of unremitting labour, Robert Moffat remained tough and resilient, unbowed by tragedy, failure or disaster. Like many who have weathered storms and overcome every conceivable adverse circumstance, it now seemed to him that those who followed in his footsteps neither knew what real hardship was nor had the necessary resolution to win through. Mary, whatever her physical weakness, her numerous pregnancies, had never failed to stand by his side, to support or, if required, act alone. He judged all other young women by her—and some of them failed badly in his estimation. He was too compassionate a man to hurt by open criticism, but every now and again, in a letter to an old friend, he would deliver himself of a crisp conclusion. 'In these days the sums required for an outfit must be enormous, and makes me look back to the first years of my companion and self as to something that existed in imagination only.' He felt that it was good to impress on a young missionary that the fewer his possessions the fewer his anxieties. He had no time for other men's pretensions. Someone in Brighton had written in admiration of John and his 'youthful devotion in going forth independent of man's arrangements'. His father thought this so ridiculous that he wrote off at once reminding the author of the 'man' Livingstone and the £150 per annum.

On the last day of January 1863 Bessie, her husband and baby, arrived unexpectedly at Kuruman. They sent a messenger on ahead with letters, to prepare the parents for their coming. He came in the back door and told the little maid, who rushed into the parlour where Mary, Robert and Jeanie were seated at their evening meal crying 'Ba-etla', 'they are coming'. Immediately there was uproar. The Prices were supposed to be a month's journey off. Jeanie walked out next morning to meet them, under a huge umbrella with her cooking apron still on. Mary issued orders about rooms, beds, food, and all the preparations for a family invasion, but when they at last arrived she was esconced in her armchair in a dark corner—she had always disliked the heat of summer—shrinking from the noise and bustle of the welcome outside.

It was her first glimpse of Bessie since her marriage and she had never seen her six-month-old grandson, Moffat. The baby, in a red travelling dress, was handed round, exclaimed over and then sat on grandma's knee to be fondled and played with. Though Robert's grave in the cemetery cast a shadow over the reunion, the little new life and Bessie's happiness and loving presence comforted Mary.

Sadly the comfort was to be short-lived. Five weeks after they had arrived Bessie's 'precious babe' died suddenly. 'It had been ailing occasionally for some time, but we little thought its latter end was so near. On Friday evening (this is Monday) it underwent a sudden change. Its little lamp grew dimmer as the night advanced and all that the affection of its parents and the skill and experience of its grandparents could do was to soothe its dying hours, but naught to prolong its life. . . . He breathed his last at 4.50 a.m. on Saturday,' Roger Price wrote.

Poor Bessie, already four months pregnant with her second. Poor Mary, suddenly again bereaved, and mourning also for her daughter's pain. It must have seemed as though Kuruman was haunted by death. Roger Price too was ill, suffering from a liver complaint which had originated during his fearful experience with the Makololo mission.

At the end of March 1863 Emily and John returned from Natal, and on April 26th his grandfather baptised John Bruce Moffat, Emily's third son, in the great stone church. In the softened atmosphere of common sorrow, and common joy, the two families had drawn closer together and, though John still looked with a critical eye on the running of his father's mission station, he kept his thoughts to himself. The friction which had marred their earlier relationship was absent. By stressing his parents' old age, the end of their active life, their son found it easier to live with them in peace.

John and Emily, Roger and Bessie all left together at the beginning of May, the one family with three children, the other with none. The young Moffats were returning to Matabele land, though Emily was still feeble and John gloomy about the future there. The Prices were going back to Shoshong and the Bamangwato. On August 29th Bessie had her second son Evan there.

Mary Moffat might be failing in strength and restricted now in her many activities, but she maintained unceasing concern for all her far-flung family. The grandchildren especially were much on her mind. Her sight was going but she continued to be able to write to them when she felt that her help and the expression of her love could be of assistance.

In the middle of 1863 she was roused out of her grief for her daughter by the news that Mary's oldest son, Robert Livingstone, aged seventeen, had arrived, unsponsored and unheralded, in Natal, 'without money, almost without clothing'—on his way to his father. She had last seen this first of all her grandsons in 1852 when he was six. He stayed in her mind as an obstinate, slender little boy, fond of doctoring any who would let him, who had picked up shells for his grandma at Lake Ngami. With his brothers and sisters he had been much in her thoughts since his mother died and his father had disappeared into the interior. That he should want to return to Africa did not surprise her, but that he should do so alone, without proper arrangements being made for him by his father's friends did.

The truth seems to be that his father did not want him, perhaps understandably, but the boy, like many others with famous and adventurous parents, needed to prove to himself that he too could undertake hazardous adventures. He got himself on to a ship, without the approval of his guardians, and arrived in Durban where he received a letter from his father forbidding him to proceed any further. 'I am now in great affliction about Robert,' Mary wrote to a friend in July 1863. 'If he had any introduction to anyone he made no use of it. Ellen [his aunt] got her brother to seek him out. He went and stopped with her till about six weeks ago when he got £1 from her to go to the Bay and get his clothes and had never since been heard of after nine days absence.'

It added to Mary's distress over this special grandchild that she had never written to him about his mother's death. Her own grief, the delay in hearing any details from Livingstone, had caused her to put off this painful duty.

By October she knew through friends that he was in Cape Town 'waiting his father's pleasure' and she wrote to him there at once. It was a loving letter full of warmth, written in the shaky hand of one whose eyes are uncertain. She neither preached at him nor recriminated, neither did she show much understanding of how he might feel about his mother's death, his father's isolation and his own lonely, adolescent uncertainties. But he lay heavy on her heart. He was the oldest grandchild, the first-born of her own dearest Mary, and she felt herself to be the only mother that he had.

'Tell me why you so soon got weary of the old fatherland, dear old Scotland, with which so many of us have been associated and which we are proud to acknowledge as the land of our ancestors. Tell us what is your aim now.' She gave him the family news of 'old Kuruman', still much as he had left it. 'Your grandfather is still the (hale) old man—steps much more lively than some who are only half his age.' 'People say you are shy and reserved,' she wrote, but she begged him to open his heart to the Lord. 'Dearest Robert—do write the very first post.'

But he did not write. In November she was in touch with Mrs Thompson at the Society's headquarters in Cape Town, thanking her for information about 'our poor unhappy grandson, Robert Livingstone'. She had had news from his father which increased her anxiety by making no mention of his son and saying that he himself was ill. Could Mrs Thompson tell her if Robert was still at the Sailor's Home and how he conducted himself and what he was going to do; would she tell him they wanted to hear from him. 'I am quite aware that he may be ashamed to do so because he cannot do it so well as he ought to be able to do. Give our tenderest love to him as the First-born of our own dear First-born.'

It is to be hoped that he got the message and knew that his grandmother cared deeply about him. Perhaps she remembered the anxieties about her own Robert when he too found it impossible to follow in his father's footsteps. She did not hear from this boy. He disappeared and no one knew where he was until news came through that he was in America fighting on the side of the North in the Civil War. He enlisted under the name of Rupert Vincent, Private, Third New Hampshire Regiment, and was fatally wounded before Richmond. He died, aged nineteen, on December 5th 1864 in the prison hospital at Salisbury, North Carolina. In 1866, writing to his sister Agnes, Mary indicated that she knew of his death as a prisoner of war. As always her concern was with his immortal soul—as he had had six weeks in hospital she hoped that he had 'fled to the Saviour'.

In January 1864 William Ashton moved to Lekhatlong. The relationship between him and Robert Moffat had never really warmed into friendship; the two men still irritated each other and neither was really sorry to part. It did, however, leave Kuruman once again in Robert's sole charge. He was active and in reasonable health, but he was nearly seventy and, more difficult, his priorities were those of an old man who has finally decided on the importance of certain aspects of the work and is indifferent to the urgency and challenge of the rest.

More clearly than Robert, Mary saw that much of their work was in danger of being undermined. Jeanie wrote of her at this time, 'Mamma cannot take a very active part in *direct* mission work *now*, but so long as she has any strength at all she will do what she can! She is hearty considering her age and the life she has led in this climate and her care for this and other missions is increasing.' Indeed by the very same post Mary herself was writing a forthright letter to the Directors whom, once again, she felt to be in danger of neglecting Kuruman.

'I do hope you will excuse what may be deemed an impertinence on my part—but were I in London I should hasten to see you—I really deplore the lack of missionaries in this part of the country—so many inviting fields and none to occupy them—except those whose sentiments lead to Rome.' '. . . my own dear husband who has not his equal for strength in this climate has begun to give way. . . .'

But it was not so much his health that worried her; she saw also that he was so engrossed in his revision of the Bible and so 'abstracted in his studies' that he failed to see where other sides of the work were being neglected and lacked a sense of urgency where the general welfare of the mission was concerned. '. . . if I have done wrong it is an error of judgement and you will treat it accordingly,' she finished her appeal for reinforcements, but in fact her strong sense of order and administration was correct. She did not criticise her husband, but she saw clearly that he should no longer be asked to undertake direction of the multifarious daily duties connected with running the station. This was for a younger man belonging to a new generation, looking towards the future—and not for one who now wished only to concentrate on the things which interested him. As she had so often set Robert's house and study in order for him when the chaos became more than her disciplined mind could stand, so she now attempted to put plans in motion for the station.

She was not very successful. Fresh starts are never easy when a long-time incumbent remains active; and the more difficult if, like Robert Moffat, he is a man of enormous reputation and strong character. One possible solution, however, seemed to be appearing on the horizon.

Both John and Emily Moffat suffered continuous ill-health, and John was depressed by the lack of any signs of life or growth in the Matabele mission. David Livingstone had written to say that he could no longer contribute to his brother-in-law's support and John opened negotiations with the LMS about his becoming, after all, one of their missionaries. In 1865 he was accepted by the Society, to his mother and father's very great pleasure, and he and Emily left the Matabele and came, temporarily, to live at Kuruman.

Robert Moffat might be old and toothless, but he still did two men's work and retained his clarity of mind and sharp humour. He was under no illusions that he had long to live (in this he was mistaken), but he did not want to have regrets in heaven that he had not done as much as he should. He suffered greatly from sleeplessness, and found his lack of teeth 'a tax on the lungs'.

The increase of white traders, searching for ostrich feathers, made for difficulties on the station. Their conduct was appalling. They not only drank too much, they had been responsible for brandy becoming a great evil among the Bechuana. One such trader was to be the cause of the last tragedy in Mary Moffat's life.

In July 1864 Bessie's second son died a month before his first birthday. It must have seemed to Bessie that she was fated never to rear a living child, and when on December 23rd of the same year she bore her third son both she and Mary prayed fervently that this precious baby might be spared. By March 20th 1866, when Bessie, again eight months pregnant, arrived at Kuruman with her healthy baby, Mary had twenty-eight living grandchildren and five dead.

On the last day of March news arrived at Kuruman of disaster at Motito. Three days before, Ann's husband, Jean Fredoux, had left the station on a pastoral visit to Morokwain some distance away. The next evening a trader, by the name of Nelson, arrived at Motito also on his way to Morokwain. At Motito he found two other traders from the Transvaal who had a quantity of brandy. Nelson got very drunk and proceeded to create havoc on the station, so much so that he was ordered by the chief to leave and a messenger was sent to warn Mr Fredoux what had happened.

Jean Fredoux considered the situation so serious that he felt it his duty to detain Nelson and take him back to Motito under escort to be judged. When the trader arrived at Morokwain, Mr Fredoux went to talk to him. Finding him still in a very belligerent mood—and certainly not willing to be tried for his behaviour—Jean Fredoux went to the chief men and asked their assistance in effecting an arrest. The chiefs agreed and with a number of their people they approached Nelson's waggon. Mr Fredoux went forward to tell the man that he must come with them. The trader waited until he was within a few yards of the waggon, then put a light to the 175lbs of gunpowder with which it was loaded and blew himself, Jean Fredoux and about forty of the Baralong men standing round sky high. The only recognisable remnant left of Ann's husband were his boots.

When the first shock of this news had worn off, Mary and Robert got into their waggon and hastened the thirty-six miles to Motito, to do what they could for their daughter and the three children that were with her. Both Moffats were extremely distressed, not only on Ann's account but by the nature of this death. For fifty years missionaries had worked in the country north of the Orange river, much of it wild and remote, and during that time none had died a violent death by the hand of man. Roger Price had long ago laid aside his suspicions of Sekeletu and the ill-fated mission to the Makololo. 'It was reserved for a European to perpetrate the atrocious murder of Fredoux,' John Moffat wrote.

Two weeks later they returned to Kuruman with Ann and the children. It was the start of a period of great unhappiness. With reluctance Ann Fredoux agreed to come back with her parents, her only desire at that moment being to remain in Motito. She was distraught, rejecting every effort on their part to offer her comfort, utterly neglectful of her children. Never a young woman of very strong mind, this tragedy drove her to the verge of madness.

It had not been a particularly happy marriage. Her parents had known this and had been sadly aware that much of the blame was their daughter's. Their son-in-law was a quiet, studious, patient man, who drove his wife to distraction by his scholarly vagueness. The small station at Motito was a barren field for a missionary and the claustrophobic atmosphere of such a situation can only have exacerbated their temperamental difference. Nevertheless, when the French Mission had offered Jean Fredoux an opportunity to join others of their Society among the Basutos, Ann resolutely refused to go. The shock and grief that she felt at her husband's untimely death must have been compounded by the pain of past unhappiness and the guilt of knowing that, but for her, he would not have met this particular fate.

From now on Ann and her family were to be a constant and heavy burden on Robert and Mary Moffat, who found themselves wholly responsible for their welfare. In her determination to go back to Motito, where she had many African friends— and maybe felt less oppressed than at Kuruman where intimate family knowledge and forbearing family kindness only added to the intolerable load of grief and guilt that she carried— Ann acted like one on the verge of insanity, refusing to speak or eat, sitting for long hours in the graveyard, roaming the field endlessly in all weathers. Perhaps she hoped for some relief in illness, even death, but she had an iron constitution and, ironically in a land where many died from lesser causes, she remained unscathed. At last, in despair and anxiety, her parents agreed that she take the children and return, temporarily, to her home.

For them, as for everybody else, life had to go on. On April 23rd Bessie had a daughter in her mother's house. She called her Isabella, after her husband's first wife. Roger, her little boy, was fifteen months and flourishing.

It was not a happy time at Kuruman. John and Emily were restive and melancholy. For the sake of their own family they had felt forced to say that they could give no help in the terrible business of Ann's tragedy. John thought that other missionaries misconstrued his being at Kuruman, imagining him to be inheriting not only the comfort of an established station but also his father's position—not through any merit of his own but simply because he was a Moffat. Though he worked quietly and amicably with the old man, relieving him of many chores, he did not find it easy.

At a time when she might legitimately have settled back, her life work done, into an honoured old age surrounded by those she loved, Mary Moffat found herself faced with as many troubles and responsibilities as she had ever known. She wrote to her granddaughter, Agnes Livingstone, who had been complaining that she did not hear from her grandmother, about the weight on her heart of so many fatherless and motherless grandchildren. She had heard from David Livingstone, in Zanzibar, anxious for information about his own family; neither he nor she knew what was happening about their prospects or future. Then, her faith reasserting itself, she added her conviction that what was really of importance was 'that they may be living stones in the great spiritual temple'. And, with a flash of her old concern for the training of young people, she impressed on Agnes the importance of reading 'in the habits of young females'.

Her own strength was small. She still had a large household to guide, and prevent waste and extravagance. Visiting families had domestics and 'they are profuse in their use of eatables'. Jeanie helped in the mornings and evenings, but she was in school all day and 'while I can toddle about I conscientiously object to her withdrawal from the school'. 'We are old,' she wrote, and Robert had too many cares on his mind— something the Directors did not seem to realise.

But the Directors *did* realise—and were already looking towards a solution. It was not, however, one that Mary could easily acknowledge, or that Robert would countenance. Quite simply it was that he should come 'home'.

It was a cruel dilemma, as yet barely discernible for the harsh necessity it was to become. For fifty years, with only a four-year leave in 1839, Kuruman had been their home. Now it was as though they had no other. They were Africans. Much of what surrounded them, the house, the garden, the orchard, the watercourse, the bustling, ordered daily life, the flourishing congregations which worshipped in the great stone church, they had planted and built together. Africa had seen the births and deaths of Mary's children. She had expected to finish her days quietly within reach of Bessie and her babies, of John and Emily and their five; to be buried beside Robert her son, in the cemetery at Kuruman, among the men and women who had watched her struggles and come to respect her faith and courage, amid the sights, sounds, scents, that were Africa and had come to mean home.

But Robert Moffat was still active, still the centre of a busy world, preaching three times on the Sabbath, undertaking all the increasing medical demands (for the nearest doctor was still 170 miles away) immersed in the immense work of revising

215

the Bible in Sechuana, overseeing the station, itinerating among the many small congregations in the country round. His father thought John a man 'of energy, patience and prudence, ready to do anything and everything'. John, for his part, felt that proceedings to replace his father were premature. It was very problematical when—or if—he would go, and as long as he remained he could not be made a cypher. The Directors said that only by his coming back to England would it be possible to see the revised Bible through the press. Robert wrote, cautiously, that he might consider a visit.

Mary watched and waited. She had never failed him and she would not do so now, but her heart must have been sore. Ann and her children remained a burden and a problem—and Ann would go nowhere other than Motito, unless it were to Britain.

Away in the north Moselekatse, king of the Matabele, died. With his death an era ended for his people. An era too was ending at Kuruman, where his old friend, Moshete, and MaMary his only wife, faced a more difficult turning on life's inexorable path. They saw plainly now the road ahead but were reluctant to accept that they must tread it. 'My old heart is warm and my step firm,' Robert wrote. '. . . when I look at the interminable regions beyond of heathen darkness, my heart melts and I wish I were young again.' But he knew that the time was rushing on now when he must 'give place to youth and energy'. The human tragedy was that it did not seem possible for him to do this and yet to remain in Africa.

Mary Moffat had arrived at Lattakoo in March 1820, a young bride with little idea of what lay before her. Fifty years later, in March 1870, she left the work and the home she had built in Africa for the last time. In the end it was Ann's continuing anguish and the necessity of her children that drove Robert Moffat to go to England—and even then only on a 'visit'.

On March 20th he preached his final sermon in the great stone church, whose roof timbers Robert Hamilton had brought from the north in 1837 when many of those on the station were poor and forlorn, the remnants of tribes broken up by the Mantatees. Now the congregation, singing to the accompaniment of the harmonium that some London ladies had presented to the Misses Moffat ten years before, numbered many hundreds. Mary, who had no ear and could only sing in church, joined in through her tears.

It was taken for granted that Jeanie would go with them, the one daughter left to care for ageing parents. For her too it must have been a wrench to see her schoolchildren, dressed in their best cotton clothes, swarming out of church across the green grass under the luxuriant fruit trees.

For the last time Mary organised her household, supervised the packing for a journey, broke one by one the living ties which bound her to Africa. For weeks now, since it had been known that they were finally going, messages of farewell, of affection and friendship, had been coming into her house—some sent verbally by those too far away or too old to come themselves, others delivered in person. It was not only the mission which recognised that an era was coming to an end—the Bechuana did likewise.

Crisis had always challenged Mary's spirit. In this, her last great occasion in Africa, she did not fail. When the time came to leave she set her house in order as thoroughly as she had ever done. Her six servants were going with her as far as Port Elizabeth. She had been offered a cart and horses, as a more comfortable way of travel than the lumbering, rocking ox-waggon, but this she refused. 'No, I will stick to my waggon as long as I can.'

They walked to their waggon, she and Robert, through a press of people, each one hoping for a last word or touch. When she had been helped up and looked for the very last time at her home, the waggons rolled out of the station into the vast country beyond followed by a great wailing crowd.

At Port Elizabeth they went on board the ship for Cape Town. Their six Bechuana servants, greatly excited at their first sight of the sea, accompanied them out in the small boat and were shown over the ship. When at last they left, receding into the distance in the rowing boat which took them ashore, Mary, watching from the deck, knew that the cable was finally cut.

They landed at Plymouth on July 24th 1870, to be met by Helen, the daughter Mary had not seen for twenty-seven years. Surrounded by kindness, it was yet a strange country that she returned to and one which offered her no function except to be

217

the 'good old mother'. Robert had his Sechuana revision still—
and he had his fame which demanded of him much in writing
and speaking. But Mary's devotion to Africa, which had pre-
dated even her devotion to Robert, had asked of her practical,
administrative, teaching gifts which were now no longer
needed. Even her household duties were taken from her by
her daughters, anxious that she should have rest and peace.
Only Robert remained for whom she came first—and she could
be satisfied that he would be well looked after.

On January 10th 1871, five months after setting foot in
Britain, Mary Moffat died quietly and peacefully in Brixton.
She was seventy-five. Watched by Jeanie and her husband, her
mind wandered back to the children left behind in Africa. So
often in the years that were gone she had thought herself on
the brink of death, and the need to live for Robert and the
mission had rallied her spirit. Now that need was gone and she
was content to die.

'For fifty-three years I have had her to pray for me,' Robert
Moffat mourned. 'The wife of my youth, the partaker of my
joys and sorrows for more than half a century has been taken
from me.' He was to live without her for another thirteen years.

EPILOGUE

Epilogue

MARY MOFFAT WAS a pioneer missionary in her own right. Looking back from a changed social standpoint a hundred years later, it is often only too easy to be critical of a previous generation's beliefs and presumptions, and of the actions that arose out of them. So too, a hundred years on, our successors may analyse us.

The early missionaries were not saints; they were men and women of strong convictions with the courage to go out and tell others of them. They were of their own time when the social climate, both in Britain and in Africa, was very different. Too often, by showing only an idealised picture of their work, a disservice has been done to their memory. What was astonishing in them was the firmness of purpose which overcame not only physical hardship but human weakness and error—from which none of us are immune. These were generally very ordinary men and women made extraordinary by the Faith in which they believed.

Mary Moffat would not have approved of personal publicity, and certainly not of exaggerated claims for her part in the Kuruman mission—or indeed for the success of that mission itself. I have tried to tell her story as she lived it, without benefit of hindsight, and in doing so have come to admire her indomitable spirit.

BIBLIOGRAPHY

Bibliography

Lives of Robert & Mary Moffat by John Smith Moffat (Fisher Unwin)

Missionary Labours by Robert Moffat (John Snow)

Matabele Journals of Robert Moffat. Vols I & II ed. J. P. R. Wallis. (Chatto & Windus)

Apprenticeship at Kuruman ed. I. Schapera (Chatto & Windus)

The Matabele Mission of J. S. & E. Moffat ed. J. P. R. Wallis (Chatto & Windus)

Robert Moffat, Pioneer in Africa by Cecil Northcott (Lutterworth Press)

Robert Moffat by E. W. Smith (Student Christian Movement)

Journals of Elizabeth Lees Price ed. Una Long (Edward Arnold Ltd)

David Livingstone, Family Letters. Vols I & II ed. I. Schapera (Chatto & Windus)

Livingstone's Private Journals 1851–1853 (Chatto & Windus)

The Zambesi Expedition. David Livingstone 1858–1863 by J. P. R. Wallis (Chatto & Windus)

Some letters from Livingstone 1840–1872 ed. Chamberlain (O.U.P.)

John Smith Moffat by R. U. Moffat (John Murray)

Ten Years North of the Orange River by John Mackenzie (Edmonston & Douglas, Edin.)

John Mackenzie, South African Missionary & Statesman by W. D. Mackenzie (Hodder & Stoughton)

Isabella Price's Journal (L.M.S. Archives)

Fathers of the London Missionary Society by J. Morison (Fisher, Son & Co)

History of the Moravian Church ed. Langton (Allen & Unwin)

REFERENCES

References

PART I: CHAPTER I

p.13 l.7 L.M.S. Archives. Personal Papers. Robert Moffat to Mrs Pitman   1879
p.15 l.12 The Journals of Eliz. Lees Price, ed. Long
p.17 l.20 Robert Moffat, Pioneer. Northcott. Rules for examination of Missionaries 1795
p.18 l.16 John Smith Moffat. Lives of Robert and Mary Moffat. pub. Fisher Unwin
p.20 l.2   ibid
p.20 l.19   ibid   Mary Moffat to Mrs Greaves
p.23 l.2   ibid   Mary Moffat to Miss Lees   May   1   1819
p.23 l.36   ibid   Mary Moffat to mother   Aug   13 1819
p.24 l.14   ibid   Charlotte Bogue to Mrs Smith   Sept   15 1819
p.24 l.27   ibid   Mary Moffat to parents   Sept   7   1819
p.24 l.39 L.M.S. Archives. Mary Smith's Journal   1819
p.25 l.24   ibid
p.25 l.32   ibid
p.26 l.14   ibid
p.27 l.18   ibid
p.28 l.32   ibid
p.30 l.30   ibid
p.30 l.35 John Smith Moffat. Lives. Mary Moffat to parents   Dec   8   1819

CHAPTER 2

p.31 l.25 John Smith Moffat. Lives. Mary Moffat to John Smith
p.35 l.37 L.M.S. Archives   Robert Moffat to L.M.S.   Jan   17 1820
p.36 l.30   ibid
p.38 l.15 John Smith Moffat. Lives. Mary Moffat to parents   Feb   17 1820
p.40 l.2   ibid   ibid   April   8   1820
p.41 l.22   ibid   ibid
p.43 l.24 L.M.S. Archives   Mary Moffat to parents   Aug   11 1820
p.43 l.31   ibid   ibid
p.44 l.3   ibid   ibid
p.44 l.23   ibid   ibid

CHAPTER 3

p.46 l.18 L.M.S. Archives   Robert Moffat to L.M.S.   July   12 1821
p.47 l.14   ibid   Mary Moffat to Mrs Philip   Sept   12 1821
p.49 l.4 The Journals of Eliz. Lees Price, ed. Long
p.49 l.24 L.M.S. Archives   Mary Moffat to Mrs Philip   Sept   12 1821
p.50 l.6   ibid   ibid
p.51 l.5   ibid   Robert Moffat to Dr Philip   Sept   12 1821
p.53 l.40   ibid   Rev. J. Campbell to R. Hamilton July   28 1821
p.54 l.29 John Smith Moffat. Lives. Mary Moffat to parents   Aug   29 1822
p.54 l.35   ibid   ibid

CHAPTER 4

p.58	l.5	Apprenticeship at Kuruman, ed. I. Schapera	Mary Moffat to parents	Feb	22 1822
p.60	l.36	John Smith Moffat. Lives.	Mary Moffat to parents	Aug	29 1822

CHAPTER 5

p.62	l.32	The Journals of Eliz. Lees Price, ed. Long			
p.67	l.33	John Smith Moffat. Lives.	Mary Moffat to parents	Sept	1823
p.68	l.20	Apprenticeship. ed. I Schapera	Mary Moffat to parents	Sept	1823
p.69	l.40	John Smith Moffat. Lives.	Mary Moffat to ?	July	1824
p.70	l.13	ibid	ibid		
p.70	l.22	ibid	Mary Moffat to Robert Moffat	July	28 1824
p.70	l.34	ibid	ibid		
p.73	l.26	ibid	Mary Moffat to ?	July	1824
p.74	l.27	L.M.S. Archives Personal Papers	Mary Moffat to James Smith	Feb	14 1825

CHAPTER 6

p.76	l.29	Rhodes Library, Oxford	Mary Moffat to Mrs Wrigley	Dec	18 1828
p.77	l.27	Apprenticeship, ed. I Schapera	Robert Moffat to parents-in-law	Sept	6 1825
p.77	l.32	ibid	ibid		
p.78	l.1	John Smith Moffat. Lives.	Mary Moffat to father	June	1826
p.78	l.37	ibid	Mary Moffat to ?	April	1826
p.79	l.9	ibid	ibid		
p.80	l.6	Apprenticeship, ed. I Schapera	Mary Moffat to father	Sept	23 1826
p.80	l.16	John Smith Moffat. Lives.	Mary Moffat to father	Sept	1826
p.80	l.23	ibid	ibid		
p.80	l.28	Rhodes Library, Oxford	Mary Moffat to Mrs Wrigley	Dec	18 1828
p.81	l.7	Apprenticeship, ed. I Schapera	Robert Moffat to Mary Moffat		
p.81	l.26	ibid	Mary Moffat to father	Aug	28 1827
p.81	l.32	ibid	Mary Moffat to John Smith	Dec	6 1827

CHAPTER 7

p.83	l.6	Rhodes Library, Oxford	Mary Moffat to Mrs Wrigley	Dec	18 1828
p.84	l.9	L.M.S. Archives	Robert Moffat to Directors		1828
p.84	l.22	ibid	ibid	Jan	1828
p.84	l.36	Apprenticeship, ed. I Schapera	Mary Moffat to father	Dec	30 1828
p.85	l.38	Rhodes Library, Oxford	Mary Moffat to Mrs Wrigley	Dec	18 1828
p.86	l.18	ibid	ibid		
p.86	l.21	ibid	ibid		
p.87	l.23	ibid	ibid		
p.87	l.39	ibid	ibid		
p.88	l.2	ibid	ibid		
p.88	l.12	ibid	ibid		
p.88	l.35	ibid	ibid		
p.89	l.17	ibid	ibid		
p.89	l.22	ibid	ibid		

CHAPTER 8

p.93 l.7 John Smith Moffat. Lives. Mary Moffat to father   Oct   1829
p.93 l.17 Rhodes Library, Oxford   Mary Moffat to Mrs Wrigley   Dec   18   1828
p.95 l.38 Missionary Labours, Robert Moffat

CHAPTER 9

p.98 l.30 John Smith Moffat. Lives. Mary Moffat to Miss Lees   Sept   15   1830
p.98 l.35   ibid   ibid
p.98 l.40   ibid   ibid
p.99 l.4   ibid   ibid
p.100 l.12 John Smith Moffat. Lives. Mary Moffat to father   Sept   15   1831
p.101 l.31   ibid   ibid   Feb   23   1832
p.101 l.34 L.M.S. Archives   Robert Moffat to Directors   Feb   1832
p.103 l.27 John Smith Moffat. Lives. Mary Moffat to father   March 20   1834
p.104 l.13   ibid   Mary Moffat to Mrs Roby   Oct   1   1833
p.104 l.16   ibid   ibid   Oct   1   1833
p.104 l.22   ibid   ibid   Oct   1   1833
p.104 l.33   ibid   ibid
p.104 l.39   ibid   Mary Moffat to father   March 20   1834
p.104 l.40   ibid   ibid
p.105 l.37 L.M.S. Archives   Robert Moffat to L.M.S.   Feb   3   1834
p.106 l.28 Missionary Labours, Robert Moffat
p.107 l.13 The Journals of Eliz. Lees Price, ed. Long
p.107 l.17 L.M.S. Archives   Mary Moffat to father   Aug   20   1834

CHAPTER 10

p.109 l.11 Rhodes Library, Oxford   Mary Moffat to Mrs Wrigley   Dec   18   1828
p.110 l.33 Matabele Journals of Robert Moffat Vol. 1
p.111 l.16   ibid
p.111 l.31 John Smith Moffat. Lives. Mary Moffat to Robert Moffat   June   25   1835
p.112 l.2   ibid   ibid
p.114 l.6 John Smith Moffat. Lives. Mary Moffat to father   April 14   1836
p.114 l.33   ibid   ibid
p.115 l.4 John Smith Moffat. Lives. Mary Moffat to Robert Moffat   May   2   1836
p.115 l.40   ibid   ibid
p.116 l.26   ibid   Mary Moffat to father   July   18   1836
p.117 l.12 L.M.S. Archives   Report to Directors   July   22   1836
p.117 l.30   ibid   Roger Edwards to Directors   July   18   1836
p.118 l.36 John Smith Moffat. Lives. Mary Moffat to father   1838
p.119 l.16   ibid   ibid

CHAPTER 11

p.127 l.25 L.M.S. Archives   Robert Moffat to Directors   Nov   3   1845
p.128 l.33 John Smith Moffat. Lives. Mary Moffat to R. Hamilton   Nov   25   1840
p.130 l.4   ibid   Mary Moffat to Mrs Unwin   Nov   1842
p.130 l.26   ibid   Mary Moffat to parents-in-law   May   1842
p.131 l.21 L.M.S. Archives   Mary Moffat to Miss Pyer   Sept   9   1842

p.135 l.5	L.M.S. Archives	Robert Moffat to Directors	Nov	3	184
p.135 l.9	ibid	ibid			
p.136 l.3	ibid	ibid	Feb	24	184
p.136 l.13	ibid	ibid			
p.136 l.30	ibid	David Livingstone to his parents	Dec	16	184
p.138 l.22	L.M.S. Archives	Robert Moffat Dr Philip			184
p.138 l.28	ibid	David Livingstone to Directors	Dec	2	184
p.139 l.1	Bruce Collection	David Livingstone to Mary Moffat	Aug	1	184
p.140 l.16	L.M.S. Archives	David Livingstone to Robert Moffat	Sept	5	184
p.140 l.23	ibid	ibid	July	18	184
p.141 l.30	John Smith Moffat. Lives.	Mary Moffat to Robert Moffat	Sept	15	184
p.141 l.38	ibid	ibid			
p.141 l.40	ibid	ibid			
p.142 l.6	ibid	ibid			
p.142 l.16	L.M.S. Archives	David Livingstone to Robert Moffat	Sept	8	184
p.142 l.21	ibid				
p.142 l.29	David Livingstone to mother, PS Mary Livingstone		May	4	184
p.143 l.10	John Smith Moffat. Lives.	Mary Moffat to father	March	17	184
p.143 l.19	ibid	ibid			

CHAPTER 13

p.144 l.17	John Smith Moffat. Lives.	Mary Moffat to father	March	17	184
p.145 l.3	ibid	ibid			
p.146 l.19	The Journals of Eliz. Lees Price, ed. Long				
p.146 l.24	ibid				
p.146 l.26	ibid				
p.147 l.7	John Smith Moffat. Lives.	Mary Moffat to father	March	17	184
p.147 l.18	ibid	ibid			
p.147 l.26	ibid	ibid			
p.147 l.31	ibid				
p.148 l.2	ibid	Mary Moffat to Robert Moffat	April	21	184
p.148 l.16	ibid	ibid			
p.148 l.28	ibid	Mary Moffat to child	May		184
p.148 l.37	ibid	ibid			

CHAPTER 14

p.150 l.1	John Smith Moffat. Lives.	Mary Moffat to child	Jan		184
p.150 l.15	ibid	ibid	March		184
p.151 l.8	L.M.S. Archives	David Livingstone to Robert Moffat	Sept	2	184
p.151 l.17	ibid	ibid	Aug	18	184
p.152 l.4	David Livingstone Family Letters Vol. II				
p.154 l.2	L.M.S. Archives	David Livingstone to Robert Moffat	March	4	18
p.154 l.25	ibid	Mary Moffat to Mrs Helmore	July	22	18
p.154 l.38	ibid	David Livingstone to Robert Moffat	Aug	24	18

p.155 l.4   David Livingstone Family Letters
p.155 l.16 L.M.S. Archives   David Livingstone to
                              Robert Moffat   Oct   27 1850
p.155 l.27   ibid   Robert Moffat to Mr Freeman   Oct   8   1850
p.155 l.30 John Smith Moffat. Lives. Mary Moffat to Mrs Sheldon   July   23 1850
p.156 l.8   ibid   ibid

CHAPTER 15

p.157 l.24 L.M.S. Archives   Wm Ashton to Mr Freeman   July   13 1850
p.158 l.17 David Livingstone Family Letters
p.158 l.32 Livingstone's Private Journals. Mary Moffat to David Livingstone
p.159 l.34   ibid   June   11 1851
p.160 l.17 L.M.S. Archives   David Livingstone to
                              Robert Moffat   Nov   29 1851
p.160 l.29   ibid   ibid   April   2   1852
p.161 l.2   John Smith Moffat   Mary Moffat to father   June   7   1851
p.161 l.32 David Livingstone Family Letters Vol II
p.162 l.21 L.M.S. Archives   Robert Moffat to Directors   April   9   1852
p.163 l.38 David Livingstone Family Letters Vol II   Jan   14 1853

CHAPTER 16

p.167 l.21 Matabele Journal of Robert Moffat   June   10 1854
p.167 l.32   ibid   July   22 1854
p.168 l.3   John Smith Moffat. Lives. Mary Moffat to Miss Braithwaite   June   9   1855
p.168 l.14   ibid   ibid
p.168 l.31 The Journals of Eliz. Lees Price, ed. Long
p.169 l.17 John Smith Moffat. Lives. Mary Moffat to Robert Moffat   Oct   9   1854
p.169 l.24   ibid   ibid
p.169 l.34   ibid   ibid
p.170 l.34 The Journals of Eliz. Lees Price, ed. Long
p.171 l.4   ibid
p.171 l.24 L.M.S. Archives   Mary Moffat to Rev. Thompson   Jan   2   1855
p.172 l.25 John Smith Moffat. Lives. Mary Moffat to Miss Braithwaite June   9   1855
p.172 l.30   ibid   ibid
p.173 l.14 The Journals of Eliz. Lees Price, ed. Long
p.173 l.21   ibid
p.175 l.24 L.M.S. Archives   David Livingstone to
                              Robert Moffat   Aug   17 1856

CHAPTER 17

p.180 l.11 The Journals of Eliz. Lees Price, ed. Long   July   8   1857
p.180 l.16   ibid
p.180 l.33 John Smith Moffat. Lives. Mary Moffat to John Smith Moffat July   13 1857
p.181 l.15 Matabele Journal of Robert Moffat Vol II
p.181 l.29   ibid
p.182 l.2   ibid
p.182 l.6   ibid

p.182 l.12	L.M.S. Archives	Mary Moffat to Directors	Nov	5	1857
p.183 l.40	ibid	Robert Moffat to Directors	April	19	1858
p.184 l.22	ibid	ibid			
p.185 l.25	Matabele Mission of J. S. & E. Moffat				
p.185 l.31	ibid				
p.185 l.34	ibid				
p.187 l.11	L.M.S. Archives	Mary Moffat to Mr Thompson	Dec	27	1859
p.187 l.17	ibid	John Mackenzie to Directors	July	5	1858
p.189 l.8	Matabele Mission of J. S. & E. Moffat.	Emily Moffat to father	Aug	25	1858
p.189 l.15	ibid	ibid	Oct	17	1858

CHAPTER 18

p.190 l.9	L.M.S. Archives	David Livingstone to Robert Moffat	July	8	1850
p.191 l.1	ibid	Robert Moffat to Rev. Thompson	May	9	1859
p.192 l.6	ibid	Wm. Ashton to Directors	Feb	23	1859
p.194 l.16	ibid	Records of Meeting	May	4	1859
p.194 l.25	ibid	Robert Moffat to Rev. Thompson	May	9	1859
p.194 l.40	ibid	Mary Moffat to Anne Helmore	May	22	1860

CHAPTER 19

p.196 l.12	L.M.S. Archives	Robert Moffat to Directors	Oct	18	1869
p.197 l.26	ibid	Mary Moffat to Rev. Thompson	Dec	27	1859
p.197 l.35	John Smith Moffat. Lives.	Mary Moffat to brother-in-law	Feb	22	1860
p.198 l.3	L.M.S. Archives	Mary Moffat to Directors	Jan	25	1860
p.198 l.17	ibid	Mary Moffat to Anne Helmore	May	22	1860
p.198 l.23	ibid	Jane Moffat to Olive Helmore	June	11	1860
p.198 l.37	ibid	Mary Moffat to Anne Helmore	May	22	1860
p.200 l.4	John Mackenzie. W. D. Mackenzie				
p.201 l.6	L.M.S. Archives	Mary Moffat to Mrs Stuart	Nov	12	1860
p.201 l.32	ibid	Robert Moffat to Directors	April	20	1861

CHAPTER 20

p.202 l.19	L.M.S. Archives	Mary Moffat to Ellen Moffat			1862
p.202 l.24	Matabele Mission of J. S. & E. Moffat	Roger Price to John Moffat	Oct	16	1861
p.203 l.8	L.M.S. Archives	Robert Moffat to Directors	Sept	2	1862
p.204 l.5	ibid	ibid	Sept	2	1862
p.204 l.33	Matabele Mission of J. S. & E. Moffat	D. Livingstone to John Moffat (PS by Mary Livingstone)	Feb	23	1862
p.205 l.1	ibid	ibid	May	29	1862
p.205 l.8	David Livingstone Trust, Blantyre	D. Livingstone to Lord Kinnaird	May	8	1862
p.205 l.25	National Library of Scotland	D. Livingstone to Mary Moffat	April	29	1862
p.206 l.14	David Livingstone Trust, Blantyre	D. Livingstone to Lord Kinnaird	May	8	1862
p.207 l.3	L.M.S. Archives	Robert Moffat to Directors	Dec	1	1862
p.207 l.9	ibid	ibid			
p.207 l.35	ibid	Roger Price to Directors	March	10	1863

p.208 l.35	Nat. Library of Scotland	Mary Moffat to friend	July	24	1863
p.209 l.11	ibid	ibid			
p.209 l.32	ibid	Mary Moffat to Robert Livingstone	Oct	3	1863
p.210 l.3	ibid	Mary Moffat to Mrs Thompson	Nov	28	1863
p.210 l.27	Mrs Sheila Moffat	Mary Moffat to Agnes Livingstone	Sept	5	1866
p.210 l.39	L.M.S. Archives	Jane Moffat to ?	Aug	1	1864
p.211 l.6	ibid	Mary Moffat to Directors	Aug	3	1864
p.212 l.10	ibid	Robert Moffat to Directors	Feb	15	1865
p.213 l.20	ibid	John Moffat to Directors	April	10	1866
p.215 l.5	Mrs Sheila Moffat	Mary Moffat to Agnes Livingstone	Sept	5	1866
p.215 l.8	ibid	ibid			
p.215 l.12	ibid	ibid			
p.215 l.14	ibid	ibid			
p.216 l.3	L.M.S. Archives	Robert Moffat to Mr Mullens	Dec	16	1868
p.216 l.20	ibid	ibid	April	22	1869
p.216 l.24	ibid	ibid			
p.217 l.23	John Smith Moffat. Lives.				
p.218 l.18	ibid				

235

INDEX

Index

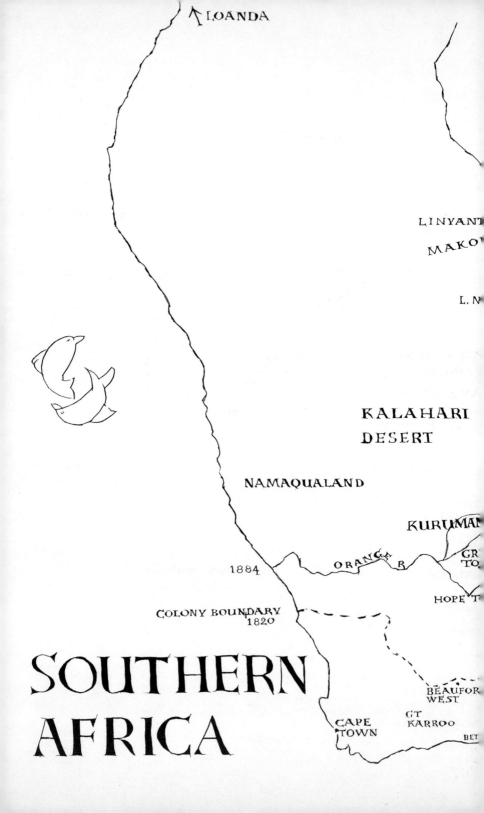

↑ LOANDA

LINYANT

MAKO

L. N

KALAHARI
DESERT

NAMAQUALAND

KURUMAN

ORANGE R.

GR
TO

1884

HOPE T

COLONY BOUNDARY
1820

SOUTHERN
AFRICA

BEAUFOR
WEST

CAPE
TOWN

GT
KARROO

BET

ZAMBEZI R

QUELIMANE

· INYATI

MATABELE

MANGWATO
SHOSHONG·

LIMPOPO R

WENA

· KOLOBENG

· CHONWANE

· MOSEGA
MABOTSA

MOSELEKATSE'S
· KRAAL
(1829-1835)

TO
TAKOO
UNG

VAAL R

HATLONG

DRAKENSBERG

COLONY BOUNDARY
1884

PHILIPOLIS

SBURG

AF
NET

ALEM· GRAHAMSTOWN

ELIZ.

LGOA
BAY

N

W   E

S